HIGHLY-DETAILED GATEFOLD ARTWORKS

MODERN
MILITARY
AIRCRAFT

HIGHLY-DETAILED GATEFOLD ARTWORKS

MODERN MILITARY AIRCRAFT

RYAN CUNNINGHAM

amber
BOOKS

First published in 2025

Copyright © 2025 Amber Books Ltd

All rights reserved. No part of this publication may be reproduced,
stored in a retrieval system, or transmitted in any form or by any
means, electronic, mechanical, photocopying, recording, or otherwise,
without prior written permission of the copyright holder.

Published by
Amber Books Ltd
United House
North Road
London N7 9DP
United Kingdom

www.amberbooks.co.uk
Facebook: amberbooks
YouTube: amberbooksltd
Instagram: amberbooksltd
X(Twitter): @amberbooks

ISBN: 978-1-83886-644-0

Project Editor: Michael Spilling
Designers: Mark Batley and Lewis Hughes-Batley
Picture Research: Terry Forshaw

Printed in China

CONTENTS

Introduction   6

Fifth-Generation Multirole Fighters   8
Feature: Lockheed Martin F-22 Raptor and
Lockheed Martin F-35 Lightning II

4.5-Generation Multirole Fighters   22
Feature: General Dynamics F-16C and McDonnell Douglas CF-18 Hornet

Fourth-Generation Multirole Fighters   62
Feature: Dassault Mirage 2000 and Sukhoi Su-27 'Flanker B'

Bombers   76
Feature: Northrop B-2 Spirit and Tupolev Tu-160

Strike and Attack Aircraft   92
Feature: Fairchild Republic A-10A Thunderbolt II and Sukhoi Su-25

Transport and Reconnaissance   108
Feature: Airbus A400M and Boeing 737 Wedgetail AEW.MK 1

Index   124

Picture credits   128

Introduction

Of all the military hardware in use today, fixed-wing aircraft are perhaps the most sophisticated, with successive generations of development since World War I. This has resulted in the most capable means of generating air power, often harnessed within relatively small physical dimensions at least where fighter jets are concerned.

Radar and other mission sensors, weapons – normally including missiles and guns – powerplant and fuel, a plethora of avionics and the pilot's cockpit and life-support systems all need to be brought together within an airframe that offers the right blend of aerodynamics and materials to guarantee the required performance. That performance also has to ensure the aircraft is effective across its mission spectrum, from take-off to aerial combat, before then returning to base, be that on land or at sea.

The fighters in operational service around the world today can be broadly categorised according to their generations, although there are of course exceptions to the rule, and the growth of mid-life upgrades and improvement programmes over the last couple of decades increasingly blur the boundaries. Today, there is no reason why a warplane designed in the 1950s can't carry a radar, for example, that is every bit as sophisticated as the types found on new-generation aircraft.

With that in mind, this book uses the broad generational definitions to classify the most important fighters in service today, before addressing some of the more specialised categories of aircraft likely to be used in operational roles, including bombers and transports.

A Sukhoi Su-57 stealth multirole fighter with pixel camouflage in flight at the MAKS 2019 air show in Moscow.

INTRODUCTION

Fifth-generation fighters

Today, only a handful of fifth-generation fighters are in service, but that number is only set to grow later this decade. While these aircraft, which typically boast stealth characteristics, high-end performance, integrated sensors, advanced cockpits and sophisticated weapons, are often the 'silver bullet' fleets within a given air force. The bulk of the world's fighter fleets is today made up of fourth-generation fighters, which can offer many of the same capabilities – especially after upgrade or further development – but which lack the same level of low-observability, making them more vulnerable to modern air defence systems.

But with upgrades, even previous-generation fighters, typified by the third-generation fighters that were originally designed and built during the Cold War, can offer capabilities that at least approach those of the fourth generation. In some cases, such as the Soviet-era MiG-29 and Su-27, continued evolution has actually allowed later versions of these jets to effectively jump from one generation to the next and remain in production today.

While fighters and, to a lesser extent, dedicated strike/attack types make up the backbone of most of the world's air forces, bombers remain an important element of a select few nations and future development programmes will ensure that there is still a place for manned (or optionally manned) bombers for many decades to come.

A product of European collaboration, the Eurofighter Typhoon was designed during the tail-end of the Cold War but only entered frontline service in the early 2000s. This pair of Italian F-2000s was taking part in the type's first operational assignment – patrolling the skies around Turin during the 2006 Winter Olympics.

Outside of these pure combat types, air forces rely equally on transport aircraft and reconnaissance and surveillance assets to ensure that the overarching mission can be achieved, whether in a contested wartime environment or a peacetime humanitarian role. Reflecting the variety of aircraft types that make up a modern air arm, later chapters in this book also look at a selection of the most important and most capable aircraft in these categories.

FIFTH-GENERATION MULTIROLE FIGHTERS

An elite group of warplanes, today's in-service fifth-generation fighters number only a handful of types but offer the most complete set of capabilities of any of their kind. These features typically include stealth design, high levels of manoeuvrability combined with supercruise performance, and highly-integrated avionics that bring together a variety of advanced sensors, information from which is rapidly converted into situational awareness and can be shared with multiple other platforms.

This chapter includes the following aircraft:
- Lockheed Martin F-22 Raptor
- Lockheed Martin F-35 Lightning II
- Sukhoi Su-57
- Chengdu J-20

An F-22 Raptor from the 95th Expeditionary Fighter Squadron, Al Dhafra Air Base, United Arab Emirates, flies over Syrian air space, 2018.

FIFTH-GENERATION MULTIROLE FIGHTERS
Lockheed Martin F-22 Raptor

The F-22A Raptor is, without question, the most capable all-around air superiority fighter in the US Air Force inventory today and, very likely, anywhere in the world.

Developed towards the end of the Cold War to meet the growing threat posed by advanced Soviet fighters, the F-22 programme was very expensive, resulting in a cost of over $130 million per aircraft, which led to the production total being trimmed to just 187 Raptors. These now serve as a highly valued 'silver bullet' fleet within the US Air Force, but the total is a far cry from the service's original ambition to field as many as 648 aircraft, which would have provided the backbone of its fighter fleet.

Designed from the ground up to achieve aerial dominance in the most contested airspace, the F-22 includes features that have come to define the 'fifth-generation fighter' appellation. Among these are all-aspect stealth qualities to reduce its chance of detection by enemy radar (or by other sensors), the ability to fly at supersonic speed without using afterburning (supercruise) as well as advanced integrated avionics.

Advanced Tactical Fighter
The F-22 emerged from the Advanced Tactical Fighter (ATF), for which a requirement was first issued in 1981, at that time envisaging a new platform to replace the F-15 and F-16 then in service with the USAF. The ATF programme yielded two rival prototype aircraft, Lockheed Martin's YF-22 and the Northrop/McDonnell Douglas YF-23, both of which recorded their first flights in late 1990.

After a competitive evaluation, the US Air Force selected the YF-22 for the engineering and manufacturing development (EMD) effort that began in 1991. The first flight of an EMD aircraft was achieved in 1997 and the F-22A entered low-rate initial production in 2001. After initial operational test and evaluation had been completed, the Raptor was approved for full-rate production in 2005. Although the F/A-22 designation was applied briefly, the new fighter was officially renamed as the F-22A in late 2005.

The stealth capabilities of the Raptor are a fundamental part of how it is intended to be employed in air combat, remaining unseen by hostile sensors long enough to fire off one or more AIM-120 Advanced Medium-Range Air-to-Air Missile (AMRAAM) to hit a target that's been detected at long range by the AN/APG-77 active electronically scanned array (AESA) radar – the so-called 'first look, first shot' advantage.

Passive receiver system
As well as the radar, the pilot can call upon the Raptor's AN/ALR-94 passive receiver system to track an emitting target without having to reveal the F-22's presence, while targeting information can also be acquired from other platforms via a fighter datalink. Using the intra-flight datalink, a team of Raptors can keep tabs on an enemy, passing targeting data to the jet that's closest to it, allowing it to make the kill without having to engage its own radar.

The low-observable characteristics of the F-22 are ensured through the use of a clean, angular airframe configuration, with jagged edges on any panels that may reflect electro-magnetic energy back to a hostile radar.

As well as being able to engage targets stealthily at long range, the Raptor is designed to be equally as capable of air combat at close quarters. This is achieved through a combination of a triplex fly-by-wire flight control system, two-dimensional thrust vectoring nozzles on the twin Pratt & Whitney F119 turbofan engines and an airframe that incorporates negative static stability. The pilot, seated below a clear-view clamshell canopy, controls the aircraft using a sidestick controller and throttle. The cockpit is configured with four colour multifunction displays as well as a wide-angle head-up display.

F-22A
Weight (maximum take-off): 37,875kg (83,500lb)
Dimensions: Length 18.92m (62ft 1in), Wingspan 13.56m (44ft 6in), Height 5.08m (16ft 8in)
Powerplant: Two Pratt & Whitney F119-PW-100 turbofans, each rated at 156kN (35,000lb) of thrust with afterburning
Maximum speed: Mach 2.25
Range: 2897km (1800 miles) with two external fuel tanks
Ceiling: 19,812m (65,000ft)
Crew: 1
Armament: One 20mm (0.787in) M61A2 Vulcan six-barrel Gatling cannon, plus up to eight air-to-air missiles carried in three internal bays, or an equivalent load of precision-guided air-to-ground munitions

---

FIFTH-GENERATION MULTIROLE FIGHTERS

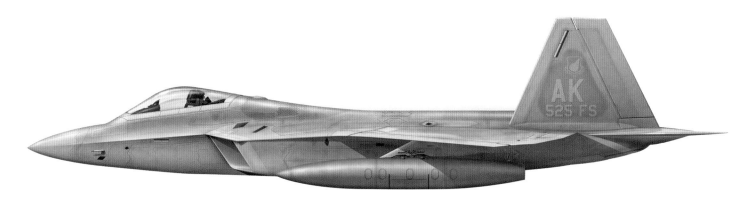

F-22A Raptor
The strategically important airspace over Alaska is defended by F-22As assigned to the 525th Fighter Squadron 'Bulldogs'. Providing 'Top Cover for America', the unit was reactivated at Joint Base Elmendorf-Richardson, Alaska, in 2007.

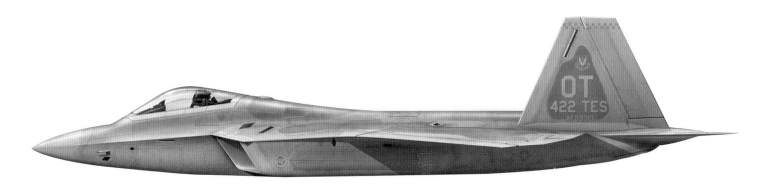

F-22A Raptor
The 422nd Test and Evaluation Squadron 'Green Bats', part of the 53rd Test and Evaluation Group, is stationed at Nellis Air Force Base, Nevada, and conducts operational testing of all fighters, as well as their munitions, before service entry with frontline units.

F-22A Raptor
This F-22A is operated by the 192nd Wing's 149th Fighter Squadron, part of the Virginia Air National Guard, stationed at Joint Base Langley-Eustis, Virginia. Although a Guard unit, the wing is operationally assigned to Air Combat Command and works closely alongside the active-duty 1st Fighter Wing at Langley.

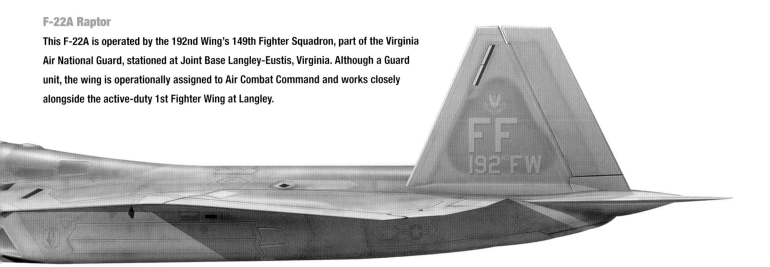

FIFTH-GENERATION MULTIROLE FIGHTERS

Air-to-ground missions

As well as its primary air-to-air mission, the F-22 has also been increasingly adapted to carry out air-to-ground missions, too, adding the GBU-32 Joint Direct Attack Munition (JDAM) and the Small Diameter Bomb (SDB) to its weapons options. Indeed, it was in the precision attack role that the aircraft was first used in combat, striking ISIS targets in Syria in September 2014.

For its air-to-air mission, the F-22A is armed with up to six AMRAAMs and a pair of short-range AIM-9 Sidewinders carried in three internal weapons bays. There are also four optional external hardpoints that can carry additional weapons if required, but which are normally utilised for external fuel to aid long-range deployments.

In 2009 the Pentagon decided to terminate production of the Raptor at just 187 aircraft – plus eight pre-production jets – despite the US Air Force pushing for more, with a stated requirement for 381 F-22s at that time. Instead, resources were pushed into the F-35 Joint Strike Fighter, which offers some similar capabilities to the F-22 but lacks the same level of high-end air dominance. The final example of the Raptor was rolled out of Lockheed Martin's Marietta, Georgia, plant in December 2011.

While the Raptor currently still rules the roost in the US Air Force fighter community, the service is already well into planning for its replacement under the multi-faceted Next Generation Air Dominance (NGAD) programme, which is expected to provide both manned and unmanned platforms that will offer capabilities in excess of even the F-22.

A USAF F-22 Raptor participates in Operation Inherent Resolve, August 2017.

FIFTH-GENERATION MULTIROLE FIGHTERS

FIFTH-GENERATION MULTIROLE FIGHTERS

Lockheed Martin F-35 Lightning II

The result of the single most expensive programme in US Department of Defense history, the F-35 Joint Strike Fighter was intended to combine high-end capabilities with a relatively low price tag.

The F-35 was intended to replace the AV-8B, F-16 and F/A-18 within the US military, as well as multiple export customers. In the event, while the F-35's 'fifth-generation' capabilities are unquestioned, the spiralling cost of the programme may very well see orders trimmed back for the US armed forces and others.

The F-35 can trace its heritage back to the Joint Advanced Strike Technology (JAST) and Common Affordable Lightweight Fighter (CALF) projects, which were brought together in the mid-1990s before being named Joint Strike Fighter (JSF).

Multiple manufacturers drafted designs for the requirement, but it was Lockheed Martin and Boeing that were finally awarded contracts to produce two demonstrators each, the X-32 and X-35 respectively. Both companies was to build one conventional take-off and landing (CTOL) version and – far more ambitiously – one short take-off and vertical landing (STOVL) model.

In 2001 the Pentagon announced that Lockheed Martin's X-35 had won the JSF fly-off competition, and the company was then awarded an $18-billion contract for the System Demonstration and Development (SDD) phase of the JSF program. While the initial demonstrators had proved the basics of the CTOL and STOVL versions, the SDD phase added the third major model, the carrier variant, intended exclusively for carrier operations by the US Navy.

Flight-test aircraft

The SDD programme eventually yielded 12 flight-test aircraft comprising four CTOL F-35As, five STOVL F-35Bs and three CV F-35Cs, together with six static test airframes.

The first of the SDD aircraft, an F-35A, began final assembly in May

---

F-35A

Weight (maximum take-off): 31,751kg (70,000lb)
Dimensions: Length 15.7m (51ft 5in), Wingspan 11m (35ft), Height 4.4m (14ft 5in)
Powerplant: One Pratt & Whitney F135-PW-100 turbofan rated at 190kN (43,000lb) of thrust with afterburning
Maximum speed: Mach 1.6
Range: 2736km (1700 miles)
Ceiling: 15,240m (50,000ft)
Crew: 1
Armament: One 25mm (0.98in) GAU-22/A four-barrel rotary cannon, plus maximum weapon load of 8050kg (18,000lb) on four internal stations, plus six underwing stations

---

F-35A Lightning II
A core tenet of the F-35 Joint Strike Fighter programme is the ambition to replace significant numbers of existing fighters, mainly F-16s, with a growing number of export customers, providing commonality and bringing down costs. Among these customers is Denmark, whose first F-35A is show here.

FIFTH-GENERATION MULTIROLE FIGHTERS

U.S. Marines with Marine Fighter Attack Squadron 121 (VMFA-121), conduct the first ever hot load on the F-35B Lightning II at Marine Corps Air Station Yuma, Arizona, 2016.

2005 and the following year the JSF was named Lightning II. The first F-35A went on to complete its maiden flight on 15 December 2006.

All three JSF variants incorporate a high degree of stealth, intended to ensure the fighter could evade enemy detection and fly combat missions in contested airspace. As a result, it primarily carries its weapons internally, but external stores can be added when flying in more permissive environments.

Fundamental to the F-35's concept of operations is its advanced sensor fusion, in which data from various different sources is brought together and presented to the pilot as a single integrated picture. This is combined with comprehensive electronic warfare capabilities that can be used to locate and track enemy forces, as well as jam hostile radars, without requiring external pods. The primary sensors include an AN/APG-81 active electronically scanned array (AESA) radar and the Electro-Optical Targeting System (EOTS) that combines infrared search and track (IRST) data collection and (forward-looking infrared) FLIR pointing and scene-tracking capabilities. The pilot is also provided as standard with a helmet-mounted display (HMD), which takes the place of a conventional head-up display (HUD) projecting vital information and FLIR imagery in its true location, with night vision display capability all around the aircraft thanks to a 360° array of sensors that form the Electro-Optical Distributed Aperture System (EODAS). Using EODAS, the pilot has the ability to 'look through' the wing or cockpit floor, for example, to see what the cameras see.

15

FIFTH-GENERATION MULTIROLE FIGHTERS

F-35C Lightning II
The 'Argonauts' of Strike Fighter Squadron 147 (VFA-147) are responsible for introducing the F-35C carrier variant to US Navy service. The US Navy's lead frontline Lightning II unit took the F-35C to sea for the first time as part of Carrier Air Wing Two (CVW-2) aboard the USS *Carl Vinson* in 2021.

F-35B Lightning II
Marine Fighter Attack Squadron 211 (VMFA-211) 'Wake Island Avengers' is one of two operational F-35B squadrons assigned to Marine Aircraft Group 13, 3rd Marine Aircraft Wing, and received its first Lightning II in May 2016. The squadron was the first in the US to fly combat missions with Joint Strike Fighters, over Afghanistan in September 2018.

Touch-screen display

The F-35's cockpit is also equipped with a large-area touch-screen display, upon which the pilot can call up data on navigation, threat warnings, target designation and others as required. The wealth of information that the F-35 can gather means that combat commanders increasingly see the aircraft as an information and communications gateway, providing a comprehensive picture of the battlespace that can be shared with ground, sea and air assets.

The F-35 is powered by a single Pratt & Whitney F135 turbofan, the most powerful fighter engine in the world. In the F-35B STOVL version, the aircraft adds a Rolls-Royce LiftFan in the mid-fuselage. An F-35B DD aircraft engaged its STOVL propulsion system in flight for the first time in January 2010, before proving short take-offs, hovers and vertical landings using the system's swivelling exhaust nozzle, which vectors engine thrust together with underwing roll ducts that provide lateral stability.

The additional weight of the LiftFan means the F-35B's internal weapons carriage is reduced to pair of 454kg (1000lb) stores plus two AIM-120 Advanced Medium-Range Air-to-Air Missiles (AMRAAMs), compared to the two 907kg (2000lb) weapons and two AMRAAMs that can be carried internally by the F-35A and C versions.

The US Air Force was the first service to receive the JSF, accepting an initial F-35A for pilot and maintainer

F-35B
Weight (maximum take-off): 27,216kg (60,000lb)
Dimensions: Length 15.6m (51ft 2in), Wingspan 10.70m (35ft), Height 4.36m (14ft 3in)
Powerplant: One Pratt & Whitney F135-PW-100 turbofan rated at 190kN (43,000lb) of thrust with afterburning
Maximum speed: Mach 1.6
Range: 2736km (1700 miles)
Ceiling: 15,240m (50,000ft)
Crew: 1
Armament: One 25mm (0.98in) GAU-22/A four-barrel rotary cannon, plus two AAMs and two bombs on four internal stations, maximum load 6800kg (15,000lb)

Lockheed Martin F-35 Lightn

This Italian Air Force F-35A is operated by the 13° Gruppo, part of the 32° Stormo, based at Amendola. This aircraft has also spent time deployed to Luke Air Force Base in Arizona, where it was used by the multinational Joint Strike Fighter training unit, within the US Air Force's 62nd Fighter Squadron, part of the 56th Fighter Wing.

RADAR
The F-35 is provided with a Northrop Grumman AN/APG-81 radar, part of a much more comprehensive sensor suite. This solid-state active electronically scanned array (AESA) radar can be used in active and passive air-to-air and air-to-ground modes and also has significant electronic warfare and intelligence, surveillance and reconnaissance functions.

BOARDING LADDER
In common with the A-10 and the F-15, but in contrast to the F-16, the F-35 features a built-in boarding ladder, seen here extended for pilot ingress/egress. The ladder is telescopic, ensuring it takes up less space within the airframe.

POWERPLANT
The F-22 Raptor is powered by two Pratt & Whitney F119-PW-100 turbofan engines, featuring thrust vectoring, supercruise capability, and high thrust-to-weight ratio for unmatched speed, agility, and stealth performance.

THRUST VECTORING
Each engine has a two-dimensional thrust vectoring nozzle, operating either symmetrically for pitch control in manoeuvring flight and additional unstick and lift forces during take-off and landing, or asymmetrically for additional roll control. Although the F-22 can 'supercruise' (sustain supersonic flight without afterburner, afterburners are incorporated for high energy manoeuvring and Mach 2-plus dash speed

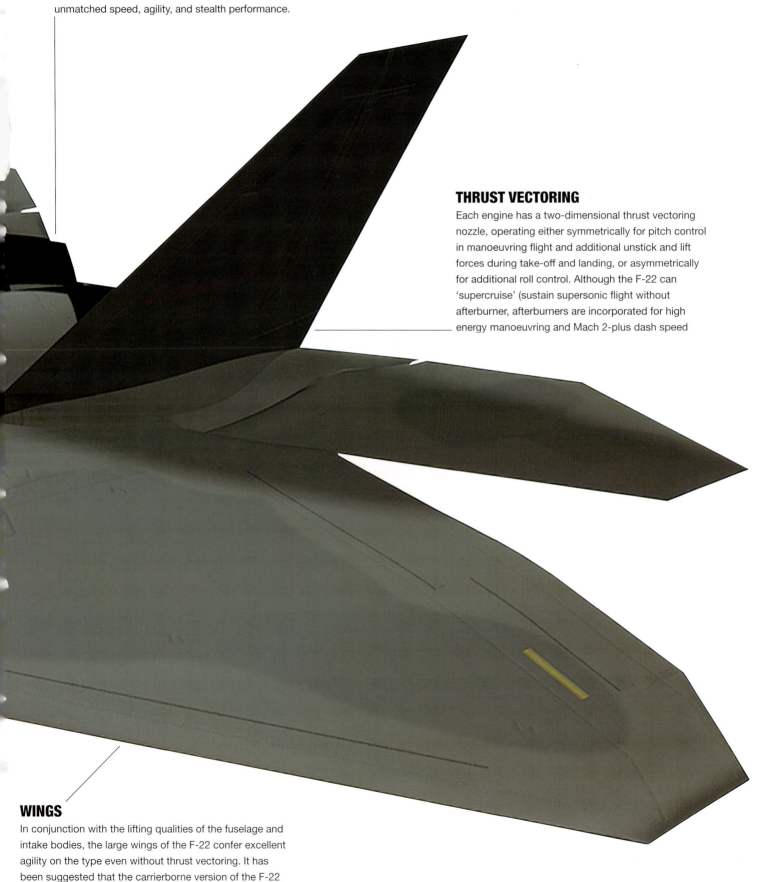

WINGS
In conjunction with the lifting qualities of the fuselage and intake bodies, the large wings of the F-22 confer excellent agility on the type even without thrust vectoring. It has been suggested that the carrierborne version of the F-22 for the US Navy would feature swing-wing technology.

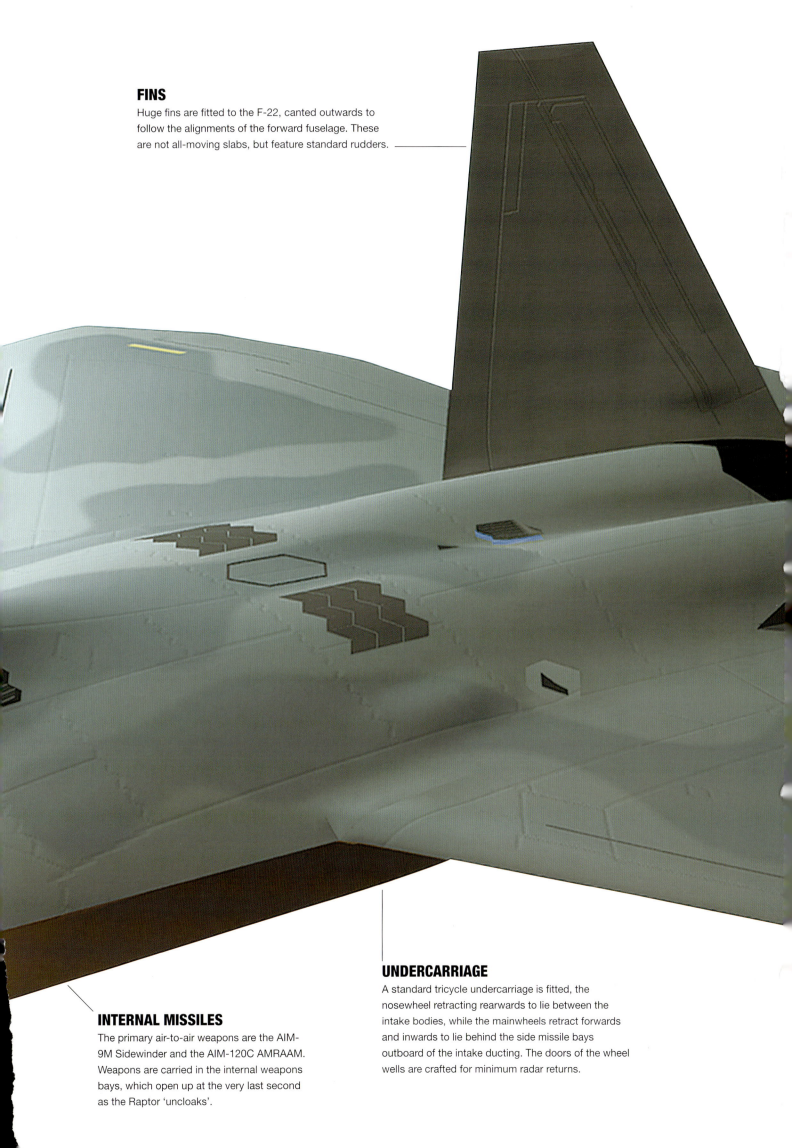

FINS
Huge fins are fitted to the F-22, canted outwards to follow the alignments of the forward fuselage. These are not all-moving slabs, but feature standard rudders.

INTERNAL MISSILES
The primary air-to-air weapons are the AIM-9M Sidewinder and the AIM-120C AMRAAM. Weapons are carried in the internal weapons bays, which open up at the very last second as the Raptor 'uncloaks'.

UNDERCARRIAGE
A standard tricycle undercarriage is fitted, the nosewheel retracting rearwards to lie between the intake bodies, while the mainwheels retract forwards and inwards to lie behind the side missile bays outboard of the intake ducting. The doors of the wheel wells are crafted for minimum radar returns.

ning II

INTERNAL GUN

The F-35A is fitted with a four-barrel 25mm (0.9in) Gatling-type cannon, designated the GAU-22/A, mounted internally in a space above the aircraft's left engine intake. The gun has a rate of fire of 3,300 rounds per minute and is fed from a 180-round magazine. To ensure the F-35A's stealth signature, the GAU-22/A is covered by a flush-mounted door, which opens when the gun is fired.

DISTRIBUTED APERTURE SYSTEM

The pilot's situational awareness is significantly enhanced by the F-35's AN/AAQ-37 Distributed Aperture System, or DAS, another Northrop Grumman product. The DAS consists of six electro-optical cameras located at various points around the aircraft. These collectively feed information into the mission systems, with critical data then presented in the pilot's helmet display.

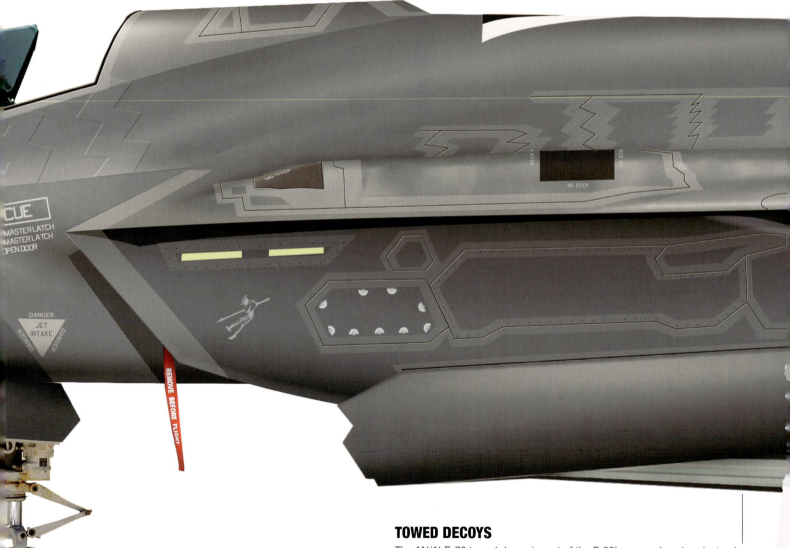

TOWED DECOYS

The AN/ALE-70 towed decoy is part of the F-35's comprehensive electronic warfare self-protection suite. The decoys are stowed in a small bay located on the right underside of the fuselage, aft of the weapons bay and infrared countermeasures doors. Four of these decoys can reportedly be carried, these being unreeled on a cable behind the aircraft, providing hostile air defence systems with a larger and more enticing target.

CONTROL SYSTEM

Combining low observables technology with a demanding operational requirement necessitated the use of artificial stability in the form of fly-by-wire controls. The central computer coordinates the actions of leading edge flaps, trailing edge flaps, ailerons, all-moving tailplanes, rudders and thrust nozzles to provide the desired control effect. Manoeuvrability is said to be phenomenal in all three planes, and high-G manoeuvres easy to sustain. High angle-of-attack flight is far more controllable than with the current generation of aircraft.

GUN

The F-22A fighter is armed with the M61A2 20mm Gatling gun system. The fixed-forward internal gun system provides maximum firing rate performance.

DATALINK

A Raptor pilot can receive information from other F-22s, allowing a radar-silent attack. A Raptor that is outside its missile envelope can thus track a target and covertly send target data to a closer Raptor to make the silent kill.

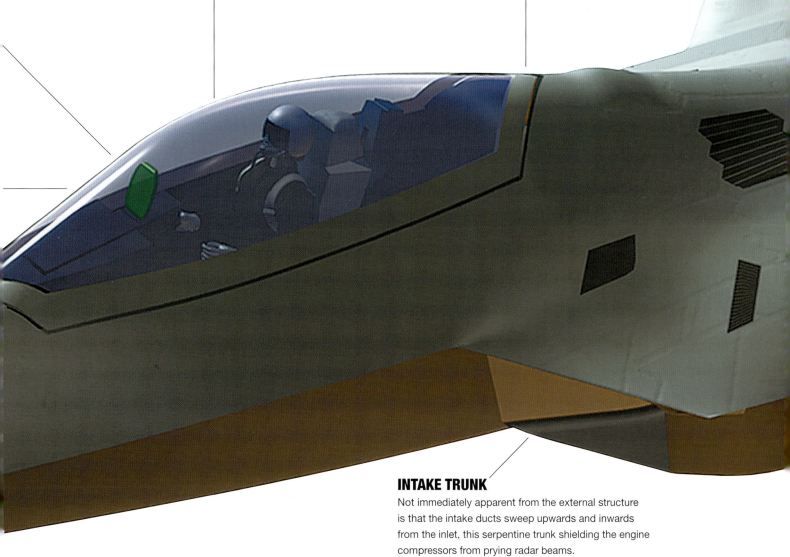

INTAKE TRUNK

Not immediately apparent from the external structure is that the intake ducts sweep upwards and inwards from the inlet, this serpentine trunk shielding the engine compressors from prying radar beams.

METEOR MISSILE

Apart from the United Kingdom, Italy is the only Lightning II operator to have chosen to arm its aircraft with the MBDA Meteor air-to-air missile (BVRAAM). The Meteor is among the most capable beyond-visual-range weapons currently available. The F-35A can carry four Meteors internally, preserving its stealth characteristics, or two Meteors as well as eight SPEAR precision-strike weapons.

NUCLEAR MISSION

As part of the NATO nuclear-sharing arrangement, the United States makes tactical nuclear weapons available to certain European air forces, including that of Italy. Eventually, the Italian F-35A will supersede the Tornado in the nuclear strike role, with the Joint Strike Fighter now cleared to carry the B61-12 freefall thermonuclear bomb.

Lockheed Martin F-22 Raptor

Widely regarded as the most potent air superiority fighter in service today, the F-22A Raptor is capable of both air-to-air and air-to-ground missions. The Raptor is described by its operator as representing 'an exponential leap in warfighting capabilities'. This revolutionary type has been designed to combine stealth, performance, agility and integrated avionics in a single airframe.

COMMUNICATIONS

The onboard communications suite features many jam-resistant and stealthy features.

RADAR

Giving first-look, first-launch, first-kill capability, the F-22's radar has long range and high resolution for the early detection of opposing fighters. It has a low passive detection signature, which allied to the aircraft's own low radar cross-section, allows the F-22 to approach very close to its quarry before being detected, thereby dramatically increasing the chance of a kill.

CANOPY

The F-22 features a beautifully crafted one-piece canopy that sits high on the fuselage. This high position gives superb all-round vision, a major consideration for air combat. The canopy is treated to not be reflective to radar energy.

FORWARD FUSELAGE

Characterized by its diamond cross-section, the forward fuselage has a distinct chined edge, which provides great stability for high angle of attack flight.

MIXED FLEET

Italy operates both the conventional take-off and landing (CTOL) F-35A variant, as seen here, and the short take-off and vertical landing (STOVL) F-35B model. The Italian Air Force and the Italian Navy are receiving 15 each of the F-35B, while the air force is set to receive a total of 60 F-35As.

F135 ENGINE

Each of the three main versions of the Joint Strike Fighter are powered by a different sub-variant of the Pratt & Whitney F135 turbofan. The land-based F-35A is fitted with the F135-PW-100, while the carrier-based F-35C uses the F135-PW-400, which differs in its use of corrosion-resistant materials to withstand the rigours of operations at sea. The STOVL-capable F-35B uses the F135-PW-600, with an articulating exhaust nozzle and other features necessary to connect it to the large lift fan in the forward fuselage.

FIFTH-GENERATION MULTIROLE FIGHTERS

training in July 2011, while the US Marine Corps received its first F-35B in the same month. In late November 2012, the Marine Corps established the first operational JSF base at Marine Corps Air Station Yuma, Arizona. The last US service to receive the Lightning II was the Navy, which accepted a first F-35C at Eglin Air Force Base, Florida, for pilot and maintainer training in June 2013.

The Marine Corps was the first of these services to declare Initial Operational Capability (IOC) for the JSF, which it did in July 2015, meaning that it considered the jet ready for combat operations, followed by the US Air Force's IOC milestone in August 2016. Since then, the US Air Force and Marine Corps have employed the Lightning II in combat, as have two export operators,

Israel and the United Kingdom. More recent milestones have included the US Navy's declaration of IOC, and the first deliveries to the US Air National Guard, both recorded in 2019.

Export orders

The US Air Force originally planned to buy 1763 F-35As, with the US Navy and Marine Corps taking a combined 680 aircraft. These figures are now likely to be reduced as these services weigh up the cost of operating the jets and ensuring that they are upgraded according to successive software standards that are required to ensure all the promised capabilities can be realised. On the other hand, the F-35 has swiftly accumulated export orders, spearheaded by the seven international programme partners – the United Kingdom, Italy, Netherlands, Australia, Norway, Denmark and Canada. In addition, there are half a dozen Foreign Military Sales customers in the process of procuring and operating the F-35 as of 2021 – Israel, Japan, South Korea, Poland, Belgium and Singapore, while Switzerland is the latest country to select the F-35 as its future fighter.

A USAF F-35 Lightning II flies over the U.S. Central Command area of responsibility, July 2020. The F-35 Lightning II is an agile, versatile, high-performance, multirole fighter that combines stealth, sensor fusion and unprecedented situational awareness.

FIFTH-GENERATION MULTIROLE FIGHTERS

Sukhoi Su-57

The latest air superiority fighter to enter service with the Russian Aerospace Forces, the Su-57 dates back to the mid-1980s when work began on potential successors to the then-new MiG-29 and Su-27.

After the Mikoyan MFI and Sukhoi Su-47 projects were abandoned, a new competition was launched in April 2001 to field the Future Air Complex of Tactical Aviation (or PAK FA in its Russian acronym). The Sukhoi T-50 was selected as the winner in 2002 and the company received a development contract to build the prototypes.

The T-50 design is optimised for manoeuvres at supersonic speed, reduced observability (as opposed to all-aspect stealth) and supercruise capability (supersonic cruise flight without afterburner). The aircraft is powered by a pair of AL-41F1 turbofans that are much-modernised versions of the AL-31F engine used in the Su-27 and Su-30 series of fighters. The pilot has a fire-control system that includes five separate, integrated active electronically scanned radar arrays plus electro-optical sensors. The radar also provides the identification friend or foe (IFF) and electronic countermeasures (ECM) functions. The aircraft is further protected by a comprehensive electronic warfare self-protection suite, including missile-approach warning sensors and, for the first time in a fighter, directional infrared countermeasures.

Weapons

Weapons are carried in two large tandem bays within the lower fuselage and two small auxiliary internal bays located in underwing fairings, but there are also underwing hardpoints for additional stores if reduced observability is no longer required. For its air-to-air mission, new missiles have been developed for the aircraft, including the infrared-guided R-74M2 for close-range combat and the active radar-guided R-77M for beyond-

Su-57
Weight (maximum take-off): 35,000kg (77,162lb)
Dimensions: Length 20.1m (66ft), Wingspan 14.1m (46ft 3in), Height 4.6m (15ft 1in)
Powerplant: Two Saturn AL-41F1 (izdeliye 117) thrust-vectoring turbofans each rated at 147.2kN (33,100lb) thrust with afterburning
Maximum speed: Mach 2.0
Range: 3500km (2175 miles)
Ceiling: 20,000m (65,617ft)
Crew: 1
Armament: One GSh-301 30mm (1.2in) cannon, plus disposable ordnance carried in two tandem weapons bays in the lower fuselage, typically up to four R-77M AAMs, Kh-58UShK or Kh-36 anti-radiation missiles, or Kh-38M or KAB-250 precision-guided munitions. Two R-74M2 AAMs carried in weapons bays in underwing fairings, plus option for external ordnance on four underwing pylons.

T-50-9

This is the ninth prototype Su-57, also known as T-50-9, and the eighth flyable prototype of the 'Felon'. It made its first flight on 24 April 2017 and wears a pixelated camouflage pattern, one of several different schemes applied to the Su-57.

FIFTH-GENERATION MULTIROLE FIGHTERS

Su-57
Although wearing the serial number 01, this aircraft is actually the second full production machine, having been renumbered following the crash of the first example on its delivery flight in December 2019. The aircraft serves with the 929th Chkalov State Flight-Test Centre and carries its insignia behind the cockpit.

visual-range engagements. The very long-range R-37M (AA-13 'Axehead') is also available. The aircraft is additionally fitted with a 30mm (1.2in) internal cannon.

Airframe problems
The initial prototype – T-50-1 – took to the air at the Komsomolsk-on-Amur factory airfield in the Russian Far East on 29 January 2010. By 2013, five prototypes had been completed but the airframe was revealing problems and design changes had to be made to strengthen it. The first of another batch of five prototypes, built according to the revised design, entered flight test in 2016. Testing continued and the aircraft was given its formal service designation Su-57 in 2017 – it also received the Western reporting name 'Felon'.

At one point, India was also involved in the programme with the aim of producing its own version, likely including a two-seat variant, but its withdrawal from the project had a knock-on effect for Russia. In 2015 Moscow decided that a smaller number of Su-57s would be procured alongside cheaper Su-30SM and Su-35 fighters.

The first pre-production Su-57 was completed in December 2019 but crashed the same month on its delivery flight. This left the second pre-production example to become the first to be handed over to the Russian Aerospace Forces, which occurred in December 2020. The initial operator is the 23rd Fighter Aviation Regiment at Dzyomgi. Ahead of the first production delivery in February 2018, two earlier Su-57s had been deployed to Syria for a two-day combat evaluation.

Ongoing development
As of early 2021, there are 76 Su-57 fighters on order for Russia while the Su-57E has been offered for export, so far without success. Should Russia place additional orders for the fighter, it will likely receive an updated version known as the Su-57M. Its most important development will be the introduction of an all-new increased-thrust engine. This powerplant, the izdeliye 30, began flight tests in December 2017.

FIFTH-GENERATION MULTIROLE FIGHTERS

Chengdu J-20

Currently the most advanced fighter operational with the Chinese People's Liberation Air Force (PLAAF), the Chengdu J-20 appeared to the surprise of most observers in late 2010.

The Chengdu J-20 made its maiden flight in January 2011 before entering service in late 2016 as the world's third operational stealth fighter (after the F-22 and F-35). In China the aircraft is known as the 'Mighty Dragon'.

Work on this advanced fighter project apparently began in China by the mid-1990s, attracting rival designs from Chengdu and Shenyang. It seems the successful proposal offered by Chengdu was more radical and today's J-20 combines a tailless delta planform with canard foreplanes, twin tails and sophisticated diverterless supersonic inlets (DSIs) to control airflow into the twin engines.

Stealth features

The initial powerplant was the Russian-supplied AL-31FN, similar to that used in the Chengdu J-10B/C. In later aircraft, these were replaced by a pair of indigenous WS-10C turbofans introduced around mid-2019 and fitted with characteristic serrated nozzles designed to reduce the aircraft's rear-hemisphere radar cross-section (RCS). Meanwhile, long-term plans call for the installation of a more powerful definitive engine, the WS-15.

Weapons

While the J-20 has underwing stores pylons, the primary armament is carried in internal weapons bays to preserve its stealth qualities. One large central bay can carry at least four medium/long-range air-to-air missiles (AAMs), while two smaller lateral bays behind the intakes can each carry a single PL-10 short-range AAM. Uniquely, the J-20 carries the PL-10s on retractable side missile launch rails, allowing the weapons' bay doors to be closed while the missile itself remains fully extended. No gun is installed but it's understood there is space to provide one in the future.

Little is known about the details of the J-20's mission avionics, but it is equipped with a Type 1475 active electronically scanned array (AESA) radar that is complemented by an infrared search and track sensor and internal electro-optical targeting and distributed aperture systems similar to those used by the F-35. The modern glass cockpit features large colour displays and the pilot controls the jet using a side-stick and throttle combination.

Successive prototypes introduced detail changes from late 2013 before the initial-production J-20As began to be handed over to the PLAAF's 176th Brigade at Dingxin in December 2016 for operational test and evaluation. The first frontline operational PLAAF unit to receive the J-20A is the 9th Brigade at Wuhu in the Eastern Theatre Command.

J-20

Weight (maximum take-off): 37,013kg (81,600lb)
Dimensions: Length 20.4m (66ft 10in), Wingspan 13.5m (44ft 4in), Height 4.45m (14ft 7in)
Powerplant: Two Saturn AL-31FN turbofans each rated at 145kN (33,000lb) thrust with afterburning
Maximum speed: Mach 2.0+
Range: 3400km (2113 miles)
Ceiling: 20,000m (65,617ft)
Crew: 1
Armament: Disposable ordnance carried in one large weapon bay in the lower fuselage, typically comprising up to four PL-15 AAMs, plus two PL-10 AAMs carried in lateral weapon bays behind the intakes. Optional additional ordnance on four underwing pylons.

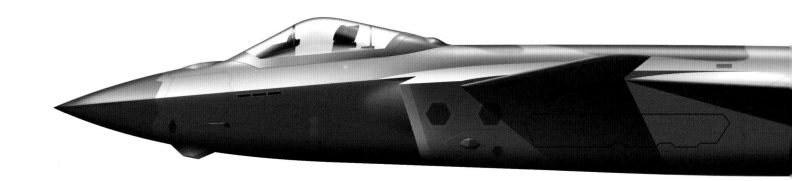

FIFTH-GENERATION MULTIROLE FIGHTERS

J-20A
J-20A serial number 78272 is among the aircraft assigned to the 176th Air Brigade at Dingxin, which also falls under the administrative control of the Flight Test and Training Base.

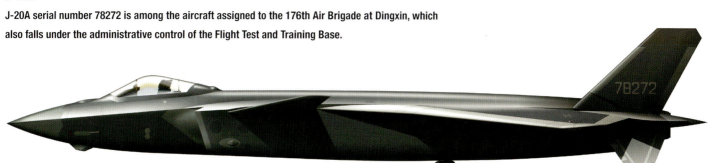

When it first appeared, some attributed a likely offensive role to the J-20, perhaps including anti-shipping strike, but there is so far no evidence that these kinds of missions are widely undertaken. Instead, the current J-20A in PLAAF service is dedicated to air defence missions, especially those of long duration, which can be further extended using aerial refuelling.

As a long-range air superiority aircraft, armed with beyond-visual-range missiles and perhaps dedicated 'AWACS-killer' missiles, the J-20 represents a significant challenge to regional rivals as well as US military assets in the Indo-Pacific region. Western sources credit the J-20 with a 1,200nm range, allowing to project power at huge distances from the Chinese mainland.

A Chengdu J-20 takes part in a flypast during the opening of Airshow China in Zhuhai, 2016.

J-20A
This J-20A serves with the People's Liberation Army Air Force's 172nd Air Brigade, part of the Flight Test and Training Base, which operates from Cangzhou. This is one of two test and training units operating the J-20.

4.5-GENERATION MULTIROLE FIGHTERS

Most of the leading air forces around the world today are spearheaded by fighters that fit broadly into the 4.5-generation category, also known as generation 4+ or 4++. Typically, these aircraft combine some of the features found in fifth-generation types, especially in regard to avionics and weapons options. However, in terms of stealth and overall performance, these designs still lag behind the fifth-generation types.

This chapter includes the following aircraft:

- Eurofighter Typhoon
- Saab JAS 39 Gripen
- Dassault Rafale
- Boeing F-15 Eagle
- Lockheed Martin F-16 Fighting Falcon
- Boeing F/A-18 Hornet and Super Hornet
- Mikoyan MiG-29K and MiG-35
- Sukhoi Su-30
- Sukhoi Su-33 and Shenyang J-15
- Sukhoi Su-35
- Chengdu J-10
- PAC JF-17 Thunder
- Shenyang J-11 & J-16
- Mitsubishi F-2
- HAL LCA Tejas

A Dassault Rafale taxis during an air display at the Aero India 2013 air show. Delivery of 36 Rafales from France to the Indian Air Force started in July 2020.

4.5-GENERATION MULTIROLE FIGHTERS
Eurofighter Typhoon

The pan-European Typhoon emerged out of a collaborative effort by Germany, Italy, Spain and the United Kingdom to produce a highly capable fighter aircraft that would be available for service from the late 1990s.

The Typhoon was intended to offer a considerable edge over the advanced variants of the MiG-29 and Su-27 then under development in the Soviet Union. In the event, the end of the Cold War saw the Eurofighter programme lose some momentum, but the aircraft is now well established in service, combat proven and has racked up some lucrative export orders, too.

EFA initiative
The origins of the Typhoon lie in the European Fighter Aircraft (EFA) initiative that explored the characteristics of the future platform, including deciding upon an unstable aerodynamic configuration with canard foreplanes, an active digital fly-by-wire control system, 'hands on throttle and stick' controls for the pilot and an advanced cockpit that included multifunction displays. In terms of structure, the aircraft would make extensive use of carbon-fibre composites and other advanced materials.

While the aircraft would be manufactured by a multinational consortium, the same would be the case for the newly developed engines, the EJ200 turbofans being the responsibility of the Eurojet concern.

Eurofighter EF2000
In 1988 a contract was signed covering design, construction and testing of eight prototypes, two of which would be completed as twin-seaters. Prototypes were built in all four partner countries, but the first to fly was the German-made DA.1, which took to the air for the first time at Manching, Germany, on 27 March 1994. By now, the EFA programme had been superseded by the Eurofighter EF2000, while the Typhoon name was formally adopted in 1998. Different prototypes were used to test various aspects of the aircraft's avionics and weapons systems and the first delivery of a Typhoon to an air force squadron followed in 2003, with the German Luftwaffe being the first recipient.

Eurofighter Typhoon
Weight (maximum take-off): 23,500kg (51,809lb)
Dimensions: Length 15.96m (52ft 4in), Wingspan 10.95m (35ft 11in), Height 5.28m (17ft 4in)
Powerplant: Two Eurojet EJ200 turbofan engines each rated at 90kN (20,000lb) thrust with afterburning
Maximum speed: Mach 2.0
Range: 3790km (2350 miles) ferry, with three fuel tanks
Ceiling: 19,812m (65,000ft)
Crew: 1 or 2
Armament: One 27mm (1.063in) Mauser BK-27 cannon, plus up to 9000kg (19,800lb) of disposable stores on eight underwing and five under-fuselage pylons

---

EF2000
This single-seat Luftwaffe Eurofighter wears a special colour scheme commemorating the NATO Tigers affiliation of Taktisches Luftwaffengeschwader 74 based at Neuburg in Bavaria. Unlike other customers, Germany does not use the Typhoon name for its Eurofighters.

4.5-GENERATION MULTIROLE FIGHTERS

Typhoon T3
The Royal Air Force's No 29 Squadron serves as the UK's Typhoon Operational Conversion Unit and therefore operates the majority of the two-seat aircraft. The unit operates from RAF Coningsby in Lincolnshire, one of five Typhoon squadrons at the base.

Typhoon FGR4
No IX (Bomber) Squadron gave up its Tornado GR4s at RAF Marham in March 2019 before being re-established at RAF Lossiemouth in Scotland as a Typhoon operator. This unit also has an aggressor role, providing high-level adversary training.

Successive new capabilities have been introduced to the Typhoon throughout its production run, while the partner nations have acquired the jets in three distinct production batches, or tranches. Initial deliveries were covered by Tranche 1, which provided 33 aircraft for Germany, 28 for Italy, 19 for Spain and 53 for the United Kingdom, plus 15 for Austria, the Typhoon's first export customer, some of which were former German jets.

Multirole capabilities
The next production batch was Tranche 2, which offered gradually enhanced multirole capabilities and covered the provision of 299 aircraft: 79 for Germany, 47 for Italy, 34 for Spain and 67 for the United Kingdom, plus 72 for Saudi Arabia, which became the next export operator, 24 of the Saudi aircraft having been diverted from the British order.

The next production block was Tranche 3, which was eventually split into two parts with only Tranche 3A actually being taken up. This provided 30 jets for Germany, 21 for Italy, 21 for Spain and 40 for the United Kingdom.

Since then, however, both Germany and Spain have decided to buy follow-on batches of Typhoons in further advanced configurations, known broadly as Tranche 4. Germany has declared its intention to buy 93 additional Tranche 4 jets. Of these, 38 will replace the Luftwaffe's early Tranche 1 aircraft, which have a limited capacity for upgrade, while the other 55 will partially replace the service's Tornado strike/reconnaissance aircraft.

Meanwhile, the Spanish government plans to replace up to 20 of its oldest F/A-18 Hornets with a similar number of Typhoons equipped to the latest standard that includes the Captor-E active electronically scanned array (AESA) radar. The same radar is now being retrofitted in most

4.5-GENERATION MULTIROLE FIGHTERS

of the Tranche 2 and 3 jets used by the partner nations and is offered as standard on new export deliveries.

RAF enhancements

Introduced primarily in an air defence role, the Typhoon has gradually embraced air-to-ground missions too, with this effort led by the United Kingdom's Royal Air Force primarily through successive software enhancements.

In this way, the RAF's Tranche 1 jets were the first to add a limited air-to-ground capability, these jets adding the Litening targeting pod and human-machine interface improvements, plus the Link 16 Multifunctional Information Distribution System (MIDS). In this form, the aircraft was able to make its combat debut over Libya in 2011.

A full multirole standard became available with the aforementioned Tranche 2, these aircraft adding more air-to-ground capabilities under the so-called Phase 1 Enhancement (P1E). This includes the Litening III pod, Paveway IV guided bomb for the RAF and the GBU-48 Enhanced Paveway II for other nations. In its definitive P1E form, the Typhoon is able to perform 'swing-role' missions, simultaneously operating in air-to-air and air-to-ground roles.

In order to replace the RAF Tornado GR4, the United Kingdom has since introduced the P2E updates, which include integration of the Storm Shadow cruise missile, Brimstone precision ground-attack weapon, Meteor beyond-visual-range air-to-air missile plus the AESA radar.

Middle East orders

In the meantime, new customers have selected the Typhoon encouraged by its progress as a true multirole fighter. Saudi Arabia followed up its initial order with another batch of 48 aircraft for a total of 72, all of which have been assembled in the United Kingdom by BAE Systems. Oman became the next to acquire the Typhoon, receiving 12 examples that were ordered in 2012. Two other Middle Eastern nations have also placed orders for Typhoons, with Kuwait and Qatar scheduled to receive 28 and 24 aircraft respectively.

A Royal Air Force Eurofighter Typhoon from No. 3 (F) Squadron fires an MBDA ASRAAM missile. The missile fired was against the flare pack towed by a Mirach target drone at the Aberporth range in Cardigan Bay, Wales.

4.5-GENERATION MULTIROLE FIGHTERS

Typhoon

Saudi Arabia ordered a total of 72 Typhoons, and these serve with three squadrons: 3, 10 and 80. This single-seat example is on the strength of 10 Squadron based at Taif/King Fahd Air Base. Weapons options are similar to the UK jets, including the AMRAAM and ASRAAM missiles shown on this jet.

Saab JAS 39 Gripen

In the early 1980s, Sweden began development of the JAS 39 Gripen as its new fighter aircraft to replace the Draken and Viggen in Swedish Air Force service and to take on fighter, attack and reconnaissance roles, as emphasised by its JAS (Jakt, Attack, Spaning) designation.

Compared to other fighters of its generation, the single-engine Gripen is notably compact, thanks to a software-driven design that exploits miniaturisation of computer systems. The jet's dimensions were also determined by the requirement to drive down overall programme costs as well as the need to operate from austere air bases, including from highways, with limited support infrastructure. The aircraft's configuration is also tailored to boost short-field performance, with all-moving canard foreplanes that can also serve as braking surfaces, and a full-authority fly-by-wire flight control system. The aircraft is powered by a General Electric F404 turbofan, built locally by Volvo Flygmotor as the RM12.

The initial Swedish Air Force requirement was for 280 aircraft, but this was scaled back to 204 (plus five prototypes) after the end of the Cold War.

After the first prototype Gripen took to the air on 9 December 1988,

JAS 39C Gripen

The C-model Gripen entered service with the Flygvapnet, or Swedish Air Force, in 2004. The last of 75 single-seat, new-build JAS 39Cs had been handed over to the service by March 2015 and there have been two attrition losses as of 2021. The air arm also received 26 two-seat JAS 39D variants.

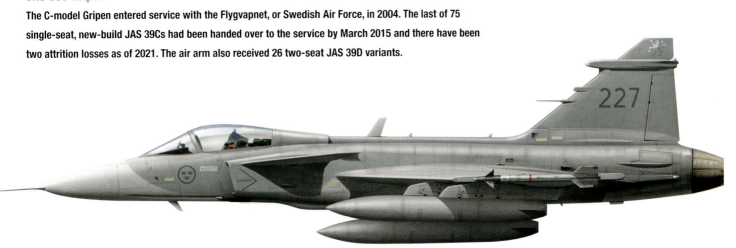

4.5-GENERATION MULTIROLE FIGHTERS

JAS 39C Gripen

The Gripen is the spearhead of the Hungarian Air Force, this example wearing a special colour scheme that was applied for participation in the 2016 NATO Tiger Meet. The Hungarian Gripen fleet – 12 single-seaters and a pair of two-seaters – was delivered between 2006 and 2007 under a 10-year leasing agreement that has since been extended until 2026.

the Swedish Air Force took delivery of three tranches of jets – Batch 1 comprising 29 single-seat JAS 39As and a single twin-seat JAS 39B; Batch 2 comprising 76 JAS 39As, 14 JAS 39Bs and 20 single-seat JAS 39Cs; and Batch 3 comprising 50 JAS 39Cs and 14 twin-seat JAS 39Ds.

Export sales

Of these 204 aircraft, 14 were diverted to the Czech Republic, while 16 airframes were used in the remanufacture of 14 Gripens for Hungary. Further exports were secured to South Africa and Thailand, which received new-build JAS 39C/Ds, acquiring 26 and 12 aircraft, respectively.

As well as being fully compatible with NATO standards, the primary difference between the first-generation JAS 39A/B and the second-generation JAS 39C/D is the latter's more advanced avionics, including a large-screen all-colour cockpit, advanced datalink plus additional radar and electronic warfare modes. The JAS 39C/D is also compatible with new weapons and adds an air-to-air refuelling probe.

With the upgrade to C/D standard complete, Saab next began work on a third-generation Gripen, with the vastly more capable Gripen E/F, which was developed under the Gripen Next Generation, or Gripen NG, programme. The resulting JAS 39E/F looks little different from the outside but boasts a new General Electric F414-GE-39E engine for improved performance as well as the ability to carry additional fuel and weapons, including on two new fuselage stations. The new fighter is also equipped with a Selex ES-05 Raven active electronically scanned array (AESA) radar and a Skyward-G infrared search and track system, and can carry the Litening laser designator pod and RecceLite reconnaissance pod. A datalink has always been part of the Gripen operating philosophy, and the Gripen E/F adds a jam-resistant 'fighter link,' together with new electronic warfare and a reduced radar cross-section to improve survivability. Other self-defence measures include missile approach warning sensors linked to automatic chaff/flare launchers.

Brazilian production

While Sweden is the primary customer of the Gripen E/F with 60 examples on order, the fighter also emerged victorious from Brazil's long-running fighter competition. Brazil will initially acquire 36 aircraft, with a portion of

---

JAS 39C

Weight (maximum take-off): 14,000kg (30,865lb)
Dimensions: Length 14.8m (49ft), Wingspan 8.4m (27ft 7in), Height 4.5m (14ft 9in)
Powerplant: One Volvo RM12 turbofan engine rated at 80.5kN (18,100lb) thrust with afterburning
Maximum speed: Mach 2
Range: 3200km (2000 miles), ferry
Ceiling: 15,240m (50,000ft)
Crew: 1
Armament: One 27mm (1.063in) Mauser BK-27 cannon, plus up to 5300kg (11,700lb) of disposable stores on eight hardpoints

---

these to be built locally. Brazil is also in charge of developing the two-seat Gripen F, with Sweden so far only committing to the single-seat Gripen E version.

4.5-GENERATION MULTIROLE FIGHTERS

Dassault Rafale

Dassault's most advanced frontline fighter, the Rafale originally emerged in the early 1980s under the ACX experimental combat aircraft programme.

Rafale M
The Aéronautique Navale, or French Fleet Air Arm, was the first operator to put the Rafale into frontline service, initially only in an air-to-air capacity, beginning in 2000. This Rafale M is assigned to Flottille 12F, one of three French Navy squadrons, all of which are land-based at Landivisiau and which deploy aboard the aircraft carrier *Charles de Gaulle*.

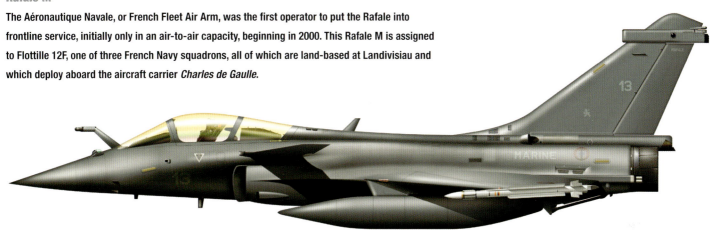

Once France had withdrawn from the European Fighter Aircraft initiative (that later produced the Eurofighter Typhoon), the manufacturer focused on developing the Rafale for the French military. A first Rafale A demonstrator aircraft took to the air on 4 July 1986. Initially powered by US-supplied General Electric F404 turbofan engines, the Rafale A was used to prove the fly-by-wire flight control system and aerodynamic configuration, as well as performing the type's first touch-and-go deck landings on an aircraft carrier.

Omni-role fighter

Described by the manufacturer as an omni-role fighter, the aircraft was designed from the outset to undertake a wide range of combat missions, including in the course of a single sorties, which it now does on behalf of the French Air Force and French Navy, as well as an increasing number of export operators.

Using a modular design philosophy, the Rafale has added successive new technologies and capabilities since its introduction to service and has yielded four distinct production tranches. The first of these was the Rafale F1 that offered air defence capabilities only, to replace the veteran F-8 Crusader with the French Navy. The first of these aircraft were delivered to the French Navy at Landivisiau Airbase, Brittany, in December 2000.

The next step was the Rafale F2, which provided a degree of precision ground-attack capability with the SCALP conventionally armed cruise missile, as well as different laser-guided bombs, and which was delivered to the French Air Force and Navy. The initial operator was the French Air Force, which began to accept F2 jets in December 2004.

The Rafale F3 was the first of the 'full-spectrum' jets, able to fly missions including reconnaissance, anti-shipping strike and nuclear deterrence. Again, examples of these went to both air arms.

The first 120 Rafales from these three production tranches were delivered with a passive electronically scanned array

Rafale M
Weight (maximum take-off): 24,500kg (54,013lb)
Dimensions: Length 15.27m (50ft 1in), Wingspan 10.9m (35ft 9in), Height 5.34m (17ft 6in)
Powerplant: Two Snecma M88-2 turbofans each rated at 75kN (17,000lb) thrust with afterburning
Maximum speed: Mach 1.8
Range: 3700km (2300 miles), ferry, with three drop tanks
Ceiling: 15,835m (51,952ft)
Crew: 1
Armament: One 30mm (1.2in) GIAT 30M791 cannon, plus up to 9500kg (20,900lb) of disposable stores on 14 hardpoints

(PESA) RBE2 radar, but in its definitive configuration the Rafale replaces this with a new active electronically scanned array (AESA) version of the same radar that is also being retrofitted to earlier jets.

Future Combat Air System
Work is now underway on the next F4 standard, which makes improvements to the sensors and self-defence suite, in particular, while a proposed F5 is expected to pave the way until the

4.5-GENERATION MULTIROLE FIGHTERS

Dassault Rafale Prototype
Rafale B01 was the two-seat prototype, which completed its initial flight in April 1993. B01 was the first Rafale to fly with the RBE2 multi-mode radar, housed within a recontoured nose.

Canard configuration
The close-coupled canard/delta wing configuration ensures the Rafale remains agile even at high angles of attack.

Refuelling probe
The refuelling probe is fixed in order to avoid any deployment or retraction problem and is a permanent fixture.

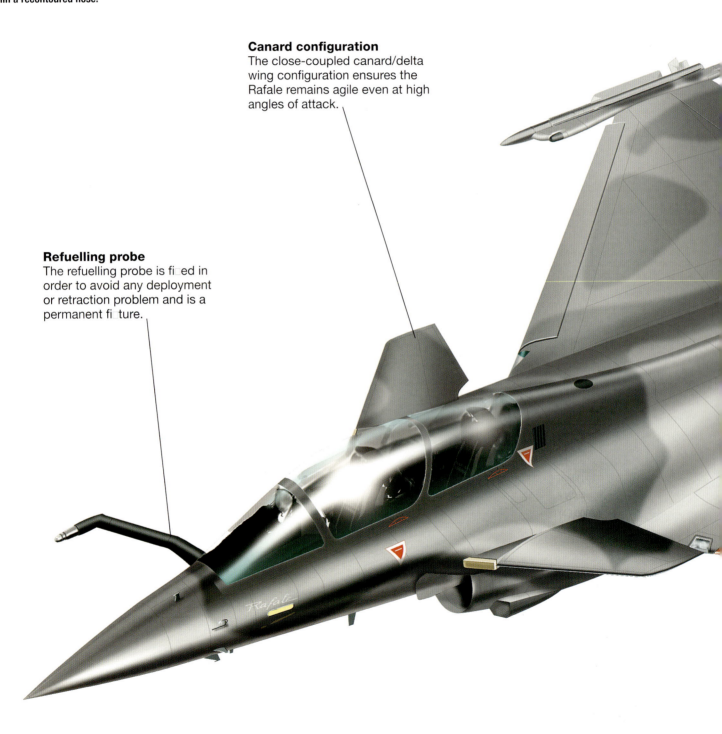

4.5-GENERATION MULTIROLE FIGHTERS

Engines
The M88-2 uses advanced technologies including integrally bladed compressor disks ('blisks'), and a low-pollution combustor with smoke-free emissions.

Stealth technology
Airframe radar cross-section is minimized by using appropriate materials and mould line, including serrated edges to the trailing edge of the wings and canards.

4.5-GENERATION MULTIROLE FIGHTERS

Rafale is finally to be replaced by a new-generation fighter under the Future Combat Air System programme. In the meantime, earlier Rafales have been successively upgraded to the F2 and then the F3 standard.

Currently, Rafale orders stand at 180 aircraft for the French Air Force divided between twin-seat Rafale B and single-seat Rafale C variants for the air force, and carrier-capable Rafale M single-seaters for the navy, which operates the jets from the aircraft carrier *Charles de Gaulle*.

The Rafale is powered by a pair of Snecma M88-2 turbofans specifically designed for the aircraft and intended to offer considerable thrust within a relatively small volume.

In terms of mission avionics, the Rafale is based around a multi-sensor suite in which data is fused together to provide a high level of situational awareness. As well as the Thales RBE2 multi-mode radar, the Rafale is fitted with the Front Sector Optronics (FSO) system mounted just ahead of the windscreen that combines an infrared search and track system with a TV sensor and laser rangefinder.

The aircraft possesses a comprehensive internal electronic warfare suite known as Spectra, which can identify threats and then use active electronic scanning arrays to jam hostile emitters. The Spectra also includes laser warning receivers.

In the cockpit, the pilot is provided with an ejection seat reclined at 29 degrees, a side-stick controller, a wide-angle head-up display, a central tactical colour display and two lateral colour touchscreens.

Targeting technology

For targeting, the Rafale was initially provided with the Damocles pod, which can also be used for intelligence-gathering, but the new-generation TALIOS (Targeting Long-range Identification Optronic System) pod is now also available. For reconnaissance missions, the Pod Reco NG can be carried on the centreline station. This features a dual-band infrared/visible sensor and can share data with other platforms in real time. Along with other improvements, the Rafale has successively added new weapons to its arsenal, with a typical air-to-air load-out comprising up to eight Mica air-to-air missiles (AAMs), which are available with either infrared or active radar seekers. From the F3R standard onwards, the Mica is complemented by the ramjet-powered Meteor beyond-visual-range AAM.

For air-to-ground missions, a wide range of conventional weapons are available, including the SCALP stealthy cruise missile, Exocet anti-ship missile, the US-made Paveway series of guided bombs and the French Armement Air-Sol Modulaire (AASM, or modular air-to-surface armament), which is a powered guided bomb available with a variety of guidance options. For the nuclear deterrence mission, the Rafale can be armed with a single ASMP-A supersonic cruise missile.

French Rafales have seen extensive combat in Afghanistan, Iraq, Libya, Mali and Syria, while export orders have been placed by Egypt, Greece, India and Qatar.

Rafale EQ
Qatar's Rafale order was announced in April 2015, with an initial batch of 24 aircraft for the Qatar Emiri Air Force (QEAF), split between 18 single-seat Rafale EQ and six twin-seat Rafale DQ aircraft. In 2017, Qatar exercised an option to buy 12 more Rafales, which will bring the QEAF total to 36 aircraft.

4.5-GENERATION MULTIROLE FIGHTERS

A French Rafale jet fighter flies a mission over Libya following a UN Security Council resolution, its underwing weapons storage and fuel tanks clearly displayed.

4.5-GENERATION MULTIROLE FIGHTERS

Boeing F-15 Eagle

The F-15 Eagle remains in production today, and despite the introduction of the fifth-generation F-22 and F-35 this is a testament to the excellence of the original design, the roots of which can be traced all the way back to the mid-1960s.

Without a competitive fly-off against any rival designs, the then McDonnell Douglas (today's F-15 is now a Boeing product) was requested to complete a series of YF-15A pre-production aircraft. The first example took to the air on 27 July 1972. Just over two years later, the first single-seat F-15A entered service with the US Air Force's 58th Tactical Training Wing at Luke AFB, Arizona.

The initial F-15A and two-seat F-15B were soon followed by the improved F-15C/D models that entered production from 1979 and became the major production versions, with 483 F-15Cs and 92 F-15Ds manufactured until 1985. In recent years, the US Air Force F-15C/D fleet has received 'Golden Eagle' upgrades including AN/APG-63(V)3 active electronically scanned array (AESA) radars.

The first export order for the Eagle came from Israel, which acquired F-15A/B models from 1976 followed by several batches of F-15C/Ds. Israeli F-15s were the first to see combat service and the type quickly gained a reputation as the preeminent air superiority fighter of its generation, Israeli jets scoring the Eagle's first aerial kills against Syrian MiG-21s in June 1979.

Operation Desert Storm
The US Air Force F-15 had its combat debut during Operation Desert Storm in 1991, when the type was credited with 36 victories against Iraqi aircraft. Also involved in Desert Storm were the F-15C/Ds of the Royal Saudi Air Force, which had in fact scored their first arial kills against Iranian F-4s in 1984. The other export operator of the original 'fighter' Eagle is Japan, which evaluated the type in the mid-1970s and then chose it to replace its F-104J Starfighter fleet. While the first two

F-15C Eagle
Weight (maximum take-off): 20,185kg (44,500lb)
Dimensions: Length 19.46m (63ft 9.6in), Wingspan 13.06m (42ft 10in), Height 5.64m (18ft 6in)
Powerplant: Two Pratt & Whitney F100-PW-220 turbofans each rated at 105.7kN (23,770lb) thrust with afterburning
Maximum speed: Mach 2.5
Range: 3900km (2400 miles), ferry, with conformal fuel tanks and three external fuel tanks
Ceiling: 18,000m (59,000ft)
Crew: 2
Armament: One 20mm (0.787in) M61A1 Vulcan six-barrel rotary cannon, plus maximum weapon load of 10,400kg (23,000lb) on four wing pylons and fuselage pylons, plus bomb racks on CFTs

F-15C Eagle
This single-seat F-15C serves with the Oregon Air National Guard's 142nd Fighter Wing, whose 123rd Fighter Squadron 'Redhawks' is located at Portland Air National Guard Base, Oregon, and has a total of 21 F-15C/Ds in its inventory. This squadron has been earmarked as the first operational unit to receive the new F-15EX, planned for 2023.

4.5-GENERATION MULTIROLE FIGHTERS

Two F-15E Strike Eagles from the 90th Fighter Squadron, which was based at Elmendorf Air Force Base, Alaska, fire a pair of AIM-7M Sparrow air-to-air missiles during a training mission over the Gulf of Mexico.

F-15Js (equivalent to the F-15C) and 12 two-seat F-15DJs were built in the US, the next eight were assembled under license by Mitsubishi, the first of these making its maiden flight in 1981. Ultimately, Mitsubishi built 163 F-15Js and 36 two-seat F-15DJs in total.

Today's in-production Eagles are derivatives of the F-15E Strike Eagle, which was intended to meet a US Air Force requirement that had begun to emerge in the late 1970s, calling for an all-weather fighter-bomber to supersede the F-111 and other types.

Strike Eagle

As F-15C/D production wound down, McDonnell Douglas switched to the F-15E, a two-seat variant that added conformal fuel tanks (CFTs), which provided not only a significant increase in range, but multiple attachment points for external weapons and stores. The Strike Eagle also incorporated a more advanced radar, the AN/APG-70 adding a high-resolution mapping capability to the existing air-to-air functions of the original AN/APG-63.

For accurate delivery of weapons day and night in all weathers, the F-15E was equipped with the LANTIRN (Low-Altitude Navigation and Targeting Infra-Red System for Night) system, which includes a terrain avoidance/terrain-following radar and forward-looking infrared (FLIR) sensors. Later modernisation added the AN/APG-63(V)4 AESA radar, Joint Helmet Mounted Cueing System (JHMCS) and AIM-9X missiles.

While the US Air Force received 236 Strike Eagles, the aircraft formed the basis of a number of advanced derivatives for export.

Having first tried to procure a single-seat F-15F fighter-bomber version, Saudi Arabia's Strike Eagle equivalent finally emerged as the two-seat F-15S, which is almost identical

4.5-GENERATION MULTIROLE FIGHTERS

F-15E Strike Eagle

The only US Air Force Eagles based permanently outside of the United States are assigned to the 48th Fighter Wing at RAF Lakenheath in England. Its squadrons comprise one of F-15C/Ds and two of F-15Es. An example of the latter is serial 98-0133, operated by the 492nd Fighter Squadron 'Bolars', which apply a blue tail flash to their jets.

F-15E Strike Eagle
Weight (maximum take-off): 36,741kg (81,000lb)
Dimensions: Length 19.46m (63ft 9.6in), Wingspan 13.045m (42ft 9.6in), Height 5.64m (18ft 6in)
Powerplant: Two Pratt & Whitney F100-PW-220 turbofans each rated at 105.7kN (23,770lb) thrust with afterburning
Maximum speed: Mach 2.5
Range: 3900km (2400 miles), ferry, with conformal fuel tanks and three external fuel tanks
Ceiling: 18,000m (59,000ft)
Crew: 2
Armament: One 20mm (0.787in) M61A1 Vulcan six-barrel rotary cannon, plus maximum weapon load of 10,400kg (23,000lb) on four wing pylons and fuselage pylons, plus bomb racks on CFTs

---

Israel's F-15I, known locally as Ra'am ('Thunder') is broadly similar to the US Air Force F-15E but adds local avionics, electronic warfare equipment, the Display and Sight Helmet (DASH) and weapons. These long-range strike aircraft are today among the most important in the Israeli Air Force fleet.

Asia-Pacific operators

Two Asia-Pacific operators have also acquired advanced Strike Eagles, with South Korea acquiring the F-15K Slam Eagle and Singapore buying the F-15SG version. The Korean F-15K is optimised for long-range precision strike and its armoury includes weapons such as AGM-84K SLAM-ER, AGM-84H Harpoon Block II and the Taurus KEPD 350 cruise missile.

Boeing unveiled a new Eagle configuration in 2009, with the F-15SE Silent Eagle that featured various stealth design modifications including outwards-canted vertical fins and conformal weapons bays. While the F-15SE didn't win any export orders, Boeing instead pressed ahead with more advanced variants that retained the same basic Strike Eagle airframe but without the low-observable features. Derived from to the US Air Force F-15E. Its export to Saudi Arabia was approved following the 1991 Gulf War. These aircraft are now being remanufactured to the F-15SA (Saudi Advanced) standard, which the country has also procured in the form of new-build airframes.

The F-15SA boasts a new fly-by-wire flight-control system that permits additional weapons carriage on new outer-wing hardpoints and the jet also harnesses the capabilities of the APG-63(V)3 AESA radar, plus a Digital Electronic Warfare System (DEWS) and infrared search and track (IRST) sensor.

4.5-GENERATION MULTIROLE FIGHTERS

A USAF F-15E Strike Eagle from 3 36th Expeditionary Fighter Squadron soars over the mountains of Afghanistan in support of Operation Mountain Lion. Its air intakes and underwing weapons stores can be clearly seen.

F-15EX Advanced Eagle

Originally known as the Advanced Eagle, and now officially named Eagle II, this is the first example of the F-15EX to be handed over to the US Air Force. Boeing formally delivered the first jet at its facility in St. Louis, Missouri, on 10 March 2021. The jet wears the tail codes of Eglin Air Force Base, Florida, from where it's flown by the 40th Flight Test Squadron.

4.5-GENERATION MULTIROLE FIGHTERS

the Saudi F-15SA, the F-15QA for Qatar is the latest and most capable export Eagle. This aircraft features Boeing's new Advanced Cockpit System with Large Area Displays and an AN/APG-82(V)1 AESA radar among other improvements. Under a $6.2 billion contract, Boeing is building 36 F-15QAs for Qatar with plans for the first examples to be delivered in 2021.

Eagle II

The F-15QA provided the US Air Force with an unlikely opportunity to buy more F-15s, decades after the last examples had been built for service. Officially known as the Eagle II, the F-15EX is based on the F-15QA and deliveries to the US Air Force began in 2021. One significant difference compared to the F-15QA is the F-15EX's Eagle Passive Active Warning Survivability System (EPAWSS) that provided enhanced self-protection capabilities.

In a significant change from previous procurement plans, the US Air Force is now buying F-15EX jets alongside the F-35A, with plans calling for a total of 144 F-15EXs to be added to its fleet, replacing F-15Cs – which have an average age of around 37 years – and filling in for delays in the F-35 programme. Initially, the F-15EX will replace the F-15Cs operated by the Florida and Oregon Air National Guards.

F-15S Strike Eagle
This F-15S is one of the 72 examples that were manufactured for the Royal Saudi Air Force (RSAF). In 2010, plans were announced that the 68 surviving aircraft would be upgraded to the improved F-15SA standard. In addition, the Kingdom has procured another 84 new-build F-15SA jets. Deliveries of rebuilt F-15SAs began in December 2016.

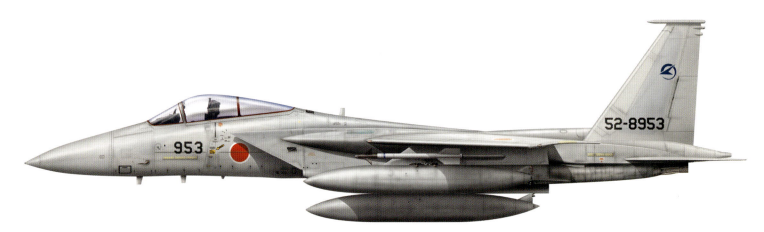

F-15J
The Eagle entered Japan Air Self-Defense Force (JASDF) in 1981 and remains the country's most important air defence fighter. This example wears the insignia of the Gifu-based Air Development and Test Command on its tailfins. Japan plans to update 98 surviving F-15Js to an advanced Japanese Super Interceptor (JSI) configuration.

4.5-GENERATION MULTIROLE FIGHTERS

Lockheed Martin F-16 Fighting Falcon

Undoubtedly the most successful Western fighter of its generation, the F-16 has accumulated more than 4500 orders to date and remains one of the most capable warplanes in frontline service.

Developed by General Dynamics as a lightweight fighter, today's F-16 is altogether more capable than first envisaged and excels as an all-weather fighter-bomber with precision attack capabilities. From the outset, however, the manufacturer decided to stress agility and performance and the F-16 was one of the first fighters to incorporate fly-by-wire controls, a sidestick control column, large bubble canopy and a reclined ejection seat.

Known colloquially, and almost universally as the 'Viper', the F-16 began life with a 1972 US Air Force request for proposals for a Lightweight Fighter (LWF), which would be optimised for daytime air-to-air combat and was initially intended to be armed only with a single 20mm (0.787in) M61A1 rotary cannon and short-range infrared-homing AIM-9

Sidewinder missiles, with even the radar being omitted.

European customers

The first prototype YF-16 made an unplanned first flight on 20 January 1974 before being selected as the winner of the US Air Force's Air Combat Fighter (ACF) project in 1975. Before long, the pure day-fighter requirement had been expanded to add air-to-ground functions and, in this form, the jet was soon selected by Belgium, Denmark, Norway and the Netherlands in the so-called 'Sale of the Century.'

In January 1979, the US Air Force's 388th Tactical Fighter Wing at Hill Air Force, Utah, became the first unit to begin converting to the single-seat F-16A, while Belgium became the first European recipient the same month

---

Block 50/52 F-16C

Weight (maximum take-off): 19,187kg (42,300lb)

Dimensions: Length 15.06m (49ft 5in), Wingspan 9.96m (32ft 8in), Height 4.9m (16ft)

Powerplant: (Block 50) one General Electric F110-GE-129 turbofan rated at 131kN (29,500lb) thrust with afterburning; (Block 52) one Pratt & Whitney F100-PW-229 turbofan rated at 131.5kN (29,560lb) with afterburning

Maximum speed: Mach 2.05

Range: 4217km (2620 miles), ferry with drop tanks

Ceiling: 18,288m (60,000ft)

Crew: 1

Armament: One 20mm (0.787in) M61A1 six-barrel rotary cannon, plus up to 7700kg (17,000lb) of disposable stores carried on six underwing, two wingtip and one centreline hardpoint

---

F-16C Fighting Falcon

This flamboyantly marked Block 42 F-16C wears the colours of the 125th Fighter Squadron, a unit of the Oklahoma Air National Guard that is assigned to the 138th Fighter Wing located at Tulsa Air National Guard Base, Oklahoma. Since the early 1990s the unit has made frequent combat deployments to the Middle East, taking part in Operations Northern Watch, Southern Watch, Iraqi Freedom and New Dawn.

4.5-GENERATION MULTIROLE FIGHTERS

when it received its first two-seat F-16B model.

The initial-production F-16A/B have since been retired by the US Air Force and upgraded by many of the original customers, while the production output switched to the improved F-16C/D. These aircraft are further subdivided into production blocks that have also introduced successive improvements.

From the Block 30/32 onwards, customers could choose between two different engines, blocks ending with a 0 being powered by the General Electric F110, while blocks ending with a 2 featured the Pratt & Whitney F100.

Today's F-16C/D is a far cry from the original LWF concept, equipped with beyond-visual-range air combat capability, multi-mode radar and AIM-120 AMRAAM missiles. As well as air-to-air missions, the F-16 is also widely used in air-to-ground combat, using advanced targeting pods to confer a night/all-weather attack ability, while optional conformal fuel tanks provide a considerable range increase. In the cockpit, the modern 'Viper' is all-digital with large, colour multifunction displays, while the pilot is provided

with the Joint Helmet Mounted Cueing System (JHMCS).

US Air Force upgrades

The most advanced versions in US Air Force service are the Block 50+/52+ models that added AN/APG-68(V)9 radar with increased air-to-air detection range and synthetic aperture function. These jets can also be fitted with advanced navigation and targeting pods, while their upgraded avionics include an improved modular mission computer, colour cockpit displays and provision for the JHMCS.

A variation is the F-16I, which is a unique version developed for Israel based on the two-seat Block 52, with an F100-PW-229 engine, conformal fuel tanks and unique Israeli avionics and weapons.

Perhaps the most capable version of all is the Block 60 Desert Falcon for the United Arab Emirates, comprising the single-seat F-16E and two-seat F-16F. These boast Northrop Grumman AN/APG-80 active electronically scanned array (AESA) radar, an Internal FLIR and Targeting System (IFTS), Falcon Edge internal

electronic countermeasures system and other advanced avionics.

With a long service career and many combat hours behind it, multiple efforts have been made to sustain many of the world's F-16 fleets through avionics and structural upgrades. For the US Air Force, this has included the Common Configuration Implementation Program (CCIP), providing common hardware and software capability to surviving Block 40/42/50/52 aircraft. In Europe, the Mid-Life Upgrade (MLU) has effectively brought F-16A/B

F-16I Sufa (Storm)

Weight (maximum take-off): 23,582kg (51,989lb)
Dimensions: Length 15.03m (49ft 4in), Wingspan 9.45m (31ft 0in), Height 5.09m (16ft 7in)
Powerplant: One Pratt & Whitney F100-PW-229 turbofan rated at 131.5kN (29,560lb) with afterburning
Maximum speed: Mach 2.05
Range: 4217km (2620 miles), ferry with drop tanks
Ceiling: 18,288m (60,000ft)
Crew: 1
Armament: One 20mm (0.787in) M61A1 six-barrel rotary cannon, plus up to 7700kg (17,000lb) of disposable stores carried on six underwing, two wingtip and one centreline hardpoint (including Rafael's Python 5 infrared-guided air-to-air missile)

F-16I *Sufa* (Storm)

The two-seat F-16I is one of the most important long-range strike assets available to the Israeli Air Force. A total of 102 of these jets were supplied to Israel, where the first examples began to arrive in 2004, while the final examples were handed over in 2009. The aircraft serve with four frontline squadrons and have seen considerable combat action, including raids on Syria.

4.5-GENERATION MULTIROLE FIGHTERS

F-16B Fighting Falcon
This two-seat F-16B – upgraded via the MLU to a standard informally known as F-16BM – belongs to the Royal Norwegian Air Force, which is now replacing its Fighting Falcons with F-35As. Norway was one of the first export customers for the F-16, acquiring 60 F-16As and 14 F-16Bs. The final operator is 331 Skvadron at Bødo.

aircraft up to a standard broadly similar to the US Air Force's F-16C/D Block 52, including AMRAAM missiles to enable, for the first time, a beyond-visual-range air-to-air capability.

Meanwhile, the latest offering from Lockheed Martin – which acquired the aerospace manufacturing arm of General Dynamics in 1993 – is the Block 70/72 F-16V (V for 'Viper'). This was launched in 2012 and is available as an upgrade configuration, as well as a new-build aircraft, with AN/APG-83 Scalable Agile Beam Radar (SABR) featuring an active electronically

A United Arab Emirates air force F-16E Fighting Falcon aircraft from Al Dhafra Air Base, UAE, lands at Nellis Air Force Base, Nevada, following a Red Flag training mission.

4.5-GENERATION MULTIROLE FIGHTERS

KF-16C Fighting Falcon

Serial number 93-065 is a KF-16C, the 'K' prefix denoting that it was one of the examples assembled in South Korea by Samsung (now Korea Aerospace Industries). In total, the Republic of Korea Air Force received 95 single-seat (K)F-16C and 45 two-seat (K)F-16D jets, completed to the Block 52 standard. This example carries AGM-88 HARM missiles for defence-suppression.

scanned array (AESA), upgraded mission computer and cockpit improvements.

So far, five nations have selected the F-16V, which also has its structural service life extended to 12,000 hours, compared to 8000 for previous jets. With F-16s today operated by more than 25 countries, and more than 13 million sorties logged to date, the future of the fighter still looks bright thanks to ongoing modernisation efforts for existing aircraft, and the F-16V production effort, which had an order book containing over 120 aircraft as of July 2021.

F-16 Fighting Falcons from the USAF's 52nd Fighter Wing line up in formation on the runway at Spangdahlem Air Base, Germany, 2019.

4.5-GENERATION MULTIROLE FIGHTERS

F/A-18F Super Hornet

The Royal Australian Air Force acquired exclusively single-seat Super Hornet variants, an initial batch of 24 F/A-18Fs, as seen here, later complemented by 12 EA-18G Growlers. The RAAF Super Hornets serve with No 1 Squadron at RAAF Amberley, which formerly operated the F-111 strike aircraft.

capability among other enhancements. Later F/A-18C deliveries provided enhanced ground-attack features, including night-vison goggles, colour multifunction cockpit displays and an AAS-38 forward-looking infrared pod for target designation.

The original, or 'legacy' Hornet, won a significant number of export orders, Canada becoming the first customer followed by Australia, Spain, Kuwait, Switzerland, Finland and Malaysia.

Two-seat versions of the Hornet began with the F/A-18B, which retains full combat capability, while the F/A-18D is the two-seat equivalent to the F/A-18C. The US Marine Corps in particular have used the F/A-18D to equip their frontline all-weather attack squadrons, replacing the A-6 Intruder.

Super Hornet

When the US Navy demanded a more capable, strike-oriented version of the Hornet to replace the A-6E Intruder and F-14 Tomcat, McDonnell Douglas (later becoming part of Boeing) developed the F/A-18E/F Super Hornet. In addition, the single-seat F/A-18E and two-seat F/A-18F have now replaced all of the US Navy's carrier-based 'legacy' Hornet fleet and, equipped with buddy refuelling pods, the two-seater has also supplanted the S-3 Viking in the carrier-based tanker role. Development of the Super Hornet included seven prototypes, which looked superficially similar to the 'legacy' jets, but which added increased fuel capacity, new engines and avionics, resulting in improved range and payload, including two more heavy weapons stations.

The initial Block I Super Hornets retained the APG-73 but this was quickly replaced by the Raytheon APG-79 active electronically scanned array (AESA) radar, which offers much increased target detection ranges and which can operate simultaneously in air-to-air and air-to-ground modes.

The Super Hornet has found some export success with Australia and Kuwait, both 'legacy' Hornet operators, acquiring these jets.

'Legacy' Hornets

Despite the arrival of the Super Hornet and Growler, the 'legacy' Hornet remains in large-scale service. Although US Navy examples no longer deploy aboard aircraft carriers, the service continues to use the first-generation F/A-18 for reserve, adversary, test and training roles, as well as with the United States Navy Blue Angels display team. The Navy has pursued various upgrades and modifications to help keep the type viable.

Marine Hornets

The situation is different for the Marine Corps, which has not acquired any Super Hornets and as a result plans to retain larger numbers of 'legacy' F/A-18s in service for much longer. To address this, Marine Hornets have undergone a more wide-ranging upgrade, including Joint Helmet Mounted Cueing System (JHMCS) helmet-mounted sights and new colour displays in the cockpit, followed by APG-79(V)4 AESA radars. Under current plans, the Marines will continue to fly 'legacy' Hornets until 2030 in an active-duty capacity, while the single reserve unit won't give up its last Hornets until 2031.

Export Hornets

As for export 'legacy' Hornets, as of 2021 these remained in service with all of their original operators, although Australia is close to retiring the type in favour of the F-35A, having already upgraded its F/A-18A/Bs to a standard closely approximating the F/A-18C/D, including APG-73 radars and JHMCS.

Some surplus Australian aircraft have

4.5-GENERATION MULTIROLE FIGHTERS

Boeing F/A-18 Hornet and Super Hornet

Developed from the Northrop YF-17 design that had lost out to the F-16 in the US Air Force's Air Combat Fighter (ACF) programme in the mid-1970s, the F/A-18 was subsequently victorious against the F-16 in the US Navy's own ACF requirement.

The aircraft has been thoroughly enhanced throughout its career, with the latest F/A-18E/F Super Hornet representing a significant overhaul of the original design concept that now serves as the backbone of the US Navy's carrier-based tactical fighter fleet.

The F/A-18 was developed as a true multirole fighter from the outset, intended to be equally proficient at fighter and strike/attack missions and allowing replacement of the US Navy's F-4 Phantom II and A-7 Corsair II fleets. While the original design can be traced back to Northrop, the responsibility for development and production was assigned to McDonnell Douglas. The company completed a total of 11 F/A-18s for trials, two of them being configured as twin-seaters. A first flight by the Hornet was achieved on 18 November 1978.

Development was swift and the first of the single-seat F/A-18A production variants were delivered in 1980 and the US Marine Corps declared the type ready for operations in 1983, the same year in which the Navy began to receive its first examples.

High-lift wing

The design of the Hornet incorporates a high-lift wing and prominent leading-edge extensions that provide excellent high-alpha capability and turn performance. The original radar was the AN/APG-73, a multi-mode unit that was capable of detecting and engaging airborne threats as well as ground targets.

The Hornet's combat debut came during the El Dorado Canyon raids against Libya in April 1986 and F/A-18s from the US Navy and Marine Corps subsequently played a significant role during Operation Desert Storm over Iraq in 1991. Hornets (and latterly Super Hornets) have since been used in combat whenever US Navy aircraft carriers have been called into action.

The original production version was superseded by the single-seat F/A-18C that added AIM-120 Advanced Medium-Range Air-to-Air Missile (AMRAAM)

F/A-18E Super Hornet
Weight (maximum take-off): 29,937kg (66,000lb)
Dimensions: Length 18.31m (60ft 1in), Wingspan 13.62m (44ft 8in), Height 4.88m (16ft)
Powerplant: Two General Electric F414-GE-400 turbofans each rated at 98kN (13,000lb) thrust with afterburning
Maximum speed: Mach 1.6
Range: 2346km (458 miles) with armament of two AIM-9s
Ceiling: 15,240m (50,000ft)
Crew: 1
Armament: One 20mm (0.787in) M61A1 Vulcan six-barrel rotary cannon, plus maximum weapon load of 8050kg (17,750lb) on six underwing pylons, three fuselage pylons and two wingtip pylons

---

F/A-18E Super Hornet

Assigned to the USS *Nimitz*, F/A-18E BuNo 166434 received this special scheme to commemorate the 90th anniversary of Strike Fighter Squadron 14 (VFA-14) 'Tophatters' in 2009. Shore-based at Naval Air Station Lemoore, California, the 'Tophatters' are the US Navy's oldest active squadron, having formed in 1919, since when it has flown 23 different aircraft types.

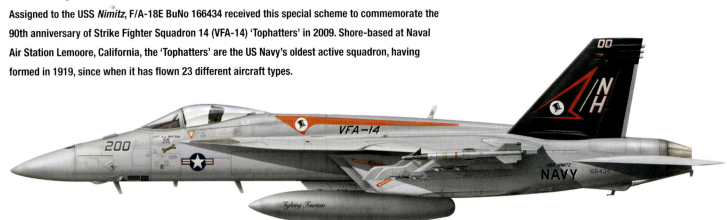

AIRBRAKE
A large, one-piece, door-type airbrake is situated in the upper section of the fuselage, between the engines. The unit is hydraulically raised to assist in low speed handling and short landings.

POWERPLANT
Located side-by-side in the rear of the fuselage are two General Electric F404-GE-400 low bypass ratio turbofan engines. They are slightly toed in to align the exhaust nozzles, and are interchangeable left and right. A feature of their excellent overall performance is a very fast spool-up time of three to four seconds from idle power to maximum afterburner.

AILERONS
The outer portion of each trailing edge flap is structurally separated to act as an aileron at low flight speeds. These relatively small items extend from just inside of the wing-fold point to just inboard of the outer wing tip.

General Dynamics F-16C Figh

This F-16 is seen wearing the markings of the 52nd Fighter Wing, stationed at Spangdahlem Air Base in Germany, in the 1990s. The wing is still based there today and is tasked primarily with defence suppression (or 'Wild Weasel' mission), having completed numerous operational taskings.

AN/APG-68 RADAR

F-16C/Ds were originally delivered with the Westinghouse AN/APG-69(V) pulse-Doppler multi-mode radar, a considerable improvement over the APG-66 fitted to earlier F-16A/B aircraft. The planar array provides numerous air-to-air modes, including range-while-search, up-look and velocity search, single-target track, raid cluster resolution and track-while-scan for up to 10 targets, and the radar also adds a very important beyond-visual-range capability.

COMMON CONFIGURATION IMPLEMENTATION PROGRAM

A significant upgrade for the US Air Force's F-16 fleet was the Common Configuration Implementation Program (CCIP), which was applied to some 650 Block 40/42/50/52 aircraft. CCIP brought these aircraft to a broadly similar standard and was undertaken in four phases, at the Ogden Air Logistics Center at Hill Air Force Base. Phase 1 provided a new modular mission computer and colour multifunction cockpit displays. Phase 1A then added the AN/APX-113 interrogator/transponder (with the characteristic 'bird slicer' antenna in front of the cockpit), as well as the Sniper targeting pod.

AGM-88 HARM

The primary defence-suppression weapon of the F-16 is the Texas Instruments (later Raytheon) AGM-88 High-speed Anti-Radiation Missile (HARM). Measuring 4.17m (13ft 8in) long and with a launch weight of 361kg (796lb), the HARM has fixed rear fins and controllable mid-set fins. A fixed seeker in the nose has a digital passive antenna that covers radar frequencies across a wide band. It can be programmed before launch to attack a specific target, or it can be launched 'blind' at longer range to acquire a target during its flight.

FLAPS
The advanced, computer-controlled leading edge and trailing edge flaps can be deflected for optimum lift and drag or manoeuvring and cruise conditions. take-off the full-span leading edge and single-slot trailing edge flaps are deflected 30° while for landing the trailing edge flaps are further deflected to 45°.

TAILFINS
The twin swept and outwardly-canted vertical tailfins and rudders are mounted ahead of the horizontal stabilators, the dual rudders providing primary directional control. The structure includes graphite/epoxy skins and steel leading edges.

WING FOLDING
To facilitate aircraft-carrier stowage the outer main wing panels can be folded upwards to reduce required stowage space. The wing-fold point consists of a long piano hinge situated across the main structural box.

...ting Falcon

COCKPIT

The cockpit design of the F-16 was tailored to support the aircraft's high level of agility, including the ability to withstand manoeuvring forces of up to 9g with a full load of internal fuel. The cockpit and its bubble canopy provide the pilot with unobstructed forward and upward vision, and greatly improved vision over the side and to the rear. The seat is angled back at 30°, as opposed to the more typical 13°, increasing pilot comfort and gravity-force tolerance.

CAMOUFLAGE AND MARKINGS

As well as its standard three-tone grey camouflage scheme, this particular F-16 wears the markings of the commander of the 52nd Fighter Wing, denoted by the non-standard full-colour shark's mouth on the nose. The fin has the 'SP' code of the wing, denoting its Spangdahlem base, and a toned-down version of the wing's crest. The fin-tip band presents the colours of the active squadrons within the wing (red for the 22nd Fighter Squadron, blue for the 23rd Fighter Squadron).

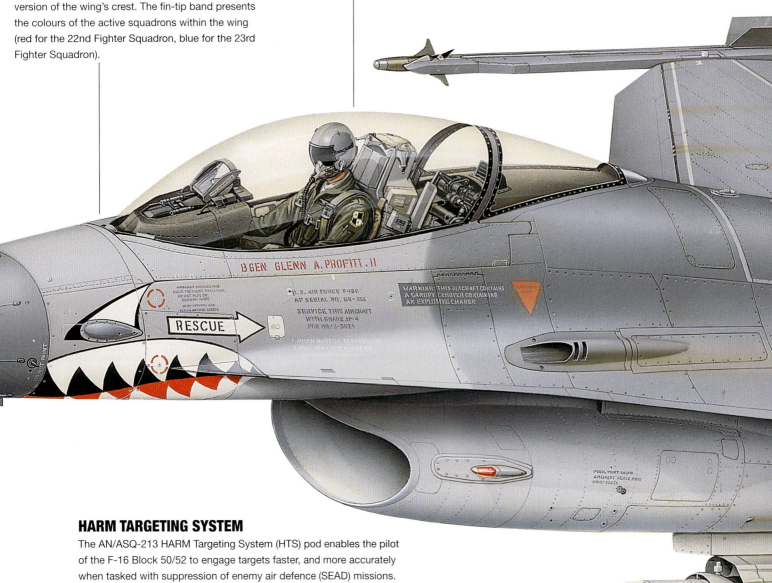

HARM TARGETING SYSTEM

The AN/ASQ-213 HARM Targeting System (HTS) pod enables the pilot of the F-16 Block 50/52 to engage targets faster, and more accurately when tasked with suppression of enemy air defence (SEAD) missions. The HTS pod is able to detect, locate and identify ground-based emitters, passing targeting information to the HARM missiles. The pod is normally carried on the aircraft's left inlet hardpoint.

ornet

CANOPY
The main canopy opens upwards and rearwards under the thrust of a hydraulic jack at the rear. The frameless structure provides excellent all-round visibility for the pilot.

EJECTOR SEAT
The current ejector seat fitted to the Hornet is the Martin-Baker Mk 14, also known as the NACES (Navy Aircrew Common Ejection Seat), this being slightly reclined for better pilot *g* tolerance during tight flight manoeuvres.

WINDSHIELD
The single-curvature windshield is a frameless moulding that hinges upwards and forwards with the forward instrument panel shroud, thus allowing easy access to the forward instruments.

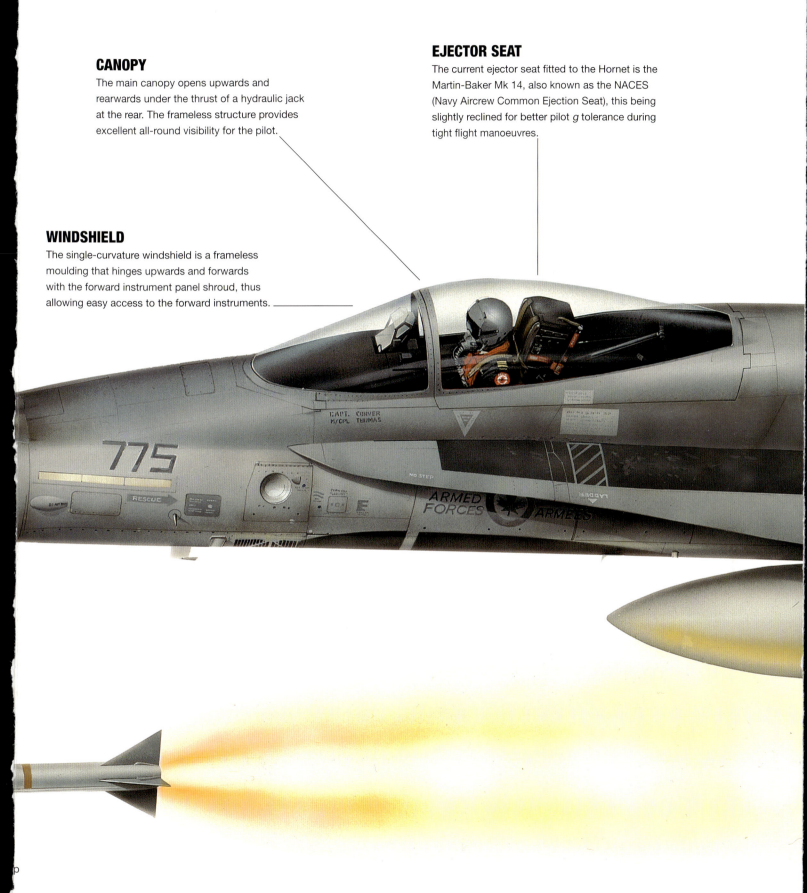

'WILD WEASEL' MISSION

The 52nd Fighter Wing initially received Block 30 F-16C/Ds that were specially configured to use the AGM-45 Shrike anti-radiation missile. From 1993, these were replaced by Block 50 aircraft, which arrived around the same time that the F-4G was being retired. The Block 50 aircraft carry out the defence suppression role in conjunction with the AGM-88 HARM and the AN/ASQ-213 HARM Targeting System (HTS) pod. This jet also carries the AN/ALQ-131 electronic countermeasures pod below the fuselage.

FLY-BY-WIRE CONTROL SYSTEM
Critical to the F-16's performance and agility is the use of a quadruplex fly-by-wire control system, in which a digital computer processes inputs from the pilot's sidestick controller and translates them into actuation of flight control surfaces, all signals being handled electronically. Unlike a conventionally controlled aircraft, the F-16 has no relaxed stability, with the location of the tail much closer to the wing, providing enhanced manoeuvrability.

ARMAMENT
Basic defensive armament of the F-16 comprises the internal M61A1 20mm (0.79in) six-barrel rotary cannon with 515 rounds of ammunition, and two AIM-9 Sidewinder or AIM-120 AMRAAM air-to-air missiles on wingtip rails. Additional fuselage and six underwing hardpoints can carry fuel tanks and additional weapons. When configured for 5.5 *g* manoeuvring, the fuselage hardpoint is stressed for 998kg (2,200lb), inboard pylons for 2,041kg (4,500lb), centre for 1,587kg (3,500lb) and the outboard for 318kg (700lb). At 9 *g* manoeuvring, these figures are reduced to 544kg (1,200lb), 1,134kg (2,500lb), 907kg (2,000lb) and 204kg (450lb) respectively.

McDonnell Douglas CF-18 Hc

The McDonnell Douglas Hornet also serves with the Canadian armed forces as the CF-18, this one flying with the No. 3 Tactical Fighter Wing, based in Cold Lake, Alberta. Canadian CF-18s took part in the Gulf War of 1991, Operation Allied Force – the 79-day Nato air campaign in the former Yugoslavia, in 1999 – and operations over Libya in 2011. Today they are primarily used to protect North American air space.

GUN

An M61 A1 20mm (0.79in) six-barrel gun is housed in the upper nose (above the radar suite) and is linked to an ammunition drum containing up to 570 rounds of ammunition. Firing rates are 4,000 or 6,000 rpm, the whole unit being pallet-mounted for easy access and rapid removal. The gun is linked to a McDonnell Douglas director gunsight with a conventional gunsight as back-up.

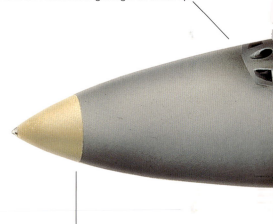

RADAR

The compact Hughes AN/APG-65 multi-mode digital tracking radar (later upgraded with an AN/APG-73) fits into a relatively small and slender area in the nose. The whole unit can be pulled forward and out on fixed rails once the nose radome has been swung through 180° to starboard via its hinge-point. The radar operates in the J-band of wavelengths for both air-to-air and air-to-ground missions, the former including auto close-combat gun director and raid assessment modes.

WEAPONS

A total of nine weapons stations are fitted to production Hornets. The wingt missile rails are joined by two pylons under each wing, a body pylon on the bottom of each engine air inlet and a centreline station. The body pylons provide near conformal carriage for AIM-7 Sparrow air-to-air missiles.

4.5-GENERATION MULTIROLE FIGHTERS

A USAF EA-18G Growler takes part in a flying display during the Finnish Air Force 100th anniversary air show at Tikkakoski Airport, Finland, June 2018.

EA-18G Growler
Weight (maximum take-off): 29,937kg (66,000lb)
Dimensions: Length 18.31m (60ft 1in), Wingspan 13.62m (44ft 8in), Height 4.88m (16ft)
Powerplant: Two General Electric F414-GE-400 turbofans, 62kN (14,000lbf) thrust each dry, 98kN (22,000lbf) with afterburner
Maximum speed: Mach 1.8
Range: 3330km (2070 miles)
Ceiling: 15,240m (50,000ft)
Crew: 2
Armament: Six under-wing and three under-fuselage with a capacity of 8,050kg (17,750lb) external fuel and ordnance, including AIM-120 AMRAAM missiles and AGM-88 HARM missiles

been sold to Canada, to boost its own Hornet fleet pending the selection of a replacement fighter type. The Canadian jets have also been upgraded with APG-73 and new mission computers, as well as JHMCS and advanced AIM-120D AMRAAM missiles, with the Spanish aircraft – locally designated C.15 and (for two-seaters) CE.15 – following a broadly similar modernisation path.

Finland, too, is yet to decide on its future fighter equipment and has put its F/A-18C/Ds through a wide-ranging upgrade programme that has emphasised long-range strike capabilities, adding the AGM-158 Joint Air-to-Surface Stand-off Missile (JASSM) stealthy cruise missile.

In 2021, Switzerland selected the F-35A to replace its Hornet fleet but in the meantime has also upgraded its jets, while Kuwaiti 'legacies' are set to be replaced by new F/A-18E/Fs. That leaves Malaysia, which has a fleet of just eight F/A-18Ds that are primarily utilised for maritime strike missions and can be armed with AGM-84 Harpoon anti-ship missiles.

EA-18G GROWLER
The two-seat F/A-18F also serves as the basis for the EA-18G Growler, a dedicated electronic attack (EA) derivative that was developed, originally as a private venture, to replace the EA-6B Prowler within US Navy carrier air wings. The Growler shares more than 90 per cent commonality with the Super Hornet, but its mission equipment is provided by Northrop Grumman and includes up to three AN/ALQ-99 radar jamming pods together with the AN/ALQ-218(V)2 antenna pods on the wingtip.

The Growler's primary role is to locate enemy communication channels and disrupt them over a wide set of frequencies using its jammer pods. Targets can also be engaged using the AGM-88 High Speed Anti-Radiation Missile (HARM).

EA-18G Growler
This brightly painted Growler is the 'CAG bird' of Electronic Attack Squadron 141 (VAQ-141) 'Shadowhawks', which is forward-based in the Pacific at Marine Corps Air Station Iwakuni, Japan. The unit provides electronic attack support for Carrier Air Wing 5 aboard aircraft carrier USS *Ronald Reagan*. 'CAG birds' are officially flown by the commanding officer of US Navy Carrier Air Groups.

4.5-GENERATION MULTIROLE FIGHTERS

Mikoyan MiG-29K and MiG-35

Unusually, the latest and most advanced versions of the prolific 'Fulcrum' family are all derived from the ship-based MiG-29K multirole fighter.

While they look superficially similar to the original MiG-29, these aircraft are actually entirely reworked with an all-new airframe including a larger wing with a different arrangement of flaps and other high-lift devices.

The original MiG-29K (internal designation izdeliye 9.31) was developed in the 1980s to operate from the Soviet Union's planned new aircraft carriers. It was first flown in 1988 and it was intended to share its airframe and N010 radar with the land-based MiG-29M (izdeliye 9.15). With the demise of the Soviet Union, both these projects were terminated in 1992.

A change in fortunes came, however, when India acquired the former Soviet aircraft carrier *Admiral Gorshkov*, which it put into service as *Vikramaditya*. In response, in late 1999 MiG launched work on an upgraded carrier-based 'Fulcrum' known as the izdeliye 9.41. This added increased-area double-slotted rear flaps, adaptive nose flaps, leading-edge vortex controllers and a digital fly-by-wire

control system. Single-seat and two-seat versions were developed, using the same basic airframe, as the MiG-29K (izdeliye 9.41) and MiG-29KUB (izdeliye 9.47) respectively. The first of these to fly was the two-seater, which took to the air on 20 January 2007.

Four aerial targets

Powered by RD-33MK turbofans providing greater thrust than the original RD-33 engines, the MiG-29K has three liquid-crystal displays in the front cockpit (and for the two-seat MiG-29KUB, four more in the rear). Avionics are based around the N041 Zhuk radar and an infrared search and track (IRST) system and the pilot also has a Thales TopSight helmet-mounted sight. The radar can simultaneously engage four aerial targets using active-radar missiles. Unlike the original MiG-29, these advanced aircraft are able to employ a wide range of precision-guided air-to-surface ordnance, including Kh-31A (AS-17 'Krypton') and Kh-35 (AS-20

'Kayak') anti-ship missiles in the case of the MiG-29K/KUB.

India ordered 12 MiG-29K and four MiG-29KUB fighters in 2004 and the first of these arrived in the country in late 2009. The following year, New Delhi signed a contract for another 29 MiG-29Ks.

In 2012, Russia ordered its own version of the carrier fighter to equip the Russian Navy's sole aircraft carrier, *Admiral Kuznetsov*. A total of

---

MiG-29K

Weight (maximum take-off): 22,400kg (49,384lb)

Dimensions: Length 17.30m (56ft 9in), Wingspan 11.99m (39ft 4in), Height 4.40m (14ft 5in)

Powerplant: Two Klimov RD-33MK turbofans, each rated at 122.5kN (19,842lb) thrust with afterburning

Maximum speed: 2200km/h (1367mph)

Range: 2000km (1700 miles)

Ceiling: 17,500m (57,415ft)

Crew: 1

Armament: One GSh-301 30mm (1.2in) cannon, plus up to 4500kg (9,921lb) of stores carried on nine hardpoints (eight under the wing and one under the fuselage)

MiG-29KR

While the Soviet Navy did not place orders for the original MiG-29K, preferring to focus on the Su-27K (later Su-33), the Russian Navy has more recently ordered the carrier-based 'Fulcrum'. In 2012, orders were placed for 20 single-seat MiG-29KR and four twin-seat MiG-29KUBR fighters. Serving aboard the carrier Admiral Kuznetsov and from a land base, these jets took part in combat operations over Syria in 2016.

4.5-GENERATION MULTIROLE FIGHTERS

MiG-29M2
The latest customer for the new-generation MiG-29 is Algeria, which placed orders for an undisclosed number of MiG-29M/M2 jets, including this two-seat MiG-29M2, serial FB-99. A contract was signed in 2019 and these aircraft are expected to replace older MiG-29S and MiG-29UB fighters in service with the Algerian Air Force.

20 MiG-29KR and four MiG-29KUBR fighters were acquired.

In parallel with the naval version, MiG developed the shore-based MiG-29M (izdeliye 9.41S) and twin-seat MiG-29M2 (izdeliye 9.47S). Early hopes of exporting this aircraft to Syria fell through, but the land-based version won its first export order in 2015 when Egypt signed for 46 MiG-29M/MiG-29M2 jets.

MiG-35
It was not until 2018 that an order was placed on behalf of the Russian Aerospace Forces for just six aircraft (four izdeliye 9.41SR single-seaters and a pair of izdeliye 9.47SR two-seaters), which are known by the alternative MiG-35S and MiG-35UB designations. Interestingly, the MiG-35 designation had earlier been used as part of an unsuccessful effort to sell the aircraft to the Indian Air Force as part of the abortive Medium Multi-Role Combat Aircraft competition. This yielded the MiG-35 (izdeliye 9.61) and the two-seat MiG-35D (izdeliye 9.67) that would have had Zhuk-AE active electronically scanned array (AESA) radar, but which didn't advance beyond the prototype stage.

Most recently, Algeria became a customer with reports from late 2020 that the first MiG-29M/MiG-29M2 aircraft had been delivered. Reportedly, a total of 14 aircraft have been acquired.

MiG-29M2
Weight (maximum take-off): 22,400kg (49,384lb)
Dimensions: Length 17.37m (57ft), Wingspan 11.4m (37ft 5in), Height 4.73m (15ft 5in)
Powerplant: Two Klimov RD-33MK turbofans, each rated at 122.5kN (19,842lb) thrust with afterburning
Maximum speed: 2200km/h (1367mph)
Range: 2000km (1700 miles)
Ceiling: 16,200m (53,150ft)
Crew: 1 or 2
Armament: One GSh-301 30mm (1.2in) cannon, plus up to 4500kg (9,921lb) of stores carried on nine hardpoints (eight under the wing and one under the fuselage)

MiG-29M2
Two-seat MiG-29M2 serial 811 is part of a major Egyptian order for the type, covering between 46 and 50 MiG-29M/M2 variants, the first examples of which were noted in Egypt in October 2017. Egypt's 'Fulcrums' can be equipped with hose-and-drogue refuelling pods and have been used as tankers for the Rafale fleet.

4.5-GENERATION MULTIROLE FIGHTERS

Sukhoi Su-30

A two-seat, highly agile heavyweight multirole combat aircraft, the Su-30 series is the most successful Russian fighter currently in production.

The Su-30 designation covers two distinct families of aircraft, which are produced by different factories in Irkutsk and in Komsomolsk-on-Amur. It began life at the end of the Soviet era as a long-range interceptor development of the Su-27UB 'Flanker-C' two-seat combat trainer. The original Su-30 utilised this airframe but added an inflight refuelling probe and a tactical display in the rear cockpit. The first prototype was flown on 30 December 1989 but only a handful of production examples were ever completed for service with what was by now the Russian Air Force.

Indian market
Development of a multirole derivative was spurred by India, which showed interest in the Su-30MK that had been developed as an improved version of the Su-30, now aimed at the export market. In 1996, the Irkutsk factory began work on the Su-30MKI for India, which added canard foreplanes,

AL-31FP thrust-vectoring engines, digital fly-by-wire and the N011M Bars passive electronically scanned array radar. The cockpits were also modernised, featuring a new head-up display in the front cockpit as well as a pair of multifunction displays for each pilot. The fire-control system combines a radar, electro-optical sighting system and helmet-mounted sight, while the radar is capable of terrain mapping with synthetic aperture, detection of warship targets and is compatible with active-radar air-to-air missiles as well as TV- and laser-guided air-to-ground munitions.

Pending availability of the full-specification Su-30MKI, India received 18 examples of the interim Su-30K, which was an export version of the basic Su-30 interceptor. Subsequently deemed surplus to requirements by India, the Su-30Ks found their way to Belarus where 12 of them were refurbished for delivery to Angola, apparently in an upgraded Su-30KN

Su-30MKI
Weight (maximum take-off): 34,000kg (74,957lb)
Dimensions: Length 21.94m (71ft 11in) without probe, Wingspan 14.7m (48ft 2in), Height 6.4m (20ft 11in)
Powerplant: Two Saturn AL-31FP thrust-vectoring turbofans each rated at 122.6kN (27,558lb) thrust with afterburning
Maximum speed: Mach 1.9
Range: 3000km (1864 miles)
Ceiling: 17,300m (56,758ft)
Crew: 1
Armament: One GSh-301 30mm (1.2in) cannon, plus up to 8000kg (17,637lb) of stores carried on 12 hardpoints

Su-30MKI
A Su-30MKI from the Indian Air Force's No. 102 Squadron 'Trisonics', based at Chabua Air Force Station as part of Eastern Air Command. In July 2020 India's defence ministry approved the purchase of another 12 Su-30MKI fighters, part of its response to heightened tensions on its borders with China and Pakistan. This brings total Su-30MKI acquisition to 284.

4.5-GENERATION MULTIROLE FIGHTERS

form. The Su-30KN had originally been developed as a low-cost upgrade adding multirole capability to the Su-30 but did not find any other customers.

In the meantime, the Indian Air Force began receiving Su-30MKIs in 2002 and is now the biggest operator of the Su-30 series, with 272 delivered by 2020 and another 12 attrition replacements on order. A substantial percentage of these aircraft have been manufactured locally at Hindustan Aeronautics Limited's Nasik facility.

International orders
The success of the Indian Su-30MKI stimulated interest in the aircraft and subsequent orders were placed by Algeria (Su-30MKA) and Malaysia (Su-30MKM). These export versions feature differences in equipment, including various items of Western avionics and Algeria reportedly has some of its aircraft modified for the reconnaissance role as the Su-30MKA(R).

Finally, in 2012 Moscow placed an order for the multirole 'Flanker' and since then has acquired successive batches of the Su-30SM version, which has been delivered to the Russian Aerospace Forces and Russian Navy.

The Su-30SM version has subsequently been adopted by export operators in former Soviet states, Armenia and Belarus having acquired four examples each by late 2019, with plans for both of these nations to field full-size squadrons (12 aircraft each) in the future. Meanwhile, Kazakhstan had received a total of 20 Su-30SMs by the end of 2020 and is expected to acquire more.

The Su-30MK/Su-30SM series retains the 30mm (1.2in) GSh-301 cannon of the original Su-27 but introduces a much greater capacity for external stores: up to 8000kg (17,637lb) of stores on 12 weapons pylons, compared to 4430kg (9766lb) of external stores on the 10 hardpoints of the basic Su-27. Air-to-air weapons include semi-active radar-guided R-27R/ER and infrared-guided R-27T/ET (AA-10 'Alamo'), active-radar R-77 (AA-12 'Adder') and short-range R-73 (AA-11 'Archer') air-to-air missiles. As well as freefall bombs and rockets, air-to-ground weapons options include Kh-59M (AS-18 'Kazoo') standoff missile, Kh-31P/A (AS-17 'Krypton') anti-radar/anti-ship missiles and Kh-29 (AS-14 'Kedge') missiles with TV or laser guidance.

While the Irkutsk Su-30 line is the most advanced, the Komsomolsk-on-Amur versions are somewhat more spartan and trace their lineage back to the Su-30MKK that was developed for China, and which used a basically unchanged Su-27UB airframe with no canards or thrust vectoring, and used a less sophisticated fire-control system. A key recognition feature are the taller tailfins, which lack the cropped tips of the Irkutsk-made Su-30 series.

After the initial batch of 76 Su-30MKKs, China acquired 24 of the more capable Su-30MK2 fighters in 2004, these being optimized for long-range anti-shipping strike with the People's Liberation Army Navy Air Force. Thereafter, however, China opted to pursue a multirole development of its own J-11, a locally produced 'Flanker' derivative, and this emerged as the J-16. Both of these Chinese developments are described separately.

Subsequent export customers for the Komsomolsk-on-Amur aircraft include Indonesia (two Su-30MKK and nine Su-30MK2), Vietnam (36 Su-30MK2V), Venezuela (24 Su-30MK2V) and Uganda (six Su-30MK2).

Russia placed a first order for Su-30M2 aircraft in 2009 and these aircraft now serve primarily as combat trainers for pilots destined to fly the upgraded Su-27SM, Su-30SM and the Su-57.

Su-30SM
A Russian Aerospace Forces (VKS) Su-30SM, assigned to the 31st Guards Fighter Aviation Regiment, based at Millerovo, under the command of the 4th Air Force and Air Defence Army, in July 2020. VKS Su-30SMs were ordered in batches of 30 in March 2012, 30 more in December 2012 and 32 in April 2016, with more on order for the navy.

4.5-GENERATION MULTIROLE FIGHTERS

Sukhoi Su-33 and Shenyang J-15

Developed during the Cold War to serve aboard an ambitious series of aircraft carriers planned for the Soviet Navy, the Su-33 eventually only went to sea aboard a single Russian Navy aircraft carrier, the conventionally powered *Admiral Kuznetsov*.

The Su-33 began life under the designation Su-27K, reflecting the fact it was a minimum-change carrier-based version of the 'Flanker-B' air superiority and air defence fighter. The changes required for carrier operations included canard foreplanes, revised wing flaps, reinforced undercarriage and an arrester hook.

To conserve space when stowed on deck or below decks, the outer wings, tailplanes, tail boom and radome all fold. The AL-31F engines feature some modifications for operations at sea and the aircraft is equipped with an inflight refuelling probe (plus optional buddy refuelling pod), unlike the land-based Su-27.

In terms of mission avionics, the fire-control system features only minor changes compared to the Su-27, retaining the N001K radar, electro-optical system and helmet-mounted sight. Armament options are the same as for the 'Flanker-B' but the naval fighter has 12 rather than 10 external hardpoints, permitting electronic countermeasures pods to be carried on the wingtips with no reduction in armament. The first prototype Su-27K, known to Sukhoi as the T-10K-1, took to the air on 17 August 1987 and made a first deck landing in November 1989. Since the 'Kuznetsov'-class carriers have no provision for catapult launch gear, the aircraft launches via an angled 'ski jump' ramp.

Naval fighter

A single example of the side-by-side two-seat Su-27KUB was completed as a prototype multirole naval fighter but ultimately Russia only procured 26 production single-seaters built at Komsomolsk-on-Amur between 1993 and 1996. These officially entered service in 1998 under the revised designation Su-33.

Shenyang J-15

After the demise of the Soviet Union, two T-10K test aircraft were left in Ukraine and one of these was sold to China in 2007. It subsequently became the pattern for the J-15 that incorporates Chinese avionics, a modern glass cockpit and has a multirole capability using indigenous weapons. The People's Liberation Army Navy Air Force took to the J-15 to sea for the first time aboard the 'Kuznetsov'-class carrier *Liaoning* in 2012. The J-15 is now also deployed on board the carrier *Shandong*, which is a Chinese version of the 'Kuznetsov' design and is likely also form the main part of the air wing of China's third carrier, which is so far unnamed.

Su-33
Weight (maximum take-off): 24,500kg (54,013lb)
Dimensions: Length 21.2m (69ft 6in) without probe, Wingspan 14.7m (48ft 3in), Height 5.72m (18ft 9in)
Powerplant: Two modified AL-31F series 3 turbofans, each rated at 122.5kN (27,558lb) with afterburning
Maximum speed: Mach 2.17
Range: 3000km (1864 miles)
Ceiling: 17,000m (55,775ft)
Crew: 1
Armament: One GSh-301 30mm (1.2in) cannon, plus up to 6500kg (14,330lb) of stores carried on 12 hardpoints

---

Su-33
Russian Navy Su-33 'Red 88', as it appeared in June 2016, on strength with the 279th Independent Shipborne Fighter Aviation Regiment. Originally, 30 Su-33s were on order but construction stopped after 26 aircraft. One more was lost prior to delivery and there have been least five accidents in service, including one lost while the *Admiral Kuznetsov* was operating in the Mediterranean during the Syrian campaign in December 2016.

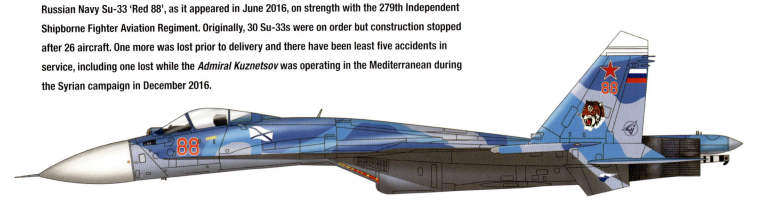

4.5-GENERATION MULTIROLE FIGHTERS

Shenyang J-15

A J-15 of the People's Liberation Army Navy Air Force (PLANAF), operating from the aircraft carrier *Liaoning* in around 2017. Equipped for short take-off but arrested recovery (STOBAR) operations from China's first carriers, at least 36 J-15 production aircraft have been completed, with as many as 60-70 examples likely planned.

With China testing an electromagnetic aircraft launch system and a steam-powered catapult, it is expected that the third carrier will permit catapult assisted take-offs, and an appropriately equipped J-15 (sometimes known as the J-15T) has been noted under test. The J-15T version also features Chinese-made WS-10 turbofans instead of the Russian-supplied AL-31 engines used in earlier J-15s.

Two other versions of the Chinese naval 'Flanker' are known to be in development. The first of these is the two-seat J-15S that combines the basic airframe of the J-15 with the cockpit section of the multirole J-16. There is also the J-15D electronic warfare version, equivalent to the US Navy's EA-18G Growler, with electronic warfare jamming pods on the wingtips. Both of these variants, or perhaps a version that unifies these two roles in a single airframe, could well enter service by the time China's third aircraft carrier is commissioned.

J-15

Weight (maximum take-off): 24,500kg (54,013lb)
Dimensions: Length 22.28m (73ft 1in), Wingspan 14.7m (48ft 3in), Height 5.92m (19ft 5in)
Powerplant: Two Shenyang WS-10A afterburning turbofans, 132kN (30,000lbf) thrust each
Maximum speed: 2,658km/h (1,652mph, 1,435kn)
Range: 3000km (1864 miles)
Ceiling: 20,000m (66,000ft)
Crew: 1 or 2
Armament: One GSh-301 30mm (1.2in) cannon, plus up to 6500kg (14,330lb) of stores carried on 12 hardpoints, including: PL-8 and PL-12 air-to-air missiles, YJ-83KH land attack missile, YJ-83K anti-ship missile

A Russian naval Sukhoi Su-33 takes off at Zhukovsky airport after modernization with the 'Gefest' system.

4.5-GENERATION MULTIROLE FIGHTERS
Sukhoi Su-35

Plans to create a much-improved and multirole-capable single-seat 'Flanker' date back to the 1980s but were frustrated by the demise of the Soviet Union.

It was only in the early 2000s that work resumed in earnest, and the result is arguably the most capable development of the original Su-27 and is likely to serve as a lower-cost complement to the advanced Su-57.

Back in 1988, Sukhoi completed the Su-27M fighter as a significantly upgraded version of the Su-27 'Flanker-B' with canard foreplanes, thrust-vectoring engines and a passive electronically scanned array radar. After a dozen test aircraft, three production fighters were completed in the mid-1990s but there was no serious interest from Russia or from export customers, the latter opting for versions of the two-seat Su-30 instead.

At the start of the new century, Sukhoi revisited the idea of an advanced single-seat 'Flanker' and developed the Su-35BM (Bolshaya Modernisatsiya, meaning 'big modernisation'). This was optimised for export but before the end of the decade Russia was showing an interest in what was now known simply as the Su-35.

Compared to the Su-27, the Su-35 incorporates an all-new quadruple-redundant digital fly-by-wire system. The new powerplant consists of two thrust-vectoring Saturn AL-41F-1S turbofans that operate in conjunction with the canard foreplanes for extreme manoeuvrability.

Radar upgrade
In terms of avionics, the Su-35 has a computer-controlled fire-control system that incorporates the N135 Irbis passive electronically scanned array radar and Khibiny-M electronic countermeasures suite. The new radar can simultaneously scan for targets while tracking up to 30 air targets, eight of which can be engaged simultaneously. The radar also incorporates air-to-ground modes and is compatible with most of the same

---

Su-35
Weight (maximum take-off): 34,500kg (76,059lb)
Dimensions: Length 21.9m (71ft 10in), Wingspan 14.7m (48ft 2in), Height 5.9m (19ft 4in)
Powerplant: Two Saturn AL-41F-1S thrust-vectoring turbofans each rated at 137.3kN (30,865lb) thrust with afterburning
Maximum speed: Mach 2.25
Range: 3000km (1864 miles)
Ceiling: 18,000m (59,055ft)
Crew: 1
Armament: One GSh-301 30mm (1.2in) cannon, plus up to 8000kg (17,637lb) of stores carried on 12 hardpoints

---

SU-35BM

The Su-35BM (Bolshaya Modernisatsiya, or 'big modernisation') was launched in the early 2000s for export, using Sukhoi funds, and the prototype, '901', first flew on 19 February 2008. After two more prototypes, plus one for static tests, the aircraft was finally selected for the then Russian Air Force as the Su-35S, the first 48 examples being ordered in August 2009.

4.5-GENERATION MULTIROLE FIGHTERS

precision ordnance as the Su-30SM (described separately). The pilot is also provided with an electro-optical sensor and helmet-mounted sight.

Air-to-air weapons are also similar to the Su-30SM, although the very long-range R-37M (AA-13 'Axehead') is an additional option and is likely intended to engage high-value targets such as enemy airborne early warning aircraft and refuelling tankers.

The fighter's self-protection attributes are significantly enhanced, with the aforementioned Khibiny-M suite supported by Pastel radar warning receivers that are also used to identify targets for anti-radiation missiles. There is also an electro-optical missile-approach warning system that makes uses of sensors distributed around the airframe for optimum coverage. While these provide the pilot with alert for missile launches from the ground or air, two laser warning sensors detect laser rangefinders that might be tracking the aircraft. As well as decoy dispensers mounted in the tail 'sting', additional jamming pods can be fitted to the wingtips to expand the capabilities of the Khibiny-M.

Russian Aerospace Forces

In August 2009, Moscow ordered 48 examples of the fighter, which are designated as the Su-35S in Russian service; the first of these were delivered from the Komsomolsk-on-Amur factory to the Russian Air Force at the end of 2011. Another batch of 50 was ordered for the newly renamed Russian Aerospace Forces in late 2015 and the last of these were handed over in late 2020. Additional orders are likely, especially bearing in mind the limited numbers of Su-57s that have been committed to so far.

The first export customer for the Su-35 was China who acquired 24 examples, the first of which arrived in December 2016, followed by Egypt, which signed a contract for the type in late 2018. By 2020 at least six Egyptian Su-35s had been delivered from a total order for at least 24 aircraft.

SU-35

In March 2019 it was reported that Egypt had signed a $2-billion contract with Russia for the delivery 30 Su-35 fighters, to be built by the Sukhoi facility at Komsomolsk-on-Amur. The first examples of which were noted prior to delivery in July 2020 and a month later it was confirmed that the contract covered 30 aircraft.

4.5-GENERATION MULTIROLE FIGHTERS

Chengdu J-10

The J-10, known in China by the popular name Vigorous Dragon, represents a milestone in the country's military aviation, as the country's first true fourth-generation multirole fighter to enter production and service.

Development of the J-10 began in the early 1980s, with Chengdu adopting a tailless delta configuration with canard foreplanes and a chin-mounted engine intake. There have been repeated suggestions that elements of the Chengdu design were derived from the Israeli Lavi fighter project and, while there was certainly contact between Chinese and Israeli engineers, this seems to have concentrated above all on the fly-by-wire flight-control system for the J-10.

People's Liberation Army Air Force
Delays to the programme meant that it was not until the early 1990s that a full-size mock-up was completed, while problems in the development of the planned WS-10 engine apparently almost led to the cancellation of the entire project.

Instead of the indigenous engine, Chengdu then opted for the Russian-made AL-31FN and it was this that powered the first prototype J-10 on its maiden flight on 23 March 1998. Flight testing then apparently proceeded fairly smoothly and the new fighter was ready for service with the People's Liberation Army Air Force (PLAAF) in June 2004.

The initial-production J-10 was swiftly followed by the J-10A with various avionics improvements, including the latest Type 1473G fire-control radar, the J-10AH for land-based naval service and the J-10AS two-seat combat trainer with tandem seating and an enlarged dorsal spine. In naval use, the trainer version is the J-10ASH. Minor modifications to the single-seater and two-seater produced the J-10AY and J-10SY versions that are operated by the PLAAF's August 1 aerial demonstration team. The J-10 was introduced to service with a relatively basic air-to-air armament based around the short-range PL-8 infrared-guided and the medium-range PL-11 semi-active radar-guided air-to-air missiles (AAMs).

The aircraft has progressively received new weapons and sensor pods, including medium-range PL-12 active-radar-guided AAMs, as well as LS-500J precision-guided bombs, used in conjunction with a forward-looking infrared/laser targeting pod, which were added later. More recently, the PL-8 and PL-12 have begun to be

---

J-10
Weight (maximum take-off): 20,500kg (45,195lb)
Dimensions: Length 16.03m (52ft 7in), Wingspan 9.25m (30ft 4in), Height 5.43m (17ft 10in)
Powerplant: One Saturn AL-31FN turbofan engine rated at 79.43kN (17,860lb) of thrust with afterburning
Maximum speed: Mach 2.1
Range: 2250km (1400 miles)
Ceiling: 17,000m (56,000ft)
Crew: 1
Armament: One 23mm (0.9in) twin-barrel GSh-23 cannon plus a maximum of 6800kg (15,400lb) of disposable stores carried on 11 hardpoints

---

A Chengdu J-10A fighter of the People's Liberation Army Air Force seen at Dyagilevo air base, Russia, during Aviadarts International Army Games, August 2019.

4.5-GENERATION MULTIROLE FIGHTERS

Chengdu J-10B
J-10B serial number 10537 of the PLAAF's 5th Regiment, 2nd Division, based at Guilin. Compared to the J-10A, the B-model can be identified by its fixed diverterless supersonic inlet (DSI), infrared search and track sensors in front of the canopy, and a revised radome featuring a different profile.

superseded by the new-generation PL-10 and PL-15, respectively.

The J-10's advanced cockpit is equipped with a wide-angle head-up display, two monochrome multifunctional displays (MFDs) and one colour MFD. The pilot is provided with a helmet-mounted sight and 'hands on throttle and stick' controls.

Fifth prototype
Unveiled in late 2008, the J-10B is a much-improved development of the fighter, characterised by its fixed diverterless supersonic inlet (DSI), a reprofiled radome, an infrared search and track sensor and a holographic wide-angle head-up display. While the first J-10Bs retained the AL-31FN, the fifth prototype appeared with the indigenous WS-10B engine in 2011, although the subsequent production batch then reverted to the Russian powerplant, presumably due to ongoing problems with the Chinese engine, although it's notable that the Chinese engine had begun to be installed in all production J-11 and J-16 fighters some years before it appeared in series-built J-10s. In 2016 the J-10B was superseded by the J-10C, which introduced the definitive radar, incorporating an active electronically scanned array (AESA). Since around 2019 the WS-10 engine has been fitted as standard in the J-10C, while one of the J-10B aircraft has also been tested with a thrust-vectoring version of the same engine, although it is unclear if this is intended for future production versions too. It may well be the case that the thrust-vectoring J-10B instead primarily serves as an engine testbed for the J-20 fifth-generation fighter.

Chengdu J-10B
Serial number 1035 is understood to be the fifth prototype J-10B and was retained by Chengdu for trials work. While the J-10B introduced a new X-band passive electronically scanned array radar, this is replaced on the definitive J-10C by an active electronically scanned array. One J-10B prototype has been tested with a WS-10B engine featuring a thrust-vectoring nozzle.

4.5-GENERATION MULTIROLE FIGHTERS

PAC JF-17 Thunder

The JF-17 fighter was developed jointly by China's Chengdu and the Pakistan Aeronautical Complex (PAC), the aircraft being tailored to a significant degree to the Pakistan Air Force's requirement for a successor to its ageing Chengdu F-7, Dassault Mirage, Nanchang A-5 and Shenyang F-6 fleets.

An agreement on co-production and co-development was signed in 1999 and work then proceeded rapidly, an initial prototype of the JF-17 flying on 25 August 2003. The aircraft is powered by a Russian-designed RD-93 turbofan engine, an improved version of the RD-33 that is found in the MiG-29, while the initial radar is a Chinese KLJ-7(V)2 radar, of the mechanically steered type, which was also co-developed and co-produced by PAC.

Pre-production models

After six prototypes had been built, there followed a batch of eight pre-production aircraft before series-built JF-17s began to be produced by PAC at its Kamra facility beginning in 2008.

Following the delivery of the first 50 JF-17s to the PAF, production switched to the enhanced JF-17 Block II version, which has improved avionics, strengthened wing roots for additional stores carriage, an inflight refuelling probe and other improved operational capabilities.

While the original Block 1 jets were all single-seaters, the Block 2s are provided in both single-seat JF-17A and two-seat JF-17B versions, the latter also being used for lead-in fighter training. Most recently, Chengdu and PAC have developed a Block 3 version of the single-seat JF-17A, which introduces a KLJ-7A active electronically scanned array (AESA) radar, as well as an improved fly-by-wire flight-control system, infrared search and track system, helmet-mounted display and a larger holographic wide-angle head-up display for the pilot.

As well as steadily re-equipping the PAF fighter force, the JF-17 has found some export success with aircraft having been delivered to Myanmar and Nigeria.

JF-17A Block 2

Weight (maximum take-off): 12,384kg (27,302lb)
Dimensions: Length 14.93m (49ft), Wingspan 9.44m (31ft), Height 4.77m (15ft 8in)
Powerplant: One Klimov RD-93 turbofan engine rated at 84.4kN (19,000lb) thrust with af-terburner
Maximum speed: Mach 1.6
Range: 1352km (840 miles)
Ceiling: 16,920m (55,510ft)
Crew: 1
Armament: One 23mm (0.787in) twin-barrel GSh-23 cannon plus up to 1500kg (3300lb) of disposable stores carried on seven external hardpoints

---

JF-17 Thunder

This Block I Thunder is operated by the Pakistan Air Force's Combat Commander School (CCS), which includes a JF-17 squadron at PAF Base Mushaf. The PAF had received eight pre-production by mid-March 2008, but the Thunder did not formally enter service until early 2010, when 26 Squadron was re-equipped with the type at PAF Base Kamra.

4.5-GENERATION MULTIROLE FIGHTERS

JF-17 Thunder

The first export operator to receive the JF-17 is Myanmar, although few details about its fleet are available. An order for an unspecified quantity of Thunders was confirmed in November 2016 and the first examples were noted prior to delivery in June 2017. The type was apparently introduced to service with the Myanmar Air Force in late 2018.

Shenyang J-11 and J-16

When the original Su-27 entered service with the People's Liberation Army Air Force (PLAAF) in the early 1990s, it provided the service with its first truly modern fourth-generation fighter.

Such was the success of the Soviet design that Beijing acquired a license-manufacturing agreement for the fighter before taking its own development path and fielding successively more capable variants with an increasing proportion of indigenous technology.

After buying three batches of single-seat Su-27SK fighters and Su-27UBK two-seat conversion trainers amounting to a total of 78 aircraft, China struck a deal worth $1.2 billion to license-build 200 Su-27SKs under the local designation J-11, with work to be undertaken by Shenyang. Engines were to be provided by Russia in the form of the standard AL-31F turbofan.

Chinese variant

Shenyang began by assembling Russian-supplied kits but as production was ramped up, a greater proportion of indigenous

---

J-11A

Weight (maximum take-off): 33,000kg (72,753lb)
Dimensions: Length: 21.9m (69ft 6in) without probe, Wingspan 14.7m (48ft 3in), Height 5.7m (18ft 9in)
Powerplant: Two AL-31F series 3 turbofans, each rated at 122.5kN (27,558lb) with afterburning
Maximum speed: 2500km/h (1600mph) at altitude
Range: 3530km (2190 miles)
Ceiling: 19,000m (62,336ft)
Crew: 1
Armament: One GSh-301 30mm (1.2in) cannon, plus disposable stores carried on 10 hardpoints

---

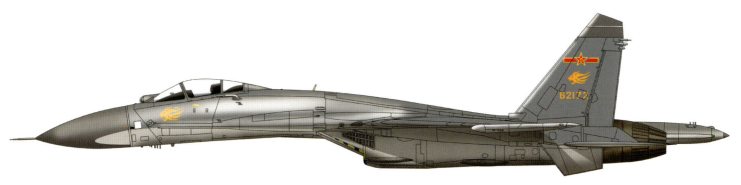

J-11A

This J-11A from the PLAAF's 16th Air Brigade at Yinchuan is unusual in that it wears unit markings on the nose in the form of a winged lion's head. The J-11A version was first flown in December 1999 and, by the end of 2006, a total of 105 were produced, including via modernisation of older aircraft. Production then switched to the J-11B.

4.5-GENERATION MULTIROLE FIGHTERS

J-16

A J-16 of the PLAAF's 98th Air Brigade, in October 2018. The J-16 is arguably the most capable multirole strike fighter in PLAAF service and is therefore one of the air arm's most prized assets. It combines features of the Russian-made Su-30MKK, including a refuelling probe and twin-wheel nose gear, with Chinese WS-10A engines and advanced indigenous avionics, among them AESA radar.

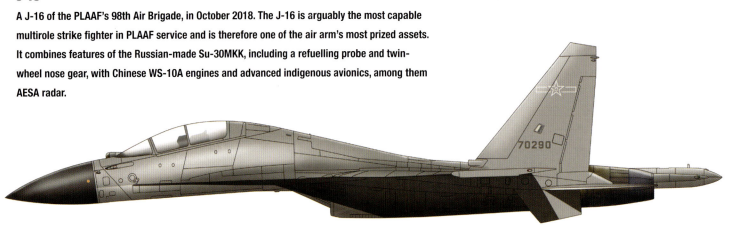

components were included, leading to full production – minus the engines. Around 95 kits were supplied by 2004, but by that date China had begun producing its first indigenous variant, the J-11A. Earlier aircraft were also brought up to the same standard, featuring a new digital cockpit with multifunction displays.

J-11B

Production then switched to the more ambitious J-11B, which added a Chinese multi-mode radar and Chinese-made WS-10A engines and was first flown in prototype form in 2004. Problems with the new engine meant that initial-production aircraft were delivered with the old AL-31F before the Chinese turbofan was introduced from late 2009.

The J-11B's Type 1493 radar can track six to eight targets and engage four simultaneously and the pilot is provided with an updated glass cockpit featuring five multifunction displays and a wide-angle head-up display. The electronic countermeasures system is Chinese, as is most of the weaponry, including PL-8 short-range infrared-guided and active-radar PL-12 air-to-air missiles.

J-16

The J-16 was revealed in 2012 and it's powered by the WS-10A turbofans that have now fully replaced the Russian AL-31Fs on Chinese-made 'Flankers'. As well as the AESA radar and a single-piece panoramic touch-screen display, the J-16 is provided with a wide range of advanced air-to-ground ordnance, including the KD-88 missile, LS-500J laser-guided bomb and standoff submunition dispensers.

Befitting a multirole fighter, the J-16 can also be armed with air-to-air missiles, including the short-range PL-10 and the medium-range PL-12 and PL-15, as well as an apparently unidentified very long-range AAM that is expected to be intended for use against airborne early warning aircraft and tankers.

There is also a J-16D version that has been developed for the suppression of enemy air defences (SEAD) role, which incorporates a new AESA radar, various electronic warfare antennas and large wingtip jamming pods.

Although there never existed a license agreement to produce the two-seater, Shenyang manufactured its own version of the Su-27UBK equipped to the same standard as the J-11B, producing the J-11BS. Both these B-versions are also operated by the People's Liberation Army Navy Air Force (PLANAF), as the J-11BH and J-11BSH respectively.

Fly-by-wire

The next variant is the J-11D, the most important feature of which is an active electronically scanned array (AESA) radar of local design. This is combined with a digital fly-by-wire control system and lightened structure featuring a greater proportion of composites. An inflight refuelling probe was also added. The exact status of this programme is unclear, and it may have been abandoned after the purchase of the Russian Su-35 or lost its priority with the introduction of the J-20.

In the meantime, work was already underway towards the two-seat J-16, an indigenous, dedicated multirole strike version of the 'Flanker'. The J-16 features both an inflight refuelling probe and AESA radar and is clearly inspired by the Russian-made Su-30MKK, with which it also shares twin-wheel nose landing gear and taller vertical tails.

4.5-GENERATION MULTIROLE FIGHTERS

Mitsubishi F-2

Looking very similar to the F-16, the Mitsubishi F-2 was developed for the Japan Air Self-Defense Force (JASDF) on the basis of that aircraft, with design work shared by Mitsubishi Heavy Industries and Lockheed Martin.

Production workshare was split roughly 60:40 in favour of Japanese industry and, although manufacture only yielded 94 aircraft (plus four prototypes) at a unit cost more closely comparable to the larger F-15, these jets today perform a vital role for the JASDF.

Intended to meet the requirement for a so-called Support Fighter, or FS-X, replacing the Cold War-era Mitsubishi F-1, the multirole F-2 was developed in the mid to late 1980s and was originally optimised for air-to-surface missions, including anti-shipping strikes to protect Japan's sea lanes, although it is also equipped for air defence missions.

The first prototype F-2 made its maiden flight on 7 October 1995 and production encompassed the single-seat F-2A and the two-seat F-2B with full combat capability, albeit with a somewhat reduced fuel load.

Increased wing area

Compared to the F-16, the F-2 features a wing area increased by around 25 per cent as well as a fuselage 'stretched' by around 43cm (17in). At one stage, it was planned to incorporate small canard foreplanes, and these were tested on a specially configured T-2, but these had been deleted by the time a full-scale mock-up was completed. The aircraft's fly-by-wire flight control system and integrated electronic warfare system were developed in Japan and the aircraft is provided with a range of indigenously developed air-to-ground and air-to-air weapons. Thanks to the larger wing, there are two additional stores stations compared to the F-16, as well as additional fuel capacity for an extended range. One other subtle difference compared to the F-16 is the F-2's two-piece cockpit canopy, a more robust construction required to provide protection against bird strikes in the low-level maritime environment.

The sensors include the J/APG-1 (later upgraded to APG-2 standard) active electronically scanned array (AESA) radar, the first of its kind to be fielded by an in-service fighter, as well as Lockheed Martin's Sniper Advanced Targeting Pod. While most of the avionics are Japanese, the cockpit of the F-2 is otherwise broadly similar to that of the F-16, including the sidestick controller.

F-2A

Weight (maximum take-off): 22,100kg (48,722lb)
Dimensions: Length 15.52m (50ft 11in), Wingspan 11.125m (36ft 6in) including wingtip pylons, Height 16ft (4.9m)
Powerplant: One General Electric F110-IHI-129 turbofan rated at 131kN (29,500lb) thrust with afterburning
Maximum speed: Mach 1.7
Range: 833km (518 miles)
Ceiling: 18,000m (59,000ft)
Crew: 1
Armament: One 20mm (0.787in) JM61A1 six-barrel rotary cannon, plus maximum weapon load of 8085kg (17,824lb)

F-2A

This single-seat F-2A, serial number 03-8509, wears the samurai insignia of the Japan Air Self-Defense Force's 3 Hikotai on the tail. After two XF-2A prototypes had been completed, the JASDF received 62 production F-2As, the last of these being delivered in September 2011. These serve with three frontline squadrons.

4.5-GENERATION MULTIROLE FIGHTERS

F-2B
Mainly employed for training, the two-seat F-2Bs, such as serial number 33-8122, are mainly assigned to 21 Hikotai, part of the JASDF's Air Training Command, and based at Matsushima. The F-2B production run encompassed two XF-2B prototypes and 32 production examples.

Weaponry

In terms of weapons, the F-1 can carry up to four indigenous anti-ship missiles, either the subsonic ASM-1 and ASM-2, with an active radar or an infrared seeker respectively, or the supersonic ASM-3 with a ramjet engine. Defensive armament includes the US-supplied AIM-7 Sparrow beyond-visual-range air-to-air missile and infrared-guided short-range AIM-9 Sidewinder, while indigenous options are the short-range AAM-3 and the beyond-visual-range AAM-4, which features an active radar seeker. Offensive weapons options have been expanded during the F-2's service career, adding, for example, the precision-guided 227kg (500lb) GCS-1 bomb, as well as the US-made Joint Direct Attack Munition (JDAM).

The JASDF F-2 force was struck a blow when Matsushima Air Base was hit by the powerful tsunami in March 2004, damaging 18 of these aircraft. Ultimately, however, all but a handful were restored to airworthy condition and the aircraft today continue to serve with three frontline and one training squadron at Hyakuri, Matsushima and Tsuiki.

Ultimately, plans call for the F-2 to be replaced by an all-new indigenous stealthy fighter, likely to be designated F-3, which is now being developed by Mitsubishi Heavy Industries under the F-X programme.

F-2 fighters from the Japan Air Self-Defense Force 8th Air Wing fly past Tsuiki Air Field, 2018.

4.5-GENERATION MULTIROLE FIGHTERS

HAL LCA Tejas

The Hindustan Aeronautics Limited (HAL) Light Combat Aircraft, or LCA, known to the Indian Air Force as the Tejas, is the first fully indigenous Indian fighter aircraft since the HAL HF-24 Marut that was designed in the 1950s.

The origins of the Tejas date back to the early 1980s, when the Indian Air Force (IAF) began planning for a successor to the MiG-21, as well as Gnat and Ajeet light fighters then in service. The project received the formal go-ahead in 1983, with plans to locally develop the turbofan engine as well as fly-by-wire technology, composite aero-structures, electronic warfare and radar systems. This ambitious undertaking inevitably led to delays, and it wasn't until 1991 that full-scale engineering and development was launched.

The first of two development aircraft took to the air on 4 January 2001 and these test aircraft were followed by another five prototypes. Ultimately, the indigenous input in the programme was scaled back, with an Israeli Elta EL/M-2032 radar and General Electric F404 engine being adopted instead of homegrown products.

Indian Air Force
After continued development work with the so-called Limited Series Production aircraft, the LCA was finally declared ready for service with the IAF in December 2013. In the meantime, a first carrier-based version – the Naval LCA – had taken to the air. Intended for service aboard Indian Navy aircraft carriers, this aircraft was ultimately rejected by the service.

The first series-production aircraft for the IAF was handed over in January 2015 and the service received 20 Tejas Mk 1 aircraft in an Initial Operating Capability (IOC) version before switching to the Full Operating Capability (FOC) model, deliveries of these 20 jets beginning in late 2019 and including the first two-seat trainers. Beyond this, the IAF is receiving another 83 aircraft completed to an improved Tejas Mk 1A standard, with active electronically scanned array (AESA) radar and improved electronic warfare self-protection equipment.

Tejas Mk 1
Weight (maximum take-off): 13,500kg (29,762lb)
Dimensions: Length 13.2m (43ft 4in), Wingspan 8.2m (26ft 11in), Height 4.4m (14ft 5in)
Powerplant: One General Electric F404-GE-IN20 turbofan rated at 90kN (20,200lb) thrust with afterburning
Maximum speed: Mach 1.6
Range: 3200km (1986 miles) with two external drop tanks
Ceiling: 16,500m (50,000ft)
Crew: 1
Armament: One 23mm (0.787in) twin-barrel GSh-23 cannon plus up to 5300kg (11,685lb) of disposable stores carried on eight external hardpoints

Tejas Mk 1
Serial number LA-5018 was the Indian Air Force's first Tejas Mk1 to be completed to the Final Operational Clearance (FOC) standard. It was delivered to No 18 Squadron 'Flying Bullets' at Sulur Air Force Station in May 2020. This is the second unit to operate the type, following No 45 Squadron 'Flying Daggers' at the same base.

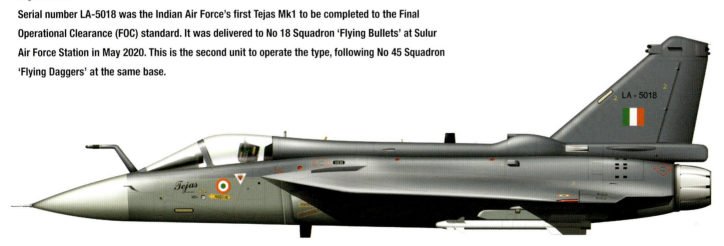

FOURTH-GENERATION MULTIROLE FIGHTERS

The fourth-generation types appeared in service towards the end of the Cold War and represented a significant technological leap over the aircraft that immediately preceded them. In general, the fourth-generation fighters introduced advanced technologies, including fly-by-wire control systems, composite materials and the first generation of true digital avionics and advanced sensors. Some of the original fourth-generation designs have continued to be enhanced and are now classified as 4.5 generation, while others remain in service today with more modest mid-life updates.

This chapter includes the following aircraft:
- Dassault Mirage 2000
- Grumman F-14 Tomcat
- Northrop F-5E/F Tiger I
- Mikoyan MiG-29
- Mikoyan MiG-31
- Sukhoi Su-27
- AIDC F-CK-1 Ching-kuo

A head-on view of a French Air Force Mirage 2000C as it approaches a U.S. Air Force KC-135R Stratotanker to refuel during a Combat Patrol mission while participating in NATO operations.

FOURTH-GENERATION MULTIROLE FIGHTERS
Dassault Mirage 2000

France's Dassault developed the Mirage 2000 as a successor to the Mirage F1, returning to the trademark delta-wing configuration that had been used so successfully on the Mirage III family but combining it with new fly-by-wire controls for much-improved agility.

After an official requirement was drawn up in 1976, Dassault launched a high-priority programme to get the new interceptor in service by the early 1980s and the first prototype took to the air on 10 March 1978.

The French Air Force was the major customer of the Mirage 2000 and as well as the air defence-optimised, single-seat Mirage 2000C, the air arm subsequently received two different dual-seat ground-attack versions as well – the Mirage 2000N for nuclear penetration and the conventionally armed Mirage 200D.

The first production Mirage 2000Cs were delivered to the French Air Force in 1983 and went into service the following year. As well as 124 single-seat Mirage 2000Cs, the service also took delivery of 30 two-seat Mirage 2000B trainers. Initially, the Mirage 2000C was powered by the interim Snecma M53-5 engine and was fitted with the RDM radar. From the 38th aircraft, the uprated M53-P2 and improved RDI radar were fitted as standard.

Nuclear capability

From 1987, the next version to enter service was the two-seat Mirage 2000N with an all-new weapons and navigation system, including terrain-following radar, fully integrated self-defence suite and the nuclear-tipped ASMP cruise missile.

While the Mirage 2000N has since been superseded by the Rafale, the Mirage 2000D remains in use. It has a revised cockpit with 'hands on throttle and stick' controls as well as a laser designator pod and improved self-defence suite.

A somewhat downgraded version of the Mirage 2000B/C was developed for export and won orders from Egypt, Greece, India, Peru and the United Arab Emirates (UAE). These aircraft were fitted with the M53-P2 engine and RDM+ radar, while the Greek aircraft added a unique anti-shipping capability with the Exocet missile. Brazil, meanwhile, acquired a dozen second-hand French Air Force Mirage 2000C/Bs as interim air defence fighters, operating them only relatively briefly while its F-5s were being upgraded.

Mirage 2000C
Weight (maximum take-off): 17,000kg (37,479lb)
Dimensions: Length 14.36m (47ft 1in), Wingspan 9.13m (29ft 11in), Height 5.2m (17ft 1in)
Powerplant: One SNECMA M53-P2 turbofan engine rated at 95.1kN (21,400lb) of thrust with afterburning
Maximum speed: Mach 2.2
Range: 3335km (2072 miles) with external fuel
Ceiling: 17,060m (55,970ft)
Crew: 1
Armament: Two 30mm (1.1in) DEFA 554 cannon, plus up to 6300kg (13,900lb) of stores carried on nine external hardpoints

Mirage F-2000C
The Brazilian Air Force operated the Mirage 2000, exclusively in the air defence role, between 2006 and 2013, under the local designation F-2000. Ten former French Mirage 2000Cs and a pair of two-seat Mirage 2000Bs were acquired under a lease arrangement, pending the Brazilian Air Force's decision to acquire the Gripen as its new fighter.

FOURTH-GENERATION MULTIROLE FIGHTERS

Mirage 2000N
Deliveries of the Mirage 2000N nuclear strike aircraft commenced in 1987 and the type entered service in April 1988. A total of 75 of these aircraft were delivered but the type was withdrawn in June 2018 and the remaining active aircraft put into storage. The French Air Force's airborne nuclear deterrence role is now handled by the Rafale.

The export success of the basic Mirage 2000 prompted the manufacturer to further develop the aircraft as the Mirage 2000-5, or Dash 5, with new avionics including an RDY multi-mode radar and MICA air-to-air missiles, as well as five cockpit displays including a wide-angle head-up display.

France updated a portion of its Mirage 2000Cs to 2000-5F standard, while Qatar and Taiwan both procured new-build Dash 5s. India subsequently also selected the Dash 5 standard when it decided to upgrade its existing Mirage 2000 fleet.

Air-to-ground missions

Since the Dash 5 was optimised for air defence, Dassault then launched the Mirage 2000-5 Mk2 – or Mirage 2000-9 – which added precision weapons such as laser-guided bombs for air-to-ground missions. The radar was updated to RDY-2 standard with increased range and new modes, including synthetic aperture, while the electronic warfare suite was also modernised. Weapons options include the MICA IR, the SCALP cruise missile and the Exocet. As the definitive Mirage 2000, the Dash 5 Mk2 – or 2000-9 – has been exported to two countries. Greece acquired new-build Mirage 2000-5 Mk2s and updated 10 of its earlier aircraft to the same standard, adding SCALP cruise missiles. Meanwhile, the UAE procured the 2000-9, which is undoubtedly the most advanced variant of the type, with an Integrated Modular Electronic Warfare System (IMEWS), Damocles targeting pod and forward-looking infrared sensor. The 2000-9 is also armed with the Black Shaheen derivative of the SCALP cruise missile.

A French Mirage 2000C taxis at Bodø Air Station, Norway. The air intakes of the SNECMA M53-P2 turbofan engine are prominent.

FOURTH-GENERATION MULTIROLE FIGHTERS

Grumman F-14 Tomcat

Still today most famous for its service with the US Navy as a carrier-based air defence fighter, the Tomcat is now only in operational use with Iran, which was its sole export customer.

The Imperial Iranian Air Force (IIAF) as it was then known received 79 examples of the F-14A that were delivered before the Islamic revolution of 1979. Today's Islamic Republic of Iran Air Force (IRIAF) continues to prize its Tomcats and, although the fleet has suffered from a lack of spare parts and serviceability issues through the years, the country has invested heavily in keeping the jets flying and has also embarked on indigenous improvement programmes with varying degrees of success.

Deliveries of F-14s to the IIAF began in 1976 and there were three frontline squadrons and one training unit active at the time of the revolution. Once the Iran–Iraq War began in September 1980, the now-IRIAF Tomcats were in the thick of the action, using their infrared-guided AIM-9J Sidewinder, radar-guided AIM-7E Sparrow and long-range AIM-54A Phoenix air-to-air missiles to good effect. Despite 64 confirmed victories in aerial combat, the Iranian Tomcat fleet was in poor shape when the war ended in 1988, with only around 30 examples still airworthy.

Arms embargoes

However, by the 1990s, the number of airworthy Tomcats had doubled but as embargoes hit in the years that followed, serviceability decreased once again and one squadron was disbanded.

Although Iran has been engineering spare parts to keep its remaining F-14s operational, the AN/AWG-9 radar and fire-control system is not fully combat-capable on many of the aircraft. Efforts were made to integrate an air-launched version of the MIM-23B surface-to-air missile, but this seems to have had only limited success, while other aircraft have been adapted to carry freefall Mk 80 series bombs, in a broad equivalent to the US Navy's own F-14 'Bombcat'.

F-14A Tomcat
Weight (maximum take-off): 32,659kg (72,000lb)
Dimensions: Length 19.10m (62ft 8in), Wingspan 19.54m (64ft 1.5in) unswept or 11.65m (38ft 2.5in) swept, Height 4.88m (16ft)
Powerplant: Two Pratt & Whitney TF-30P-414A turbofan engines each rated at 92.97kN (20,900lb) thrust with afterburning
Maximum speed: Mach 2.38
Range: 3200km (2000 miles) with two external drop tanks
Ceiling: 15,240m (50,000ft)
Crew: 2
Armament: One 20mm (0.787in) M61A1 Vulcan six-barrel Gatling cannon, plus up to 6600kg (14,500lb) of ordnance and fuel tanks carried on 10 external hardpoints

---

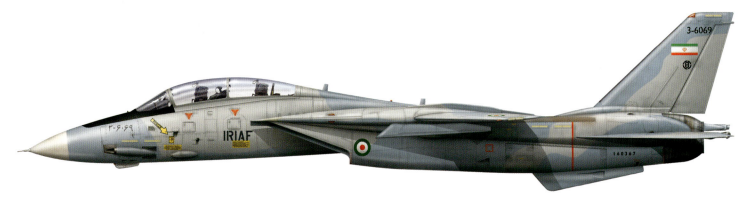

F-14A Tomcat
The Islamic Republic of Iran Air Force (IRIAF) is today the sole operator of the F-14, with three squadrons still equipped with the survivors from a total of 79 aircraft originally delivered. Operating units are the 81st Tactical Fighter Squadron (TFS), 82nd TFS, and the 83rd TFS, all based at Esfahan, in central Iran.

DEFENSIVE SYSTEMS

The Su-27 is protected by an L-006 (SPO-15) Beryoza passive radar warning receiver system, with antennas on the trailing edges of the tailfins. This gives 360° coverage and classifies, prioritizes and displays threats using a built-in threat library, and indicates bearing, range and system type. The aircraft also has a Parol identification friend-or-foe (IFF) set and an S0-69 transponder. The internal electronic countermeasures (ECM) system can be used in the rear hemisphere only when the Su-27's own onboard radar is in use.

TAILCONE AND ENGINE NACELLES

The long tailcone projecting aft from between the engine nacelles reduces drag and accommodates the twin braking parachutes and a variety of other equipment items. Perhaps most obviously, there is the APP-50 chaff/flare dispenser system, comprising 32 groups of chaff/flare dispensers above the tailcone, each containing three launchers. The engine nacelles are anchored beneath the mid-fuselage and, together with twin side-mounted tailbooms and a central boom, form the rear fuselage.

SHORT-RANGE MISSILES

For close-range engagements, the basic Su-27 can carry up to four R-73 (AA-11 'Archer') infrared-guided air-to-air missiles (AAMs) on the wingtip and outboard underwing pylons. One of the first of a new generation of close-range AAMs that appeared toward the end of the Cold War, the R-73 featured what was, for the time, a new level of agility and was capable of off-axis launch from all aspects.

Dassault Mirage 2000

The Mirage 2000 has had considerable export success, being sold to Egypt, Greece, Peru, Qatar, Taiwan and India. This Mirage 2000 flew with No. 1 Squadron, Central Air Command, Maharajpura Air Force Base, in Gwailor, India. The No. 1 'Tigers' Squadron is mainly an air defence unit, but can also undertake ground-attack missions.

RADOME
The glass fibre radome is designed for high bird strike and erosion resistance. The strike Mirage 2000N has a similar radome covering its ESD Antilope terrain-following radar scanner.

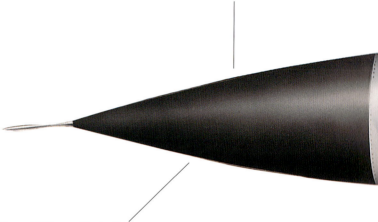

RADAR
Early French Mirage 2000s are fitted with the Thomson CSF RDM multi-mode pulse-Doppler radar, a generally improved version of the Cyrano IV fitted to the Mirage F1. This set was originally intended to be for export aircraft only. All French 2000s will eventually receive the newer RDI radar.

MATRA SUPER R530D
This missile has a body of steel and steel honeycomb and a ceramic radome that give great strength and temperature resistance and allow speeds of up to Mach 4.6. The missile has a 56-km (35-mile) range and can be used against targets up to 9150m (30,000ft) above or below the launch aircraft.

COMBAT PERSISTENCE
One area where the Su-27 still excels is its ability to engage many targets during the same mission. With a typical combat load of six R-27 medium-/long-range missiles, four short-range R-73s and an internal cannon, the Su-27 can engage several targets before having to return to base and refuel and rearm.

STRAKE
A small fixed strake with marked dihedral on each intake trunk produces a similar effect to a canard foreplane, improving manoeuvrability and angle of attack (AOA) performance.

EJECTION SEAT
The aircraft is fitted with Martin-Baker F10Q zero-zero capable ejection seats to allow safe escape at all altitudes and airspeeds.

WINDSHIELD
The curved one-piece windscreen gives the Mirage 2000 pilot an excellent, unobscured forward view.

ENGINE AIR INTAKE
The semi-circular section air intakes are fitted with moveable half-cone centrebodies which adjust airflow to the engine in different flight regimes.

WING ROOT FAIRINGS
Karman fairings give extra internal fuel capacity, and allow a semi-blended wing/body junction.

MAIN UNDERCARRIAGE
The Messier-Hispano-Bugatti single-wheel main undercarriage units retract into the wing roots. Hydraulically-actuated carbon composite disc brakes are fitted.

GSH-301 CANNON
Provided with 150 rounds, the internal 30mm (1.18in) cannon is the same highly accurate GSh-30-1 as is carried by the MiG-29 'Fulcrum' series and by other members of the 'Flanker' family. Combat capability during air combat is boosted significantly by the integration of a helmet-mounted weapon cueing system for the pilot.

LONG-RANGE MISSILE ARMAMENT
The Su-27's primary armament is the R-27, known to NATO as the AA-10 'Alamo'. This is a family of missiles with long and short range infrared-guided and semi-active radar guided variants. The Su-27 carries R-27s on its inboard underwing pylons, on pylons below the engine intake ducts, and in tandem between the engine nacelles. The basic semi-active radar homing (SARH) R-27R is usually carried between the nacelles or underwing, as is the IR homing R-27T. Long range versions of both SARH and IR-homing variants are the R-27RE and R-27TE, with a boost sustain motor. They are usually carried under the intakes.

AIRBRAKES
Typical Mirage airbrakes are located above and below each wing, set close in to the wing root

LEADING EDGE FLAPS
These two-section, full-span flaps are retracted during the cruise or acceleration, and operate in conjunction with the elevons to enhance lift and/or manoeuvrability.

DELTA WING

The Mirage 2000 has a low-set, cantilever multi-sparred wing with a traditional delta wing planform. There is 58° of sweep on the cambered leading edge.

RUDDER

The inset rudder is actuated by the fly-by-wire control system via hydraulic servos. There is no manual reversion. The rudder has a light alloy honeycomb core and a boron/epoxy/carbon composite skin.

POWERPLANT

Most Mirage 2000s are powered by the SNECMA M53-P2 turbofan, rated at 6560kg (14,462lb st) dry and 9700kg (21,385lb st) with afterburning. Older French Mirage 2000Cs may still be fitted with the less powerful M53-5.

ELEVONS

The trailing edge of the wing consists of twin section full span elevons, actuated by the fly-by-wire control system. They can operate symmetrically as elevators or flaps, or differentially as ailerons.

ENGINE NOZZLE

A variable area exhaust nozzle is provided for the afterburning turbofan engine.

Sukhoi Su-27 'Flanker-B'

This single-seat 'Flanker-B' was part of the Soviet (and later Russian) military presence in Poland, flying from the airfield at Chojna in the northwest of that country. The operating unit was the 582nd 'Guards' Fighter Aviation Regiment, part of the 4th Air Army (Northern Group of Forces), Frontal Aviation. The regiment was one of two Poland-based Su-27 units withdrawn to Russia during 1992 as part of the general withdrawal of Russian forces from Europe.

INDIVIDUAL MARKINGS

This aircraft carries seven red stars under the cockpit, denoting live missile firings during exercises. The 'dart and pentagon' emblem below these is an excellence award, applied to individual aircraft in recognition of their condition as a reward to the crew chief.

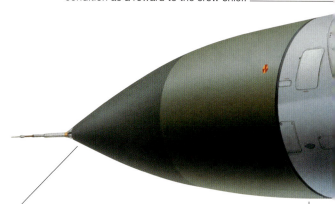

EARLY PRODUCTION BATCH

This aircraft, 'Blue 24', was one of several from the early production batch of Su-27s that were based at Chojna. These could be identified on account of their dark green radomes and dielectric panels. These were changed to white for later 'Flankers'.

FLIGHT CONTROL SYSTEM

While the Su-27 has a partial fly-by-wire (FBW) flight control system, the aircraft is statically unstable only in pitch, since this is necessary to achieve the benefits of high manoeuvrability, low drag, high lift and reduced weight. The Su-27's SDU-21 system controls the aircraft in pitch but provides only stability augmentation to the mechanical lateral and yaw control circuits. The control system consists of four computers, each fed from a separate air data source, with quadruple-redundant transducers and signal paths.

FOURTH-GENERATION MULTIROLE FIGHTERS

Northrop F-5E/F Tiger II

The F-5E/F was one of the most successful US export fighters of the Cold War and it continues in service today with a diminishing number of operators, its frontline status a testament to its suitability for a range of avionics, aerodynamic and weapons upgrades.

Developed as an improved version of the F-5A/B Freedom Fighter, the first single-seat F-5E took to the air on 11 August 1972. In total, Northrop completed over 790 F-5Es and 140 two-seat F-5Fs, plus 12 RF-5E reconnaissance variants. Another 90 examples were built under license in Switzerland, which continues to use the type for air defence.

Today, the US Navy and Marine Corps employ 44 former Swiss F-5Es (redesignated as F-5Ns) and F-5Fs as adversary aircraft, ideally suited for simulating types such as the MiG-21. Other Tiger IIs also perform similar duties in the hands of private contractors.

The F-5E/F remains the primary frontline fighter for the Brazilian Air Force and also continues to serve with Chile. The Brazilian jets have been upgraded to F-5EM/FM standard with Leonardo Grifo-F radar, Rafael Derby beyond-visual-range air-to-air missiles (AAMs) and short-range Python 3 and 4 AAMs. Chile's F-5E Tigre IIIs are similarly upgraded, with Elta EL/M-2032B multi-mode fire-control radar, Derby and Python missiles, Elop head-up display, 'hands on throttle and stick' controls and the Elbit Display And Sight Helmet (DASH). Mexico and Honduras also retain a handful of F-5E/Fs, but these have not received significant capability upgrades.

In the Middle East, Bahrain and Iran are the remaining F-5E/F operators, the Islamic Republic of Iran Air Force retaining the survivors from what was once the world's second largest F-5 fleet. A number of these aircraft have further passed through indigenous modification programmes, some of these adding twin vertical stabilisers.

Kenya's Tiger IIs remain operational in limited numbers, while Royal Moroccan Air Force F-5E/Fs have also been modernised with Grifo-F/X Plus radar, new electronic warfare systems and precision-guided bombs. The final African operator is Tunisia, whose aircraft have been modernised by Northrop Grumman.

The largest remaining operator of the F-5E/F is South Korea, with around 120 examples that have undergone a service-life extension programme with Korea Aerospace Industries. The F-5E/F also remains in service with Taiwan's air force, which mainly uses the type for lead-in fighter training, as well as flying a handful of RF-5E Tigereye variants for reconnaissance. Taiwan is the third Asian operator of the type and its jets have also been extensively modernised, featuring a new cockpit, electronic warfare systems, DASH and Python 4 missiles.

F-5EM Tiger II
Weight (maximum take-off): 11,214kg (24,722lb)
Dimensions: Length 14.4m (47ft 4.7in), Wingspan 8.1m (26ft 8in), Height 4.1m (13ft 4.25in)
Powerplant: Two General Electric J85-GE-21C turbojet engines each producing 22.24kN (5,000lb) of thrust.
Maximum speed: Mach 1.64
Range: 1328km (825 miles), clean
Ceiling: 15,240m (50,000ft)
Crew: 1
Armament: None

Northrop F-5EM Tiger II
The Brazilian Air Force operates some of the most heavily upgraded Tiger IIs anywhere in the world. The upgrade is built around a Leonardo Grifo pulse-Doppler radar with multi-aircraft targeting capability, while an Embraer datalink allows information to be exchanged with other F-5s within the same formation.

FOURTH-GENERATION MULTIROLE FIGHTERS

Mikoyan MiG-29

While the original MiG-29 is now of diminishing importance in the Russian Aerospace Forces, the fighter remains in widespread service around the world.

MiG-29SE
The MiG-29SD and MiG-29SE were produced as export derivatives of the 9.12 and 9.13, respectively, and combine N019ME radar with R-77 beyond-visual-range AAMs, plus some Western navigation and communication equipment. Sudan received a batch of 10 MiG-29SD aircraft, plus a pair of MiG-29UBs, in 2004.

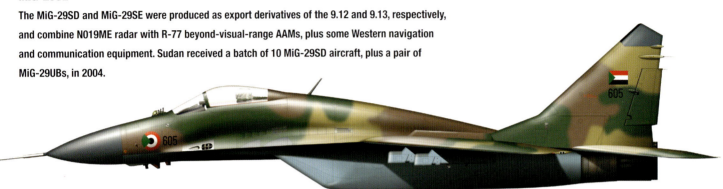

With the Western reporting name 'Fulcrum', the MiG-29 serves with several NATO air arms and a number of upgrade programmes have been initiated to ensure it remains active on the frontline for the foreseeable future.

The MiG-29 was originally designed in the early 1970s and it was decided that the Soviet Air Force would adopt the fighter as a 'lightweight' counterpart of the 'heavyweight' Su-27. The first MiG-29 prototype took to the air on 6 October 1977 and a total of 14 aircraft were completed for development work before pre-production aircraft began to join the test campaign in 1979. Finally, the initial series-production aircraft flew in 1982.

In its initial single-seat fighter form, the MiG-29 'Fulcrum-A' (factory designation izdeliye 9.12) was powered by a pair of RD-33 afterburning turbofans and its pilot was provided with analogue cockpit instruments. The airframe made some use of composites and featured a large, blended fuselage/wing centre section and wing leading-edge root extensions that provided considerable lift. Unlike in the Su-27, the original flight-control system was not fly-by-wire. An unusual feature were the auxiliary air intakes above the wing roots that were activated for operations on rough airstrips, the main engine intakes being blanked off by large doors to prevent foreign object damage.

Targeting and navigation
The fire-control system was based around an N019 pulse-Doppler radar with lookdown/shootdown capability, coupled with an infrared search and track (IRST) system with the sensor mounted in front of the cockpit that provided targeting and navigation. The pilot was also provided with a helmet-mounted sight for target designation. Using the radar, the pilot could track 10 targets simultaneously while searching for more and could engage one of them.

While the single-seat MiG-29 was built in Moscow, a separate factory in Gorky (today Nizhny Novgorod) handled production of the two-seat MiG-29UB 'Fulcrum-B'. This retained a limited combat capability, with the 30mm (1.2in) GSh-30-1 cannon and underwing pylons and IRST, but lacked radar.

Standard armament, as well as the cannon with 150 rounds of ammunition, comprised two medium-range R-27R

MiG-29 'Fulcrum-C'
Weight (maximum take-off): 14,200kg (31,306lb)
Dimensions: Length 17.32m (56ft 10in), Wingspan 11.41m (37ft 5in), Height 4.73m (15ft 6in)
Powerplant: Two Klimov RD-33 turbofans each rated at 81.4kN (18,300lb) with afterburning
Maximum speed: Mach 2.3
Range: 2100km (1305 miles) with drop tank
Ceiling: 18,000m (59,050ft)
Crew: 1
Armament: One GSh-301 30mm (1.2in) cannon, plus up to 4000kg (8818lb) of stores carried on eight hardpoints

(AA-10 'Alamo') semi-active radar-guided air-to-air missiles (AAMs) plus up to four R-73 (AA-11 'Archer') or R-60M (AA-8 'Aphid') short-range infrared-guided AAMs. Air-to-ground weapons included a range of unguided bombs and rockets, or tactical nuclear bombs for Soviet-operated aircraft.

The next major production version of the Soviet era was the izdeliye 9.13 that retains the MiG-29 name in service but received the Western reporting name 'Fulcrum-C.' Its major difference is increased internal fuel capacity and optional underwing fuel tanks to address the limited range of the initial model, as well as a new electronic jammer.

FOURTH-GENERATION MULTIROLE FIGHTERS

Radar upgrade

While the 'Fulcrum-C' became the major production version, it was joined shortly before the collapse of the Soviet Union by the MiG-29S (9.13S) that features a more advanced N019M Topaz radar that offers extended range and compatibility with the medium-range R-77 (AA-12 'Adder') AAM with active radar guidance. Only a small batch was ever completed before production came to an end in 1993, with more than 1300 of all variants having been built.

In the immediate aftermath of the end of the Soviet Union, MiG made several efforts to offer more advanced versions of the MiG-29 for export. These included the MiG-29SD and MiG-29SE that were based on the 9.12 and 9.13 airframes respectively, both with export-optimised N019ME radar, R-77 AAMs and some Western avionics. Customers included Eritrea, Myanmar, Peru and Sudan. Adding an inflight refuelling probe to the MiG-29SD created the special MiG-29N that was delivered only to Malaysia.

Further advanced was the MiG-29SM that added an N019MP radar with air-to-ground capability and could carry a range of precision-guided munitions. Peruvian MiG-29s were upgraded to this standard and, reportedly, Syrian 'Fulcrums' have also been brought up to a similar standard.

A more extensive reworking of the basic design created the MiG-29SMT (izdeliye 9.17) and the two-seat MiG-29UBT (izdeliye 9.52), adding a large conformal fuel tank in the spine of the aircraft as well as a completely revised avionics suite. This included the N019MP radar with air-to-ground modes, a glass cockpit with two multifunction displays and hands on throttle and stick (HOTAS) controls. An inflight refuelling probe was by now fitted as standard. While the 9.17 and 9.52 found little interest and never proceeded beyond prototypes, the MiG-29SMT (izdeliye 9.18) has been more successful, this lacking the conformal fuel tank but adding more advanced avionics including an export version of the N010M radar. It has been sold to Yemen.

Algeria then placed an order for a different iteration of the MiG-29SMT (izdeliye 9.19) with a dorsal fuel tank reinstated. However, the Algerian aircraft were ultimately rejected by the customer and returned to Russia, which then put them into service itself.

Probably the most advanced of all the upgraded 'Fulcrums' is India's MiG-29UPG (izdeliye 9.20), which adds a 9.19-style dorsal fuel tank, new RD-33 series 3M engines, Zhuk-M2E radar with additional modes and an updated IRST. It also features India-specified electronic warfare equipment, including items from local production.

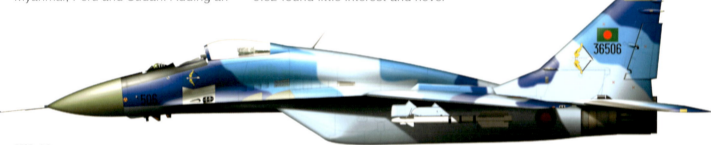

MiG-29
Although Bangladesh offered its MiG-29 fleet for sale in 2002, citing excessive operating costs, type remains in service today. The Bangladesh Air Force received six single-seat MiG-29 (9.12B, non-Warsaw Pact export standard) fighters and a pair of two-seat MiG-29UB combat trainers. These entered service with 8 Squadron in 1999.

MiG-29UPG
Serial number KBU3123 is one of the Indian Air Force's upgraded MiG-29UPG jets, in this case assigned to 8 Wing. India placed a contract for the upgrade of 57 jets, based on 50 existing single-seat MiG-29s and seven two-seat MiG-29UBs. The last two examples started the upgrade process in September 2019, after which another 21 second-hand jets were ordered from Russia.

FOURTH-GENERATION MULTIROLE FIGHTERS

Mikoyan MiG-31

The MiG-31 took shape in the Cold War as a long-range interceptor intended to defend the Soviet Union's northern regions against attack, especially by cruise missiles.

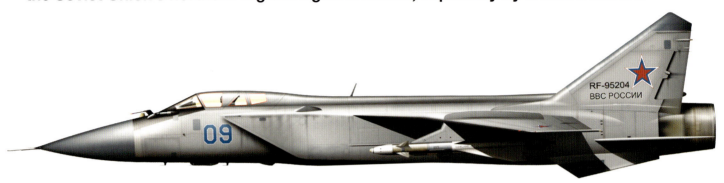

MiG-31DZ
This 'Foxhound' is one of a dwindling number of active Russian Aerospace Forces examples that have not yet undergone the MiG-31BM modernisation. RF-95204 is an inflight-refuelling-capable MiG-31DZ that's operated by the 764th Fighter Aviation Regiment based at Bolshoye Savino near Perm. A long-range infrared-guided R-40TD (AA-6 'Acrid') missile is seen below the wing.

The MiG-31 programme was launched in 1968 to replace the MiG-25 'Foxbat' and the resulting aircraft shared some similarities with its predecessor. However, major differences included two crew seated in tandem and a powerful Zaslon electronically scanned radar able to engage multiple targets simultaneously. The initial MiG-25MP prototype took to the air on 16 September 1975 and was followed by a first production MiG-31 a little over a year later. Deliveries of the first MiG-31 'Foxhound-A' aircraft commenced soon after and the first unit was declared operational at Pravdinsk, near Gorky, in 1983.

Meanwhile, improvements were made on the avionics side, after details of the Zaslon radar and R-33 (AA-8 'Amos') long-range air-to-air missiles (AAMs) were compromised during a spy scandal. The MiG-31B variant introduced the enhanced Zaslon-A radar and modified R-33S AAMs in response. The MiG-31 and MiG-31B were also complemented by the MiG-31DZ variant that added an inflight refuelling probe for extended-duration missions and which entered production in 1989. Meanwhile, earlier aircraft were also modernised to the improved MiG-31B standard, resulting in the MiG-31BS that was produced using existing MiG-31 or MiG-31DZ airframes.

Advanced derivatives
Towards the end of the Soviet era, work was underway on two yet more advanced derivatives, the MiG-31D that carried an anti-satellite missile and the MiG-31M 'Foxhound-B' that was an improved version of the original interceptor, with Zaslon-M radar, additional internal fuel and new AAMs. While several test aircraft were completed, no quantity production was undertaken.

After the demise of the Soviet Union, Russia embarked on a mid-life upgrade of its existing 'Foxhounds' under the MiG-31BM programme. This includes an improved Zaslon-AM radar with increased range and the ability to track 24 targets and engage six of them simultaneously. New weapons include the very long-range R-37M (AA-13 'Axehead') AAM that was originally developed for the MiG-31M. The twin cockpits are also outfitted with new liquid-crystal displays and new navigation and communication equipment is fitted.

More recently, Russia has developed the MiG-31 to undertake new roles, beginning with the MiG-31K strike aircraft that carries a single Kinzhal ballistic missile under the fuselage and which was first seen in public during

MiG-31B
Weight (maximum take-off): 46,200kg (101,853lb)
Dimensions: Length 20.62m (67ft 8in) without probe, Wingspan 13.46m (44ft 2in), Height 6.15m (20ft 2in)
Powerplant: Two Aviadvigatel/Perm D-30F-6 turbofans each rated at 152kN (34,172lb) thrust with afterburning
Maximum speed: Mach 2.83
Range: 3300km (2051 miles) unrefuelled
Ceiling: 20,600m (67,585ft)
Crew: 2
Armament: One six-barrel GSh-6-23 23mm (0.9in) cannon, four semi-active radar-guided R-33 AAMs below the fuselage, plus two medium-range R-40TD or four R-60M AAMs on wing pylons

FOURTH-GENERATION MULTIROLE FIGHTERS

MiG-31BM
RF-92385 is an upgraded MiG-31BM that was delivered to the 3958th Aviation Base at Savasleyka, a long-term 'Foxhound' operating location. Compared to the original jets, the MiG-31BM features different underwing weapons pylons, optimised for carriage of the R-73 (AA-11 'Archer') short-range missiles, which replaced the older R-40s and R-60s.

the Victory Day parade in Moscow in 2018. Based on the Iskander surface-to-surface missile, the Kinzhal can carry a nuclear or conventional warhead over a reported range of more than 2000km (1243 miles) at hypersonic speed.

Anti-satellite role
Russia has also turned its attention back to an anti-satellite version of the MiG-31 under the Burevestnik programme. This involves a single large, two-stage solid-fuel rocket carried below the interceptor's fuselage. It is expected that the Burevestnik will launch small interceptor satellites into orbit to defeat enemy satellites.

The 'Foxhound' remains in service with the Russian Aerospace Forces and Russian Navy, with aircraft being processed through the MiG-31BM upgrade programme. As of 2020, Russia operated around 120 examples of the MiG-31BM, plus a much smaller number of non-upgraded aircraft along with dozens more in a non-airworthy status. The only foreign operator is Kazakhstan, which inherited aircraft on its territory after the collapse of the Soviet Union.

A Mikoyan MiG-31 interceptor prepares for the 2018 Victory Day Parade in Russia. A Kinzhal ('dagger') nuclear-capable, air-launched ballistic missile is prominent on the underside of the aircraft.

FOURTH-GENERATION MULTIROLE FIGHTERS

Sukhoi Su-27

Today's successful 'Flanker' series of combat aircraft – the Su-30, Su-33, Su-34 and Su-35 are all described separately – started out in the form of the Su-27, a single-seat, long-range, air-superiority fighter.

Work on what became the Su-27 began under the Perspektivnyi Frontovoi Istrebitel, or future tactical fighter programme that was launched in the Soviet Union in 1969, Sukhoi's T-10 design being chosen in 1971. The first prototype of the T-10 made its maiden flight on 20 May 1977 and received the Western reporting name 'Flanker-A,' but after seven examples had been completed it was decided that a major redesign was required.

The reworked design was the T-10S and this took to the air for the first time in April 1981. The aircraft was of all-metal construction with a wide, blended fuselage/wing centre section similar to that chosen for the MiG-29. The twin, uncanted tailfins were supplemented by twin ventral fins. Power was provided by two AL-31F afterburning turbofans and there was considerable internal fuel capacity, including in the tailfins, to provide a very respectable range. A distinctive long boom projecting aft between the engines carried more fuel, as well as

countermeasures dispensers and a drag chute. An analogue fly-by-wire flight control system was also fitted, helping the Su-27 retain controllability during extreme manoeuvres.

Combat trainers

Production of the initial single-seat Su-27 'Flanker-B' began in 1982 and was later complemented by two-seat Su-27UB 'Flanker-C' combat trainers. While single-seaters were built in Komsomolsk-on-Amur in the Far East, almost all the two-seaters came from the factory in Irkutsk.

The basic Su-27 features a conventional cockpit with analogue instruments and, as well as a 30mm (1.1in) GSh-301 cannon, armament can be carried on 10 external pylons. In its primary air-to-air role, the maximum weapons load comprises six medium-range R-27 (AA-10 'Alamo') air-to-air missiles (AAMs) plus four R-73 (AA-11 'Archer') short-range infrared-guided AAMs. The 'Alamos' are provided in semi-active radar-guided and infrared-

homing variants, and these can also comprise extended-range versions. Air-to-ground missions were very much secondary for the original Su-27, but various combinations of unguided bombs and rockets could still be carried.

Weapons are acquired and controlled using a fire-control system based around an N001 pulse-Doppler lookdown/shootdown radar, an infrared search and track (IRST) system and a

---

Su-27 'Flanker-B'

Weight (maximum take-off): 28,300kg (62,391lb)
Dimensions: Length 21.94m (72ft) without probe, Wingspan 14.7m (48ft 3in), Height 5.93m (19ft 6in)
Powerplant: Two Saturn AL-31F turbofans each rated at 122.58kN (27,558lb) thrust with afterburning
Maximum speed: Mach 2.35
Range: 3720km (2312 miles)
Ceiling: 18,500m (60,700ft)
Crew: 1
Armament: One GSh-301 30mm (1.1in) cannon, plus up to 4430kg (9766lb) of external stores on 10 weapons pylons

---

Su-27P

RF-92407 is one of the Russian Aerospace Forces' surviving Su-27P interceptors, delivered in the original air defence standard and not subsequently significantly upgraded. Since it was intended for the Soviet Air Defence Forces, the Su-27P sub-variant had no provision for air-to-ground rockets or bombs.

FOURTH-GENERATION MULTIROLE FIGHTERS

A Ukrainian Air Force Sukhoi Su-27 'Flanker' takes part in the Royal International Air Tattoo at RAF Fairford in the UK, 2017.

helmet-mounted sight. The radar has a search range of around 85–100km (53–62 miles).

Export models

There were no Cold War-era exports of the Su-27, but after the demise of the Soviet Union, China emerged as the first foreign customer for the fighter, buying the export-optimised Su-27SK and two-seat Su-27UBK (China's J-11s and subsequent developments are discussed separately).

The post-Soviet era also saw some efforts to upgrade the basic Su-27, leading to the Su-27SKM, another export fighter with a more advanced fire-control system. For Russia, the focus was on mid-life upgrades to in-service 'Flanker-Bs,' firstly with the Su-27SM that also added a new fire-control system and a revised cockpit that replaced the analogue instruments of the basic Su-27 with two multifunction displays. Next came the Su-27SM(3) that added still more improved equipment, including R-77 (AA-12 'Adder') active-radar AAM. The Su-27SM(3) was produced for Russia by upgrade and a small production batch was completed.

As well as former Soviet states that inherited Su-27s, other export customers include Angola, Eritrea, Ethiopia, Indonesia (the only customer for the Su-27SKM variant) and Vietnam, with some of these operators receiving surplus aircraft from ex-Soviet stocks.

Su-27SK

The Vietnam People's Air Force has been an enthusiastic 'Flanker' customer. This Su-27SK is among the first of those acquired by Vietnam and serves with the 925th Fighter Regiment. The country acquired seven single-seat Su-27SK and five two-seat Su-27UBK jets in the mid-1990s, followed by 36 of the more advanced, multirole Su-30MK2V fighters in several batches.

73

FOURTH-GENERATION MULTIROLE FIGHTERS

AIDC F-CK-1 Ching-kuo

Work began on Taiwan's first homegrown fighter aircraft in the early 1980s, when the decision was taken to field a replacement for the Northrop F-5 and Lockheed F-104 then in service.

F-CK-1C
Single-seat IDF Ching-kuo serial number 1455 is on strength with the 3rd Tactical Fighter Group/1st Tactical Fighter Wing that operates from Tainan Air Base. This aircraft is configured with wingtip AIM-9P Sidewinder missiles, as well as drop tanks.

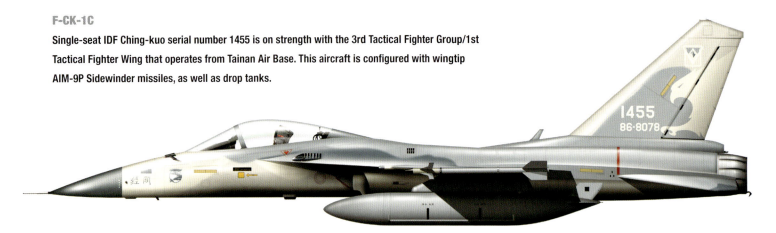

The resulting Indigenous Defense Fighter (IDF) was given the go-ahead in 1982 and the Aerospace Industry Development Center (AIDC) took the lead in the project. The ambitious nature of the programme led to it being broken down into four separate development areas: airframe (in which AIDC was assisted by General Dynamics), engines (Garrett), avionics (General Electric, Westinghouse and others) and air-to-air missiles.

Four prototypes of the F-CK-1 were completed, the CK standing for Ching-kuo, the name of the former Taiwanese president. The first flight was recorded on 28 May 1989 and a total of 10 pre-production aircraft were then delivered for test work between 1992 and 1993.

At one time, the air force expected to receive as many as 250 F-CK-1s to re-equip its fighter force, but numbers were cut to 130 after the United States granted permission to export the F-16A/B to Taiwan in the early 1990s.

The first production models – single-seat F-CK-1A and two-seat F-CK-1B – were delivered to the Ching Chuan Kang Air Base, Taichung, in 1992, replacing the unit's ageing F-104s. As well as a 20mm (0.787in) M61A1 Vulcan six-barrel rotary cannon, the F-CK-1 carried a primary air-to-air armament of indigenous Tien Chien 2 (TC-2) medium-range air-to-air missiles (AAMs) with active radar homing, two of which could be mounted in tandem below the fuselage. These were complemented by short-range TC-1 AAMs with infrared guidance, or US-made AIM-9P Sidewinders.

At first, the F-CK-1 was primarily used as an air defence fighter, operating mainly at low level. This was due to the relatively limited power output of the F125 turbofans, the United States being unwilling to provide more potent engines at this time. While the F-CK-1 retains this powerplant, efforts soon began to increase its capabilities in other ways, including adding radar warning receivers (RWRs) early in its career.

Mid-life upgrade
A more extensive modernisation effort then began in the early 2000s, which was to be conducted in two phases. The first of these addressed avionics, including the cockpit, onboard computers, radar and identification friend or foe system. The second phase dealt with the weapons and stores, including new conformal fuel tanks (CFTs). Lockheed Martin assisted in these efforts and a first prototype of the mid-life upgrade was flown in October 2006. Early testing revealed the CFTs were too heavy for the aircraft's limited thrust and these were omitted.

F-CK-1C
Weight (normal take-off): 9072kg (20,000lb)
Dimensions: Length 14.21m (46ft 7.5in) including probe, Wingspan 8.53m (28ft), Height 4.65m (15ft 3in)
Powerplant: Two ITEC (Garrett/AIDC) TFE-1042070 (F125) turbofans each rated at 42.08kN (9460lb) thrust with afterburning
Maximum speed: more than 1275km/h (792mph) at sea level
Range: 1100km (680 miles)
Ceiling: 16,760m (55,000ft)
Crew: 1
Armament: One M61A1 Vulcan 20mm (0.787in) rotary cannon, plus a typical air-to-air armament of two Tien Chien 2 and two TC-1 AAMs, or alternative air-to-ground stores

FOURTH-GENERATION MULTIROLE FIGHTERS

F-CK-1D
Two-seat Ching-kuo serial number 1624 belongs to 1st Tactical Fighter Group/1st Tactical Fighter Wing at Tainan Air Base. This jet is armed with the indigenous Wan Chien cruise missile. The 1st TFG serves as an operational conversion unit for the fighter.

Taiwan designates the upgraded jets as the F-CK-1C (single-seat) and F-CK-1D (two-seat) and these feature three multifunction displays in the cockpit, rather than the previous two, plus a new flight-control computer and a revised GD-53 Golden Dragon radar with additional operating modes.

Eventually, all surviving aircraft were updated to the new configuration under a program known as *Hsiang Zhan*. The last two upgraded aircraft were redelivered in late 2017.

Among the significant advantages offered in the F-CK-1C/D is a long-range standoff attack capability, prosecuted using the Wan Chien cruise missile that has a range of around 400km (250 miles) and is armed with a submunitions warhead. The upgraded fighter can also carry four TC-2 air-to-air missiles, including the TC-2C version with longer range.

An AIDC F-CK-1D Ching-kuo multirole combat aircraft takes off at Taichung, Taiwan, June 2020.

75

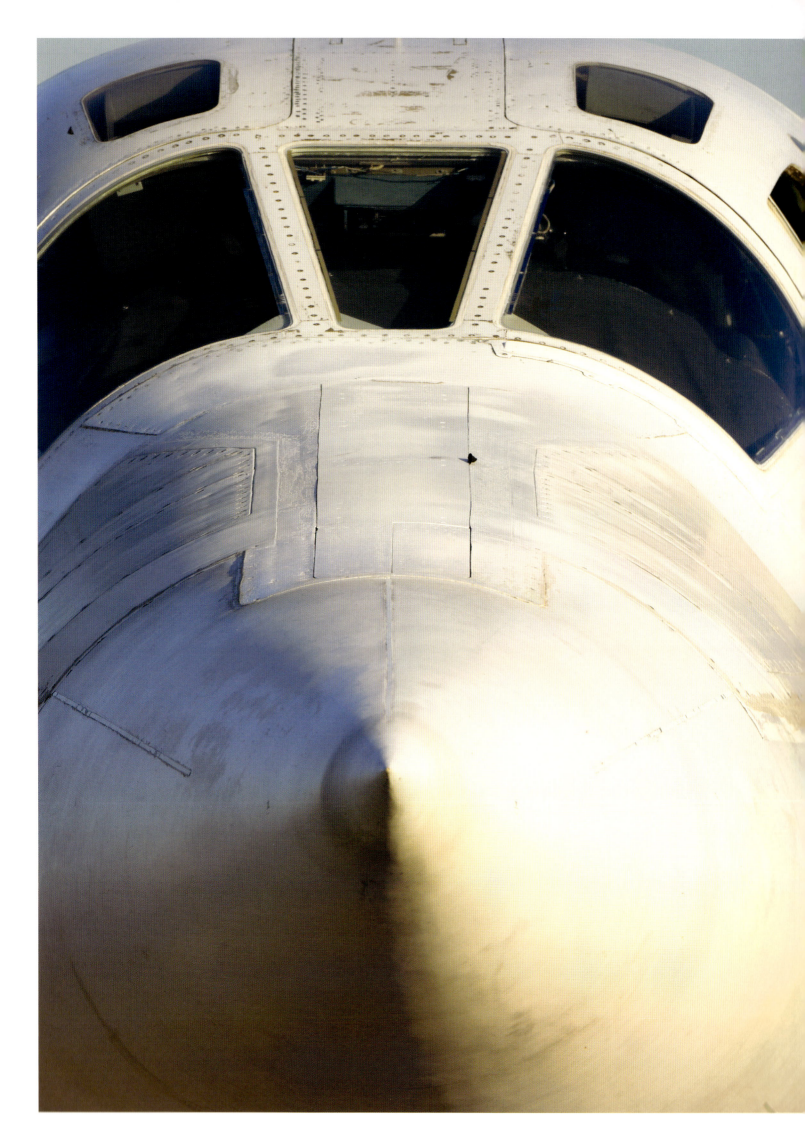

BOMBERS

BOMBERS

For many years, bombers have been an elite category of warplanes operated by only a handful of the most capable air arms with true strategic ambitions. Today, genuine bombers are flown only by China, Russia and the United States. In the United States, the B-52H Stratofortress, B-2 Spirit and B-1B Lancer make up a bomber triad within Air Force Global Strike Command, but only the first two still have a nuclear mission. Russia has moved its entire bomber inventory to Aerospace Forces command, having previously operated these aircraft within Naval Aviation, too. In China, the Xi'an H-6 is deployed primarily as a missile carrier. This chapter includes the following aircraft:

- Rockwell B-1B Lancer
- Northrop Grumman B-2 Spirit
- Boeing B-52H Stratofortress
- Tupolev Tu-22M
- Tupolev Tu-95MS
- Tupolev Tu-160
- Xi'an H-6

Russian Air Force Tupolev Tu-160 RF-94109 stands at Zhukovsky International Airport, Moscow, during the MAKS-2015 air show.

BOMBERS
Rockwell B-1B Lancer

Although its days in US Air Force service are now numbered with plans to retire the B-1B in the future in favour of the forthcoming B-21 Raider, the 'Bone' remains a prized asset in the inventory.

Today's Lancer has its origins in the B-1A that was developed in the early 1970s as a replacement for the B-52 and which first flew on 23 December 1974. After four prototypes of this long-range, Mach 2.2-capable variable-geometry bomber had been completed, the programme was cancelled in 1977. However, the Reagan administration then relaunched the bomber's development in revised B-1B form in 1981, this aircraft instead being optimised for low-level penetration missions. In addition, the radar cross-section was considerably reduced to improve its survivability, while the avionics were updated to include adding an advanced AN/APQ-164 multi-mode offensive radar.

A first production B-1B flew in October 1984 and a total of 100 were completed for the US Air Force, which received its first operational example at Dyess Air Force Base, Texas, in June 1985.

Variable-geometry wings

The B-1B's design incorporates a blended body/low-wing configuration, with variable-geometry wings and four afterburning turbofans in podded pairs below the fixed centre section of each wing. The crew of four comprises a pilot, co-pilot, offensive systems operator and defensive systems operator.

Self-protection equipment includes electronic jammers, radar warning receivers and chaff and flare countermeasures, as well as a towed decoy. These components operate as part of the ALQ-161 electronic countermeasures system that detects and identifies threat emitters and can then respond to them automatically.

As initially delivered, the B-1B had a primary nuclear penetration mission, but the nuclear capability was removed in 1994 after the end of the Cold War saw the bomber's missions reassessed. Thereafter, the

---

B-1B Lancer
Weight (maximum take-off): 163,300kg (360,000lb)
Dimensions: Length 47.8m (147ft), Wingspan 41.8m (137ft) unswept or 24.1m (79ft) fully swept, Height 10.24m (33ft 7.25in)
Powerplant: Four General Electric F101-GE-102 turbofan engines each developing 133.45kN (30,000lb) of thrust with afterburning
Maximum speed: Mach 1.2
Range: 11,675km (7255 miles)
Ceiling: Around 10,668m (35,000ft)
Crew: 4
Armament: Up to a maximum of 56,250kg (125,000lb) ordnance, including 84,227kg (500lb) Mk 82 or 24,907kg (2,000lb) Mk 84 conventional bombs, the entire family of USAF laser- and satellite-guided munitions as well as AGM-158 JASSM and LRASM missiles

---

B-1B Lancer

This B-1B, serial number 85-0075, named 'Scorpion Pride', and operated by the 419th Flight Test Squadron at Edwards Air Force Base, California, was involved in the first external carriage tests of the AGM-158 JASSM missile, seen here mounted on a pylon below the forward fuselage. The demonstration flight was conducted over Edwards on 20 November 2020.

BOMBERS

B-1B Lancer
Carrying a Sniper targeting pod on its external hardpoint, this Lancer makes an interesting contrast to the other example on this page, with the wings on this jet fully forward, and those on the Edwards example swept back for high-speed flight. This aircraft, serial number 85-0073, is assigned to Dyess Air Force Base, Texas, and its tail markings denote the resident 7th Operations Group.

B-1B's external missile pylons were deactivated and other nuclear-related interfaces removed.

Operation Desert Fox

In its new conventional guise, the B-1B first saw combat during Operation Desert Fox, a series of airstrikes mounted against Iraq in December 1998. The following year, the aircraft was employed during Operation Allied Force, the NATO campaign against Serbia. Since then, the B-1B has been a regular contributor to US military campaigns in Afghanistan, Iraq, Libya and Syria, successively adding new conventional weapons capabilities to improve its utility, initially as part of the Conventional Mission Upgrade Program (CMUP). Meanwhile, avionics improvements have seen the aircraft add a GPS-aided inertial navigation system that is used in conjunction with the synthetic aperture radar, as well as a Fully Integrated Data Link (FIDL) with Link 16 capability that, together with the AN/AAQ-33 Sniper targeting pod, greatly improved situational awareness over the battlefield.

Among the different types of conventional weapons that the B-1B can now deploy is the AGM-158 Joint Air-to-Surface Stand-off Missile (JASSM) – up to 24 internally, with plans to add another 12 on external hardpoints – a stealthy weapon that provides a long-range precision attack capability. The formidable payload of the Lancer means that it is also being adapted to carry some even more exotic weaponry, including the AGM-158C Long Range Anti-Ship Missile (LRASM) for maritime strike, and potentially even future hypersonic missiles.

Despite its enormous utility, the US Air Force has already begun retiring the B-1B, with plans to remove 17 from service before the end of fiscal year 2021. This will leave a force of 43 frontline B-1Bs, plus two more for test and evaluation, and these will then be phased out once the B-21 begins to be delivered beginning in the mid-2020s.

79

BOMBERS

Northrop Grumman B-2 Spirit

Developed under the highly secretive Advanced Technology Bomber programme, work on the future B-2 stealth bomber was authorised by President Jimmy Carter in 1979, with the Northrop/Boeing design being selected in 1981 over the Lockheed and Rockwell proposal.

In 1988 the B-2 emerged from the 'black world' before completing a first flight on 17 July 1989. At one time, it was expected that 132 aircraft would be manufactured for the US Air Force, but the demise of the Soviet threat saw that number reduced to just 21, each of which is thought to have cost at least $1.2 billion.

The US Air Force describes the B-2's low observability, or stealthiness, as being 'derived from a combination of reduced infrared, acoustic, electromagnetic, visual and radar signatures. These signatures make it difficult for the sophisticated defensive systems to detect, track and engage the B-2. Many aspects of the low-observability process remain classified; however, the B-2's composite materials, special coatings and flying-wing design all con-tribute to its stealthiness.'

Stealth bomber force

In December 1993, the first B-2A was delivered to Whiteman Air Force Base, Missouri, which today is home to the entirety of the US frontline stealth bomber force. The service announced full operational capability for the B-2 force a decade later in December 2003.

Initially designed to carry freefall nuclear bombs deep into Soviet territory, the end of the Cold War has seen the B-2 adapted to conduct a wider range of conventional missions.

In its initial Block 10 configuration, the ordnance capability comprised 997kg (2000lb) Mk 84 conventional bombs or gravity nuclear weapons.

Ordnance

An early effort to add conventional weaponry, Block 20 provided the interim GBU-37 GPS-Aided Munition (GAM), which was quickly replaced by the Joint Direct Attack Munition (JDAM). Today, under Block 30 weapon options include up to 80 independently targeted 227kg (500lb) GBU-38 JDAMs, 16,997kg (2000lb) Mk 84 general-purpose bombs,

B-2 Spirit

Weight (maximum take-off): 152,634kg (336,500lb)
Dimensions: Length 21m (69ft), Wingspan 52.4m (172ft), Height 5.18m (17ft)
Powerplant: Four General Electric F118-GE-100 turbofans each rated at 76.95kN (17,300lb) of thrust
Maximum speed: high subsonic
Range: 7480 miles (12,038km) without refuelling
Ceiling: 15,240m (50,000ft)
Crew: 2
Armament: Up to 18,144kg (40,000lb) of conventional or nuclear weapons, including preci-sion-guided munitions and gravity bombs

B-2A Spirit

This Spirit, serial number 82-1068, is named 'Spirit of New York' and is currently operated by the 13th Bomb Squadron 'The Devil's Own Grim Reapers', part of the 509th Bomb Wing at Whiteman Air Force Base.

BOMBERS

Boeing B-52H Stratofortress

The remarkable B-52 first entered service with the US Air Force in 1955 and is set to survive on the front line longer than the B-1 or B-2, both of which were developed, at least in part, to replace it.

Today's B-52H is the most modern of the Stratofortress line, but even the youngest of these airframes was delivered as long ago as October 1962. It is therefore not improbable that these aircraft will eventually remain in service for close to a century. The reason for this longevity is the adaptability of the B-52, which although subsonic can perform strategic attack, close air support, air interdiction, offensive counter-air and maritime operations all with equal efficiency.

Loiter time

As well as offering long range, vital for global deployments, the B-52 also has very generous loiter time, meaning it can remain on station in less-contested airspace for long periods and then deliver a wide range of ordnance, in considerable quantities, when required.

The first B-52A took to the air on 15 April 1952 and the then Strategic Air Command received the first 102 of the definitive B-52H model in May 1961. These aircraft are today capable of carrying either nuclear or precision-guided conventional ordnance, the nuclear option comprising up to 20 AGM-86 Air-Launched Cruise Missiles (ALCMs) after the last freefall nuclear bombs were removed from the type's armoury.

Avionics upgrade

While the airframe may be old, avionics upgrades ensure the crew of five (two pilots, electronic warfare officer, radar navigator and navigator) can call upon advanced sensors to aid their mission, including electro-optical sensors, a forward-looking infrared and advanced targeting pods. The pilots are also provided with night-vision goggles, or NVGs, while the Combat Network Communications Technology (CONECT) has added new digital avionics for increased situational awareness, including multifunctional colour cockpit displays and beyond line-of-sight secure communications.

The B-52H was widely employed in Operation Desert Storm over Iraq in 1991, striking targets while flying from bases in both the United Kingdom and the United States and dropping around 40 per cent of all coalition air-delivered weapons in that conflict. In 1996, another mission over Iraq was the longest recorded by any bomber to that date, taking a pair of B-52Hs from Barksdale Air Force Base,

---

B-52H Stratofortress

Weight (maximum take-off): 219,600kg (488,000lb)
Dimensions: Length 48.5m (159ft 4in), Wingspan 56.4m (185ft), Height 12.4m (40ft 8in)
Powerplant: Eight Pratt & Whitney TF33-P-3/103 turbofans each rated at 75.62kN (17,000lb) thrust
Maximum speed: Mach 0.84
Range: 14,162km (8800 miles)
Ceiling: 15,151m (50,000ft)
Crew: 5
Armament: Up to a maximum of approximately 31,500kg (70,000lb) of mixed ordnance including bombs, mines and cruise missiles

---

BOMBERS

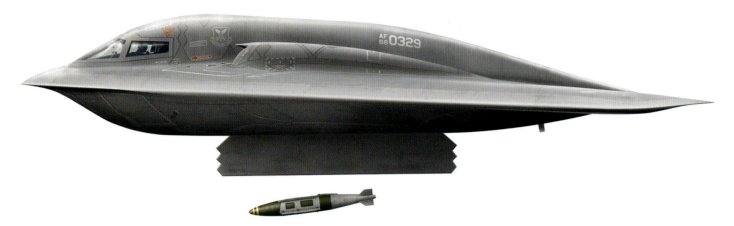

B-2A Spirit
B-2A Spirit serial number 88-0329 'Spirit of Missouri', also now flown by the 509th Bomb Wing's 13th Bomb Squadron. This aircraft is shown dropping a single 2,000lb (907kg) JBU-32 JDAM precision-guided weapon, one of the type's most important conventional stores.

16 AGM-154 Joint Stand-Off Weapons (JSOWs) or 16 AGM-158 Joint Air-to-Surface Stand-off Missiles (JASSMs). One unique weapon in the stealth bomber's inventory is the GBU-57A/B Massive Ordnance Penetrator (MOP), a 13,608kg (30,000lb) 'bunker-busting' weapon intended to destroy hardened targets.

The Spirits have received numerous other upgrades since entering service, including expanded communications capabilities and radar improvements under the Radar Modernization Program (RMP).

Operation Allied Force
The B-2 was first used in combat during Operation Allied Force in 1999 when it was credited with destroying 33 per cent of all Serbian targets in the first eight weeks of the campaign. During this conflict the B-2 established a reputation for flying very long nonstop sorties from its home base in Missouri. The same pattern of missions was continued during Operation Enduring Freedom in Afghanistan, Operation Iraqi Freedom in 2003 and Operation Odyssey Dawn over Libya in 2011. The Libyan mission was typical of the kinds of tasks the B-2 is now called upon to undertake. On the first night of the operation, three B-2s were assigned 48 high-priority targets and 45 of these were hit during flights that lasted over 25 hours. The targets included hardened aircraft shelters that were destroyed using JDAMs.

Despite the B-2's unique capabilities, plans are afoot for the aircraft to be replaced by another stealth platform, the forthcoming Northrop Grumman B-21 Raider.

This new aircraft, equally secretive as the B-2 was in the early years of its development, is expected to adopt a similar basic configuration. At least 100 of these new aircraft are expected to enter service following a first flight planned for 2022.

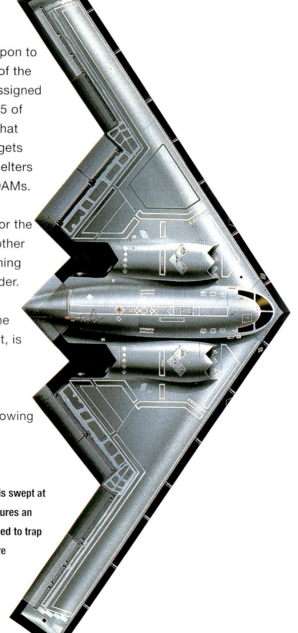

The leading edge of the wing platform is swept at 33 degrees, while the trailing edge features an unusual sawtooth configuration designed to trap radar energy. The engine intakes feature S-shaped curves.

FIN

The large fin incorporates a long dorsal fin for structural integrity and additional keel area. At approximately third-span is a fairing that houses the actuators and spindle joints for the tailerons, and which extends beyond the trailing edge for housing ECM equipment. Above this fairing is a one-piece all-moving rudder. All control is handled by a fly-by-wire system.

TAILPLANE

Mounted on the fin proud of the fuselage is the all-moving tailplane. The two halves operate as tailerons, i.e., simultaneously for pitch control and differentially for roll control. These are augmented at low speed for the latter by wing ailerons.

WING SURFACES

For use at the 20° wing sweep setting are extensive outer wing surfaces. Across the full span of the leading edge is a slot flap, while the trailing edge has a double-slotted flap inboard. Forward of the flaps are 'interceptors' that raise into the airflow to block a small portion and so improve flap effectiveness. Drooping ailerons are incorporated in the trailing edge outboard for roll control.

Northrop B-2 Spirit

This B-2 Spirit is one of those operated by the 393rd Bomb Squadron as part of the 509th Bomb Wing at Whiteman Air Force Base, Missouri. The 393rd was the first operational squadron within the wing. It was followed by the 394th Combat Training Squadron, which was a conversion training unit, although this was deactivated in 2018 and its mission transferred to the 13th Bomb Squadron.

FLYING WINGS

Aircraft with a flying wing planform date back to at least World War II and this design feature was selected for the B-2 since it provides the optimum combination of stealth as well as payload-carrying capability, while weighing less and using less fuel. The wing structure itself is far more efficient because the weight of the aircraft is spread across the wing rather than concentrated in the centre.

FUEL

Most of the aircraft's fuel is housed in the large wing centre-section, and is sufficient to provide a range of about 14000km (8,700 miles). Mission endurance is further extended by inflight refuelling, a probe for which is located in the nose ahead of the cockpit. This is retractable, covered by long double doors when not in use.

WINGS

The Tu-160 has short, thick inboard sections to which are mounted thin, slender variable-geometry outer sections. The wing sweep is manually selected to any of three sweep angles, these being 20° for take-off and landing, 35° for cruising and 65° for supersonic flight.

POWERPLANT

Located in two nacelles under the inner wing section, the four engines of the Tu-160 are Kuznetsov-designed NK-32 turbofans (Type R). Developed for the Tu-22M 'Backfire', these develop 245kN (55,055lb) thrust each in full afterburner.

MAIN UNDERCARRIAGE

Each main undercarriage strut holds a six-wheel bogie with three pairs of wheels. These retract backwards to lie in the wing centre-section between the fuselage and engine nacelles. Each wheel measures 1.26m (4ft 1½in) in diameter and 0.425m (1ft 4½in) in width. The wheel track is narrow at 5.4m (17ft 8½in).

MAINTAINING THE FLEET

In all, only 21 B-2s were ever built, these being completed at Plant 42 starting in the late 1980s. One example was lost in a crash at Andersen Air Force Base on Guam in 2008 and another written off after an emergency landing and fire at Whiteman Air Force Base in Missouri in 2022. Each B-2 passes through a programmed depot maintenance cycle every nine years, including a general overhaul and a complete reapplication of the special RAM skin.

DEFENSIVE MANAGEMENT

The B-2 has undergone various upgrades, among the most important being the Defensive Management System Modernization (DMS-M) programme. The upgrade adds new defensive systems and means crews are less reliant on rigid mission planning, being able to change their routes and tactics in response to emerging situational threat information. DMS-M also brings a secondary electronic intelligence capability.

B61-12

The B61-12 is the latest nuclear bomb to be introduced in the US stockpile and it was first cleared for operational use on the B-2. The B61-12 makes use of components from multiple existing B61 types but adds various new and improved features – most significantly, a precision guidance package. The bomb's reported maximum yield setting is 50 kilotons.

WEAPON BAYS

Like its B-1B counterpart, the Tu-160 has two bomb bays located in the central fuselage. Each can accommodate a rotary launcher or be configured for clips of free-fall weapons. Missiles are launched downwards from the bays before the motors ignite. Bomb bay dimensions are a length of 12.80m (42ft), width of 3.05m (10ft) and depth of 3.80m (12ft 6in).

CRUISE MISSILE

One of the Tu-160's principal weapons is the RK-55 cruise missile, known to NATO as AS-15 'Kent'. The weapon is 8.09m (26ft 6½in) long, weighs 1700kg (3,747lb) and has a range of 3000 km (1,865 miles) carrying a 200-kT nuclear warhead. The Russian designation is derived from *raketa krylataya*, which translates as winged missile. The weapon is in the class of the USAF's AGM-86B, but is not thought to be as accurate.

NOSEWHEEL

The heavy nosewheel retracts backwards from a point behind the crew compartment. It has two large wheels, which measure 1.08 m (3ft 6in) in diameter and 0.4m (1ft 3½in) in width.

CREW ACCESS

The four-man crew enter the 'Blackjack' via a ladder extended from the rear of the nosewheel bay. A walkway leads forward to the flightdeck.

RCS CONTROL MEASURES
To preserve the B-2's stealth qualities, the doors and other apertures around the airframe have serrated edges, a technique devised by Northrop in around 1977. In the B-2, sharp edges are combined with curved surfaces on the lower surfaces. Together with its continuous curvature, this ensures radar energy flows around the aircraft.

MOP
Currently a weapon unique to the B-2 is the GBU-57/B Massive Ordnance Penetrator (MOP), a bomb in the 13,608kg (30,000lb) class. This precision 'bunker-buster' is specially designed to penetrate very deeply buried and fortified targets. The MOP uses a 'smart fuse' to help improve the weapon's effectiveness, even when the exact depth and positioning of the buried target are not definitively known. A single B-2 can carry just two of the huge bombs.

B83 NUCLEAR BOMB
As designed, the B-2's primary strategic weapon was the variable-yield B83 megaton-class bomb. The B83 was the first US strategic-yield weapon designed for low-level laydown deliveries, replacing the B28, B43 and B57 weapons. The bomb can be used from as low as 46m (150ft) and has fully-variable fusing and yield, this being programmed by the crew in flight. The B83 is primarily targeted against hardened military targets such as ICBM silos, underground facilities and nuclear weapons storage facilities.

Tuplolev Tu-160 'Blackjack'

This Tu-160M2 'Blackjack' is one of those modernized by the Russian Aerospace Forces since an upgrade programme was begun in 2018. The 'Blackjack' is flown by a crew of four, comprising two pilots sitting side-by-side, and two navigators behind. One of the latter is known as a 'navigator-operator', and is responsible for the weapons aiming, while the other navigator is responsible for en route navigation.

COCKPIT
The two pilots have a standard analogue cockpit with dial instruments. No head-up display or multi-function display CRTs are incorporated, but like the B-1B they are provided with fighter-style control columns. The thrust levers are offset to the right and are primarily the responsibility of the co-pilot.

NAVIGATION
The principal navigation aid is an astro-inertial system tied into the auto-pilot system. The navigator has a map display which constantly shows the aircraft's position. A terrain-following radar in the nose allows safe low-level flight, although the reliability and capability of this unit remains unknown.

TV CAMERA
The angular fairing under the Tu-160's nose contains a forward/downward-facing TV camera, which aids the crew during weapon aiming. The fairing has a flat pane window in the front. A TV screen is located at the navigator-operator position.

RAM COATING

In addition to its shape, a key component of the B-2's radar cross-section-reduction techniques is the use of special coatings that absorb radar energy and transmit it around the aircraft's surface. The materials themselves can suffer from adverse climatic conditions. As a result, specialized facilities were initially required to maintain the B-2's stealth properties, although improvements to the RAM coating have reduced the down-time needed between missions and made the bomber deployable to other airfields without recourse to building specialized facilities.

STEALTH SHAPE

The B-2's distinctive shape was the result of Northrop's low radar-cross-section (RCS) design philosophy. Before the bomber developed, this was tested on the Tacit Blue demonstrator. Fundamentally, the design approach relies on the principle that a flat plate has both the largest and smallest RCS of any simple shape. If the entire skin of the aircraft comprises one surface, with curving contours of constantly changing radius and direction, the number of edges is reduced to a minimum, avoiding any 'hotspots' in the RCS.

BOMBERS

Boeing B-52H
Wearing Air Force Reserve Command titles on its tail, B-52H serial number 61-0031 is operated by the 93rd Bomb Squadron 'Indian Outlaws', part of the 307th Bomb Wing also at Barksdale and one of only two reserve bomber squadrons in the US Air Force.

Louisiana, to Baghdad over a 34-hour period, covering 25,750km (16,000 miles) in the process.

Operation Allied Force

The B-52H was back in combat in 1999 for Operation Allied Force over the former Yugoslavia, and the bomber has since been an almost permanent fixture in the various campaigns fought in the Middle East and in Afghanistan that began in 2001 with Operation Enduring Freedom. Such was the demand for the bomber's services that in 2016 the aircraft were also forward deployed to the Central Command area of responsibility in order to join the campaign against ISIS forces in Syria and Iraq, providing round-the-clock close air support.

The US Air Force's active fleet of 58 B-52Hs is assigned to two wings, the 2nd Bomb Wing at Barksdale Air Force Base, Louisiana, and the 5th Bomb Wing at Minot Air Force Base, North Dakota, while the type is also operated by Air Force Reserve Command's 307th Bomb Wing, also at Barksdale.

Re-engineering program

Under current plans, the US Air Force expects to continue to operate its B-52Hs until 2050 and is embarking on a re-engining programme that will replace the current Pratt & Whitney TF33 turbofans to keep the aircraft viable until the end of its prodigious career.

Boeing B-52H
B-52H serial number 60-0054 is shown in the markings of the 2nd Bomb Wing's 11th Bomb Squadron, at Barksdale Air Force Base, Louisiana. This aircraft has since been transferred to the 20th Bomb Squadron 'Buccaneers' at the same location.

83

BOMBERS

Tupolev Tu-22M

Known in the West by the codename 'Backfire', the Tu-22M was developed by Tupolev as a supersonic intermediate-range bomber and missile carrier to supersede the Tu-22 'Blinder'.

Carrying nuclear and conventional weapons the Tu-22M was expected to strike targets both on land and at sea – the latter, during the Cold War, would have included the US Navy's aircraft carrier battle groups.

It has variable-geometry wings with large fixed 'gloves' at the centre section into which the main landing gear retracts. The crew of four are provided with ejection seats, with two pilots at the front and a navigator and weapons system officer behind them. The powerplant comprises a pair of Kuznetsov NK-25 afterburning turbofans and there is also provision for rocket-assisted take-off gear to reduce take-off distance. An inflight refuelling probe was originally installed in the nose but was later removed to comply with arms treaty legislation.

Automatic flight
Targets are located and prosecuted using a navigation/attack radar in the nose and an optical TV bombsight below the cockpit. Automatic pre-programmed flight can be undertaken at high or low altitudes, using a computer-controlled navigation system that includes an inertial navigation system and Doppler radar. For self-protection, the Tu-22M3 is equipped with radar warning receivers, infrared missile-launch and approach sensors, active jammers, noise jammers and countermeasures dispensers. In addition, defensive armament is provided in the form of a 23mm (0.9in) twin-barrel cannon in the tail, although this is normally also loaded with decoys.

When first deployed, the primary armament of the Tu-22M was the Kh-22 (AS-4 'Kitchen') supersonic missile that can carry a nuclear or conventional payload and is available in different versions for anti-ship or land attack, with active radar or inertial guidance. The improved Kh-32 was made available in the early 2000s, although this is outwardly similar to

---

Tu-22M3
Weight (maximum take-off): 124,000kg (273,373lb)
Dimensions: Length 42.46m (139ft 4in), Wingspan 23.3m (76ft 5in) fully swept or 34.28m (112ft 6in) fully spread, Height 11.05m (36ft 3in)
Powerplant: Two Kuznetsov NK-25 turbofans each rated at 245.18kN (55,115lb) thrust with afterburning
Maximum speed: 2000km/h (1243mph) at high altitude
Range: 6800km (4225 miles) subsonic at high altitude
Ceiling: 14,000m (45,932ft)
Crew: 4
Armament: One twin-barrel GSh-23M 23mm (0.9in) cannon, plus up to 24,000kg (52,911lb) of stores carried internally and externally. Primary armament is up to three Kh-22 or Kh-32 missiles on the centreline and under the wing gloves. Freefall bombs can be carried in the bomb bay and on racks under the engine intakes and under the wing gloves

---

Tu-22M3
Shown with its wings swept back, and with unusual 'shark' markings applied to the engine intake, RF-34079 wears the tactical identification ('Bort') number '57 Red'.

BOMBERS

Tu-22M3

Tu-22M3 RF-94221 '58 Red' is shown armed with a Kh-22 anti-ship missile below the wing glove and with its wings swept forwards for cruise flight.

the earlier weapon. Three of these big missiles can be carried, but one is a more typical load.

Development of the original Tu-22M began in 1967 and the first of a small batch of Tu-22M0 development aircraft made its maiden flight on 30 August 1969. There followed small numbers of the Tu-22M1 version with a revised wing before the Tu-22M2 that became the initial quantity-production model was first flown in 1973. The Tu-22M3 'Backfire-C' that is currently the only version in service appeared in 1977 and features larger, wedge-type air intakes, NK-25 engines and further revisions to the wing.

Over 500 of all variants of the 'Backfire' were completed between 1969 and 1993 and although some of these were inherited by Ukraine after the fall of the Soviet Union, Russia is today the only operator. Although previously divided between the air force and navy, the current Tu-22M3 fleet is operated exclusively by the Russian Aerospace Forces, which have around 60 examples in use.

Equipment refit

As well as the aforementioned Kh-32 missile, there have been other efforts to upgrade the bomber, the most important being the Tu-22M3M that was first flown in 2018. It features a new radar and navigation system compatible with new weapons, a glass cockpit, digital flight-control system and revised self-protection equipment. Of all Russia's current bombers, the Tu-22M has seen the most combat, firstly in Afghanistan and later over Chechnya and Georgia, with one example being shot down in the latter theatre. Since 2015 the Tu-22M3 has been periodically employed over Syria, and in 2021 examples of the bomber made a first combat deployment to an air base in that country's Latakia Province.

BOMBERS
Tupolev Tu-95MS

The origins of the aircraft known in the West as the 'Bear-H' can be traced back to the days of Stalin in the early 1950s, when Tupolev was tasked to develop a new strategic-range bomber, the Tu-95.

First flown on 12 November 1952, the Tu-95 entered production three years later with major versions during the Cold War including standoff missile carriers and maritime reconnaissance aircraft. Of these earlier 'Bears', a total of 173 were completed at Samara by 1969, after which production focused on the Tu-142 long-range maritime patrol aircraft, which incorporated a much-revised airframe and was built in Taganrog.

The Tu-142 became the basis for the Tu-95MS 'Bear-H' that's now in service with the Russian Aerospace Forces. This was developed as a carrier for a new generation of air-launched cruise missiles that became available in the late 1970s.

Crew of seven

First flown in prototype form on 14 September 1979, the Tu-95MS was to be armed with the Kh-55 (AS-15 'Kent') nuclear-tipped cruise missile and retained the key features of the original 'Bear,' including a mid-mounted swept wing mounting four NK-12MP turboprops, each driving two four-blade co-axial contra-rotating propellers. The main undercarriage units retract into distinctive fairings on the wing trailing edges. The fuselage was shortened compared to the Tu-142 and had accommodation for a crew of seven including two pilots, a navigator, navigator/defence system operator, communications operator, flight engineer and a tail gunner.

Deliveries of the Tu-95MS to the then Soviet Air Force began in December 1982 and a total of 88 examples were completed by the time production ended in 1992. With the collapse of the Soviet Union, some aircraft were left in Kazakhstan and Ukraine, most of which were eventually handed over to Russia.

Long-range missiles

The Tu-95MS was produced in two sub-variants, the basic version using the original Kh-55 missiles and Osina missile-guidance system, while the later aircraft had a more modern Sprut missile-guidance system capable of

---

Tu-95MS
Weight (maximum take-off): 185,000kg (407,885lb)
Dimensions: Length 49.13m (161ft 2in), Wingspan 50.04m (164ft 2in), Height 13.30m (43ft 8in)
Powerplant: Two Kuznetsov/Samara NK-12MP turboprops, each developing 11,185kW (15,000hp) at maximum power
Maximum speed: 830km/h (516mph)
Range: 10,500km (6524 miles) unrefuelled with six internal cruise missiles
Ceiling: 10,500m (34,450ft)
Crew: 7
Armament: One twin-barrel 23mm (0.9in) GSh-23 cannon in the tail turret, plus a maximum weapons load of 21,000kg (46,297lb) typically consisting of six Kh-55 or Kh-55SM cruise missiles in an internal weapons bay, with the option to carry 10 more missiles under the wings on some aircraft. After upgrade, other options included six Kh-555s internally or up to eight Kh-101/Kh-102s

---

Tu-95MS

In recent years, Russian Aerospace Forces Tu-95MS bombers have begun to receive individual names, this example, RF-94124 '16 Red', being named 'Veliki Novgorod', in honour of the city of the same name in the far west of Russia. This aircraft equips the 184th Heavy Bomber Aviation Regiment at Engels.

BOMBERS

Tu-95MS
Another 184th Heavy Bomber Aviation Regiment aircraft, Tu-95MS RF-94117 '27 Red' is named 'Izborsk', after the site of an important historical fortress in western Russia.

operating the long-range Kh-55SM missile, plus revised self-defence and communication systems. While some of the bombers could carry six missiles in the internal weapons bay, others had pylons below the wings to accommodate another 10 missiles. The Kh-55 and Kh-55SM were exclusively nuclear and the aircraft later added the Kh-555, which is a conventional modification of the same weapon, six of which can be carried internally.

More recently, the Kh-55 and Kh-55SM have been complemented by new-generation Kh-101 and Kh-102 cruise missiles, which utilise stealthy design features and are armed with conventional and nuclear warheads, respectively. These missiles are significantly larger than the Kh-55 family so have to be carried externally, with a maximum of eight mounted on new external pylons.

Separate to the missile upgrade, surviving Tu-95MS aircraft are also being upgraded to the 'deeply modernised' Tu-95MSM standard. This features a new radar, a revised navigation suite and a cockpit outfitted with five liquid-crystal displays. In addition, the self-defence suite is improved, a new flight-control system is installed and the engines upgraded to extend their service life and improve efficiency.

Since it was originally restricted to the use of nuclear weapons, the Tu-95MS was first used in combat in November 2015, by which time it had received Kh-555 missiles that were used to strike targets in Syria. These long-range missions involved the bombers flying direct to their missile launch area from their base at Engels, flying over the Caspian Sea and Iran in the process.

BOMBERS

Tupolev Tu-160

Developed by Tupolev towards the end of the Cold War, the Tu-160 is a supersonic missile carrier and bomber with an intercontinental range.

Tu-160 Kusnetzov
Named 'Nikolai Kuznetsov', this Tu-160, RF-94100 '10 Red', is another of the 121st Heavy Bomber Aviation Regiment's fleet at Engels. This is the sole operational unit flying the 'Blackjack' today, with one more example of the bomber assigned to Tupolev for test duties.

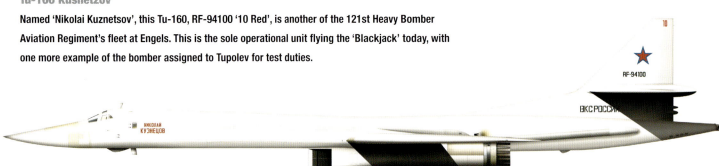

Although production of the Tu-160 was curtailed by the demise of the Soviet Union, more recently manufacture of a new version of the 'Blackjack' has been launched at the same factory in Kazan in southwest Russia.

As originally drafted, the swing-wing Tu-160 was primarily intended to carry strategic cruise missiles and these, in updated form, remain its primary armament today with both nuclear and conventional warheads available. Unlike the American B-1B, the Tu-160 is designed to enter enemy airspace by either flying on a low-level mission profile or a high-level approach towards the target at speeds as high as 2000km/h (1243mph).

The Tu-160 is operated by a crew of four, comprising a pilot, co-pilot, navigator/offensive weapons operator and a navigator/electronic warfare operator, all provided with ejection seats. Powered by four Kuznetsov NK-32 turbofans mounted in widely spaced pairs below the fuselage, the aircraft has variable-geometry wings and a blended fuselage/wing centre section that also includes two weapons bays in tandem.

Although the Tu-160 programme was launched as early as 1967, the first prototype did not take to the air until 18 December 1981. In the years that followed, the Tu-160 established 44 world records and the

Tu-160
Weight (maximum take-off): 275,000kg (606,270lb)
Dimensions: Length 54.1m (177ft 6in), Wingspan 35.6m (116ft 9in) at 65° sweep, 50.7m (166ft 4in) at 35° sweep and 55.7m (182ft 9in) at 20° sweep
Height: 13.1m (44ft)
Powerplant: Four Kuznetsov NK-32 turbofans each rated at 245.18kN (55,115lb) thrust with afterburning
Maximum speed: 2000km/h (1243mph)
Range: 13,950km (8668 miles)
Ceiling: 15,600m (51,181ft)
Crew: 4
Armament: Two tandem weapon bays in the fuselage initially accommodated 12 nuclear-armed Kh-55SM (AS-15 'Kent') cruise missiles on two rotary launchers, or up to 24 Kh-15 (AS-16 'Kickback') short-range attack missiles on four rotary launchers. Subsequent upgrades have added provision for up to 12 Kh-555 conventionally armed missiles or 12 Kh-101/Kh-102 series conventionally/nuclear-armed missiles

BOMBERS

first series of production examples were delivered to a frontline unit in April 1987. After the collapse of the Soviet Union, only six operational Tu-160s were stationed on Russian territory, with another 19 left in Ukraine. Of the Ukrainian aircraft, eight were subsequently bought back by Moscow, arriving in 1999–2000. After two previous losses, the Russian Aerospace Forces was left with a fleet of 16 Tu-160s, all based at Engels in central Russia.

Mid-life upgrade

Despite these relatively small numbers, the Tu-160 has always been a highly prized asset and in the mid-2010s work began on a mid-life upgrade for the surviving aircraft. This work has been implemented in two stages. Firstly, aircraft have received a new autopilot, navigation and communication systems during routine overhaul. Next, a first

flight was completed of a 'deeply modernised' Tu-160M in February 2020, which incorporates a complete overhaul of the mission systems and avionics. This includes a new Novella radar and a glass cockpit, as well as an improved flight-control system, navigation and self-defence suites.

At the same time, work began to reinstate the Tu-160 production line and in 2018 an order was placed for 10 new-build Tu-160M aircraft that would be completed to a similar standard as the definitive mid-life upgrade. These aircraft are also receiving improved NK-32-02 engines that offer a longer service life for the same thrust output.

The first new-production Tu-160M (as opposed to a mid-life upgrade) was expected to be rolled out at Kazan in 2021. Ultimately, the Russian Aerospace Forces may have a requirement for as many as 50 new-build 'Blackjacks,' although this will

likely also depend on progress made with the new-generation PAK DA strategic bomber.

Syrian airstrikes

The Tu-160 was first used in combat in November 2015, during Russian airstrikes against targets in Syria. These missions involved Tu-160s flying over the Caspian Sea before launching Kh-101 and Kh-555 cruise missiles from locations over Iranian airspace.

On another occasion, the Tu-160s routed around Norway and the British Isles before launching their weapons from over the Mediterranean.

The 'Blackjack' has also been used in a number of high-profile long-range deployments, including visits to South Africa and Venezuela, as well as operating off the coast of Alaska, over waters close to Japan and over the Bay of Biscay, all with the aid of aerial refuelling tankers.

Tu-160 Kopylov

Tu-160 RF-94115 '08 Red' is named Vitali Kopylov and is one of the more recent aircraft to join the fleet. It was completed using an unfinished airframe at the Kazan plant and took to the air in December 2007, joining the then Russian Air Force the following April. It serves with the 121st Heavy Bomber Aviation Regiment.

BOMBERS
Xi'an H-6

The early Cold War-era Tupolev Tu-16 'Badger' was the template for the H-6, which remains the primary long-range bomber in the Chinese inventory, although local development means the latest versions of this aircraft are far removed from the original design.

As early as 1956, China came to an agreement with the Soviet Union to establish an assembly line for the Tu-16 at Harbin in China, where the aircraft would be known as H-6. Moscow provided a pair of Tu-16s as pattern aircraft in early 1959, followed by another in kit form. At the same time, work began to produce the Mikulin RD-3 turbojet engine under licence as the WP-8. A first Chinese-assembled H-6 took to the air in September 1959.

Hydrogen bomb

Two years later, production of the Chinese 'Badger' switched to Xi'an, but this proved to be a considerable undertaking, and it wasn't until December 1968 that an H-6 built at the new production centre finally took flight. The original Xi'an-built aircraft was known as the H-6A and began to enter service with the People's Liberation Army Air Force (PLAAF) in 1970. In the meantime, one of these aircraft was used to drop China's first hydrogen bomb in 1967. Production of the H-6A continued into the mid-1980s, by which time around 140 had been completed.

By the mid-1970s, work was also underway on a variant for the People's Liberation Army Navy Air Force (PLANAF). This was the H-6D that was equipped to launch the YJ-6 anti-ship missile, and which featured a large target-acquisition radar below the nose. This initial naval variant entered service from 1985.

Paralleling 'Badger' developments in the Soviet Union, China also fielded inflight refuelling tanker versions of the aircraft. Work on these began in the mid-1980s, although service entry did not occur until the 1990s.

H-6K

Weight (maximum take-off): 95,000kg (209,439lb)
Dimensions: Length 34.8m (114ft 2in), Wingspan 33m (108ft 3in), Height 10.36m (34ft)
Powerplant: Two Soloviev D-30KP-2 turbofan engines each rated at 118kN (27,000lb) thrust
Maximum speed: 1050km/h (650 mph)
Range: 6000km (3700 miles)
Ceiling: 12,800m (42,000ft)
Crew: 4
Armament: Six underwing pylons for air-launched KD-20 or KD-63 land-attack cruise missiles

These aircraft include the HU-6 that was built as a tanker from the outset and features a solid nose with no chin radome. In contrast, the HU-6D

H-6K

This H-6K is operated by the People's Liberation Army Air Force's 108th Air Regiment, part of the 36th Bomber Division, which has operated successive variants of the H-6 since the mid-1960s. The 108th Air Regiment flies both the H-6K and the H-6M from Wugong, in the province of Shaanxi.

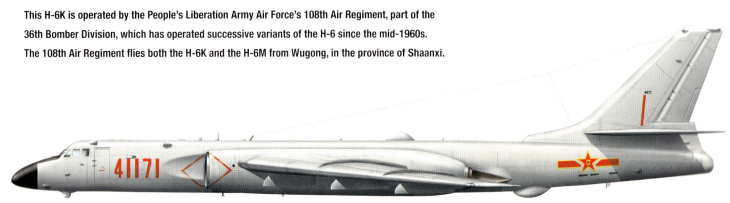

BOMBERS

H-6N
An H-6N assigned to the 106th Air Brigade, another component of the 36th Bomber Division, this time based at Nanyang-Neixing air base in Henan province. This base includes caverns carved into the neighbouring mountain to provide protection for the resident H-6K and H-6N bombers.

Freefall bombers
While the H-6E/F added new navigation and electronic countermeasures equipment, they were still freefall bombers, while the H-6H appeared in the late 1990s with a new long-range missile capability in the form of the KD-63 land attack cruise missile. The H-6M is broadly similar but was apparently converted from H-6E/F bombers and also features a more comprehensive self-protection suite, as well as newer KD-20 air-launched cruise missiles.

PLANAF variants continued, meanwhile, with the H-6G, a successor to the H-6D but armed with more modern YJ-83K anti-ship missiles or YJ-91 anti-radiation missiles on four underwing pylons. The H-6L derivative is capable of launching supersonic YJ-12 anti-ship missiles.

New design
There then followed a major overhaul of the basic H-6 design to produce a family of new versions, characterised by their airliner-style nose without glazing, larger radome and redesigned air intakes that feed Russian-supplied D-30KP-2 turbofan engines. These new-look aircraft include the PLAAF's H-6K missile carrier with six cruise missiles under the wings, the PLANAF's H-6J armed with the YJ-12 and the H-6N that is a dedicated carrier for an air-launched ballistic missile, which also features an inflight refuelling probe.

tanker was produced via conversion of existing PLANAF H-6Ds and retains the glazed nose and radome. Both these tankers feature a hose and drogue system to refuel probe-equipped fighters.

While the PLANAF continued to receive the H-6B, the PLAAF instead chose to upgrade its H-6As to a variety of different, improved configurations with new onboard systems, producing the nuclear-capable H-6E and conventional H-6F.

An H-6K strategic bomber of the People's Liberation Army Air Force seen at Dyagilevo airfield, Russia, during Aviadarts contest, 2019.

91

STRIKE AND ATTACK AIRCRAFT

During the Cold War, much effort was given to developing combat jets that would be optimised for strike or ground-attack missions. Since the 1990s, there has been a much greater emphasis on multirole fighters, which are able to fly strike missions as well as air defence. There is also a newer category of light combat aircraft. Often based on advanced trainer airframes, these are more affordable and have less impressive performance, but can fly many of the roles of the 4.5 generation types. The L-159 ALCA and TA-50 Golden Eagle are typical of these designs. This chapter includes the following aircraft:

- Panavia Tornado
- SEPECAT Jaguar
- AMX International AMX
- Aero Vodochody L-159 ALCA
- McDonnell Douglas AV-8B Harrier II
- Fairchild Republic A-10 Thunderbolt II
- Sukhoi Su-24
- Sukhoi Su-25
- Sukhoi Su-34
- Xi'an JH-7
- TA-50 Golden Eagle

A pair of Russian Air Force Sukhoi Su-25 ground attack aircraft prepare for the annual Victory Day parade at Kubinka air base, Moscow region, 2015.

STRIKE AND ATTACK AIRCRAFT
Panavia Tornado

The Tornado, which survives in service with three operators, was once one of Europe's most important combat aircraft, fulfilling a primary nuclear strike role in the latter years of the Cold War.

While its status has diminished since the United Kingdom retired the last of its Tornado GR4s in early 2019, the type has continued to be upgraded and the last of the line remain highly capable frontline assets. Development began in 1968, with Italy, the United Kingdom and West Germany leading the Multi-Role Combat Aircraft (MRCA) programme, and the first prototype of the variable-geometry, two-seat all-weather Interdictor Strike (IDS) aircraft made its first flight on 14 August 1974. In total, there were nine prototypes and five pre-series aircraft, followed by production deliveries from manufacturing facilities in all three countries.

Defence suppression

Upgrades for the fleet of German Tornados, which include both IDS variants and the specialised Electronic Combat and Reconnaissance (ECR) models used primarily for defence suppression, will ensure that the German Air Force can keep flying approximately 85 of these jets until at least 2025. The fleet is operated from two bases, Schleswig-Jagel and Büchel, the latter still having a nuclear strike role using US-supplied B61 gravity bombs.

German Tornado modernisation has been undertaken via the Avionics System Software Tornado Ada (ASSTA) series of upgrades, which began with the introduction of features including a new main mission computer, a laser inertial navigation system/global positioning system, Rafael Litening laser designator pod and new precision-guided weapons, including the Taurus KEPD 350 standoff cruise missile. ASSTA 2 followed with the Display System Upgrade (DSU) and the Tornado Defensive Aids Subsystem (TDASS). This standard was quickly superseded by ASSTA 3, incorporating new radios, upgraded main computer and the Multifunction Information Distribution System (MIDS) for Link 16 datalink,

---

Tornado GR4
Weight (maximum take-off): 20,240kg (44,622lb)
Dimensions: Length 16.72m (54ft 10in), Wingspan 13.9 m (45ft 8in) at 25° sweep or 8.6m (28ft 3in) at 67° sweep, Height 5.95m (19ft 6in)
Powerplant: Two Turbo-Union RB199-34R Mk 103 turbofans each rated at 76.8kN (17,300lb) thrust with afterburning
Maximum speed: Mach 2.2
Range: 3890km (2420 miles), ferry
Ceiling: 15,240m (50,000ft)
Crew: 2
Armament: One 27mm (1.063in) BK-27 cannon, plus up to 9000kg (19,800lb) of ordnance and fuel tanks carried on four underwing and three under-fuselage hardpoints

---

Tornado IDS
Although an IDS rather than an ECR version of the Tornado, this Luftwaffe aircraft is shown carrying AGM-88 HARM missiles, with which it is also compatible. The aircraft wears the markings of Taktisches Luftwaffengeschwader 51 'Immelmann', which operates both variants from Schleswig-Jagel, as well as reconnaissance-configured examples.

STRIKE AND ATTACK AIRCRAFT

as well as Laser Joint Direct Attack Munition (LJDAM) compatibility. Beyond that, ASSTA 3.1 addressed further cockpit upgrades as well as a new chaff/flare dispenser pod and improvements to the Tornado ECR's Emitter Locator System (ELS).

German Tornados have recently seen operational use in the Middle East, flying reconnaissance missions as part of Operation Inherent Resolve and before that they were employed in the same role in Afghanistan. Italy's Tornado fleet, which is now concentrated in a single wing at Ghedi Air Base, has also flown reconnaissance sorties in support of the counter-ISIS mission, as well as over Afghanistan and Libya.

Italian upgrades

The Italian jets have followed similar series of upgrades to their German counterparts, with both IDS and ECR variants in use. Around 60 Tornados remain in Italian service in three different upgrade standards: RET 7 (used only for training) and the operational RET 6 and RET 8 jets. The Italian Tornados can also carry B61 nuclear bombs, and the aircraft are expected to serve until at least 2025 when they will be superseded by the F-35.

A first Italian upgrade included improved communications and navigation equipment as well as new avionics, operational software and additional precision-guided weapons, including the GBU-31 Joint Direct Attack Munition (JDAM) and the MBDA Storm Shadow cruise missile. By contrast, the latest RET 6 and RET 8 configurations feature the Thales Convertible Laser Designation Pod (CLDP) and the Rafael RecceLite reconnaissance pod, as well as much-improved cockpit displays and interfaces.

A Saudi Arabia Air Force Panavia Tornado IDS takes off from Malta on its way back to Saudi Arabia after undergoing an upgrade program at BAe Systems in the UK.

Final operator

The third and final operator is Saudi Arabia, which acquired Tornado IDS variants in the mid-1980s together with Tornado ADV interceptors that have since been retired. Procured in two batches of 48 aircraft, the Tornado IDS were supplied with JP233 runway denial system, Sea Eagle anti-ship missiles and ALARM anti-radar missiles, and were broadly equivalent to Royal Air Force aircraft.

These planes have since been upgraded to a standard similar to the RAF's definitive GR4 models under the Tornado Sustainment Program (TSP). This includes the Thales Damocles targeting pod, dual-mode Paveway IV laser/GPS-guided bombs plus Brimstone anti-amour weapons, as well as the Storm Shadow cruise missile.

STRIKE AND ATTACK AIRCRAFT

SEPECAT Jaguar

The Cold War-era Jaguar was developed from the early 1960s by France and the United Kingdom as a tactical strike aircraft and advanced trainer. Today it serves exclusively with the Indian Air Force, providing it with one of its most important offensive assets.

India selected the Jaguar as its Deep Penetration Strike Aircraft (DPSA), a requirement that was formulated following the 1971 Indo–Pakistan War, and initial orders were placed in 1978. Initial deliveries comprised 18 Jaguars provided from British Royal Air Force stocks as an interim measure, followed by 40 produced by British Aerospace (in single-seat Jaguar IS and two-seat Jaguar IB variants) and another 110 to be completed under licence by Hindustan Aeronautics Limited (HAL). Ultimately, HAL's production run included 128 Jaguars, the last of which were ordered in 2006.

In the meantime, the Indian Jaguar saw its first major combat during the 1999 Kargil Conflict between India and Pakistan.

Most HAL-built Jaguars received the standard Ferranti Laser Ranger and Marked Target Seeker (LRMTS), but eight were modified with a Thomson-CSF Agave radar for the maritime strike role, coupled with Sea Eagle missiles. The Agave radar was later replaced by the Israeli-supplied Elta EL/M-2032.

Multi-phase upgrades

From early on in the type's career, India embarked on a multi-phase upgrade programme for its Jaguars, known as Display Attack Ranging and Inertial Navigation, or DARIN. This has added new avionics including, at first, a Head-Up Display and Weapon Aiming Computer (HUDWAC).

Successive phases of DARIN added another new head-up display (HUD), multifunction displays (MFD) and a new Thales LRMTS in a re-profiled nose. As well as avionics improvements, the weapons and stores available to the Indian Jaguar have been progressively increased and Israeli and Indian electronic warfare equipment has been added too.

SEPECAT Jaguar
Weight (maximum take-off): 15,700kg (34,613lb)
Dimensions: Length 15.52m (50ft 11in), Wingspan 8.69m (28ft 6in), Height 4.89m (16ft 1in)
Powerplant: Two Rolls-Royce/Turbomeca Adour Mk 102 turbofans each rated at 32.5kN (7300lb) thrust with afterburning
Maximum speed: 1700km/h (1056mph)
Range: 1408km (875 miles)
Ceiling: 12,192m (40,000ft)
Crew: 1
Armament: Two 30mm (1.2in) DEFA cannon, plus up to 4536kg (10,000lb) of disposable stores on seven external hardpoints

Jaguar IS

This Jaguar IS version is operated by the Indian Air Force's No 14 Squadron 'Bulls' at Ambala Air Force Station, part of the Western Air Command. A total of 125 Jaguar IS aircraft were delivered to India, the last 20 of which were delivered in 2006 and 2007 and were provided already equipped with the DARIN (Display Attack Ranging Inertial Navigation) system.

STRIKE AND ATTACK AIRCRAFT

AMX International AMX

A lightweight fighter-bomber and reconnaissance aircraft, the programme to develop the subsonic AMX was launched by Brazil and Italy in the late 1970s with production lines in both countries.

In total there were six prototypes built, which were produced by Aeritalia and Embraer and the first of these took to the air on 15 May 1984. The aircraft is powered by a licence-built Rolls-Royce Spey turbofan and, in its original form, the pilot is provided with 'hands on throttle and stick' controls, as well as head-up and head-down displays. A removable inflight refuelling probe can be fitted on the forward fuselage.

Operation Inherent Resolve

Eventually 187 examples were built for the Italian Air Force and 79 for the Brazilian Air Force in both single-seat and two-seat (AMX-T) forms. The AMX features good short-field performance and advanced nav/attack systems and has been used in combat by both operators. Italian examples have been employed on reconnaissance missions in the Middle East as part of Operation Inherent Resolve, while the Brazilian jets have been used during counter-narcotics operations and against other illegal activities in the country.

While the AMX failed to secure any export orders, the type remains in service with both Brazil and Italy as of mid-2021, with the surviving Brazilian aircraft known locally as A-1A (single-seat) and A-1B (two-seat) having undergone an upgrade programme that provides a modernised cockpit as well as precision-guided munitions. A Brazilian reconnaissance version, the RA-1, can be equipped with the Rafael RecceLite pod.

Meanwhile, the Italian jets that were previously designated as the A-11A and TA-11A have undergone their own upgrade, resulting in the A-11B and TA-11B. However, plans call for the last of the Italian AMX fleet to be retired before the end of 2021.

AMX

Weight (maximum take-off): 13,000kg (28,660lb)
Dimensions: Length 13.23m (43ft 5in), Wingspan 8.87m (29ft 1in), Height 4.55m (14ft 11in)
Powerplant: One Rolls-Royce Spey 807 turbofan rated at 49.1kN (11,000lb) of thrust
Maximum speed: 1053km/h (654mph)
Range: 3336km (2073 miles), ferry
Ceiling: 13,000m (43,000ft)
Crew: 1
Armament: One 20mm (0.787in) M61A1 Vulcan six-barrel Gatling cannon (Italy) or two 30mm (1.1in) cannon (Brazil), plus up to 3800kg (8378lb) of ordnance and fuel tanks carried on five external hardpoints

---

A-1AM

This Brazilian Air Force AMX has been upgraded to A-1AM standard and is in service with the 1°/10° Grupo de Aviação stationed at Base Aérea de Santa Maria. The upgraded AMXs are flown by two squadrons at the base and can be equipped with Rafael RecceLite pods, as well as Elbit Lizard laser-guided bombs designated by the Rafael Litening III pod.

STRIKE AND ATTACK AIRCRAFT

Aero Vodochody L-159 ALCA

The L-159 ALCA traces its origins back to the enormously successful L-39 Albatros advanced jet trainer that was developed in the late 1960s and which became a standard aircraft of its type across much of the Warsaw Pact and for many of its allies.

L-159 ALCA

The 21. základna taktického letectva – the 21st Tactical Aviation Base – at Čáslav. After transfers, conversions to two-seat standard and attrition, the Czech Air Force today operates 16 L-159A aircraft, with several more in storage.

Developed from the early 1990s, the subsonic Advanced Light Combat Aircraft (ALCA) is fully optimised for combat missions and available in single-seat L-159A and two-seat L-159B forms. Initially intended to replace the Czech Air Force's ageing MiG-21 fleet, the ALCA introduced a US-made Honeywell F124 powerplant and NATO-standard avionics. These advanced avionics are centred around an Italian-supplied Grifo multi-mode radar.

First flight

The L-159 took to the air for the first time in two-seat form on 2 August 1997, and the country placed orders for 72 examples, although only 24 of these were eventually put into service. While some of these jets were later sold for export, the Czech Air Force later decided to convert six of the single-seat L-159As into two-seat L159T1 versions to fulfil a need for additional training.

The first export customer for the ALCA was Draken International, a US-based aggressor firm that used 21 of the jets for adversary training, flying against US and allied air arms and simulating advanced threat aircraft and missiles.

Iraqi order

In 2015, Iraq also placed orders for the ALCA with a contract for 15 examples, which were delivered in L-159A and L-159T variants. Since their delivery to Iraq in the same year, the ALCAs have seen considerable combat action against ISIS militants in the country. Meanwhile, the Czech L-159T1s, delivered without radar, are now being updated to a combat-capable L159T+ standard, with Grifo radar, radar warning receivers and chaff/flare dispensers.

L-159A
Weight (maximum take-off): 8000kg (17,637lb)
Dimensions: Length 12.72m (41ft 9in), Wingspan 9.54m (31ft 4in) with tip tanks, Height 4.87m (16ft)
Powerplant: One Honeywell/ITEC F124-GA-100 turbofan engine rated at 28.2kN (6300lb) thrust
Maximum speed: 936km/h (582mph)
Range: 1570km (980 miles)
Ceiling: 13,198m (43,300ft)
Crew: 1
Armament: Seven hardpoints under the wing and fuselage for a range of stores including 20mm (0.787in) gun pods, bombs, rockets and AIM-9 Sidewinder air-to-air missiles up to a total weight of 2340kg (5159lb)

STRIKE AND ATTACK AIRCRAFT

McDonnell Douglas AV-8B Harrier II

The iconic 'jump jet' began life with the British-developed Hawker Siddeley Harrier that first appeared in the early 1960s and soon attracted interest from the US Marine Corps (USMC), which acquired the first-generation AV-8A Harrier beginning in 1968.

AV-8B Harrier II Plus

BuNo 166287 is a 'radar bird' AV-8B that is shown as it appeared in April 2021, while serving with Marine Attack Squadron 223 (VMA-223) 'Bulldogs'. This is scheduled to be the final Harrier operator in the US Marine Corps, retaining its jets until it begins its transition to the F-35B in Fiscal Year 2028.

The USMC then sponsored the development of the much-improved AV-8B Harrier II, which eventually saw the basic aircraft mature from a day-only ground-attack to a much more capable multirole attack platform carrying a heavier weapons load over far longer distances. The aircraft incorporated an all-new wing of larger size and supercritical aerofoil section, made more extensive use of composite materials and also introduced 'hands on throttle and stick' controls as part of an entirely revised cockpit layout. The Harrier II took to the air in YA-8B prototype form on 9 November 1978.

The USMC eventually received three distinct versions of the single-seat Harrier II, the original baseline AV-8B being followed by the AV-8B Night Attack model (from the 167th aircraft onwards) with forward-looking infrared sensor, an improved head-up display and other cockpit improvements. However, the most capable of the jets is the AV-8B Harrier II Plus, which added the Raytheon AN/APG-65 pulse-Doppler radar, featuring both air-to-air and air-to-ground modes. This version became standard from the 205th production aircraft onwards and earlier aircraft were retrofitted with the same capabilities.

As well as the first-generation AV-8A, the Harrier II also superseded the A-4M light attack aircraft in USMC ranks. According to the USMC, the official mission profile of the AV-8B is to "attack and destroy surface and air targets, to escort helicopters, and to conduct other such air operations as may be directed." For training, the Marines also received the two-seat TAV-8B version.

Operation Desert Storm

After testing four pre-production AV-8Bs, the USMC took delivery of its first example in 1983. Ultimately, a total of 286 aircraft were built, including attrition replacements added after Operation Desert Storm in 1991.

Export operators of the Harrier II are Italy and Spain, both of which operate small fleets from their own aircraft carriers. The Spanish Navy, which previously flew the first-generation AV-8S, received the EAV-8B – known locally as the VA.2 Matador II – as well as the TAV-8B for training. The Italian Navy, which didn't previously operate jump-jets, procured AV-8Bs and TAV-8Bs, and both services have upgraded their single-seat jets to the USMC's radar-equipped Harrier II Plus standard. While Italy is introducing the F-35B to replace its Harriers, Spain currently has no direct successor planned for its Matador IIs.

AV-8B Harrier II+

Weight (maximum take-off): 14,100kg (31,000lb) vertical take-off or 9,415kg (20,755lb) rolling take-off

Dimensions: Length 14.12m (46ft 4in), Wingspan 9.25m (30ft 4in), Height 3.55m (11ft 8in)

Powerplant: One Rolls-Royce Pegasus F402-RR-408 (Mk 107) turbofan rated at 105kN (23,500lb) of thrust

Maximum speed: Mach 0.9

Range: 3300km (2100 miles), ferry

Ceiling: 11,582m (38,000ft)

Crew: 1

Armament: One 25mm (0.98in) GAU-12 Equaliser five-barrel rotary cannon, plus up to 4200kg (9200lb) of stores carried on seven external hardpoints

99

STRIKE AND ATTACK AIRCRAFT

VA.2 Matador II
Known locally as the Matador II, this is one of the Spanish Navy's AV-8B Harrier II Plus jets. Spain has received 13 of these jets, comprising eight newly built aircraft delivered from 1996, plus five that were upgraded from existing EAV-8B airframes. One has since been lost to attrition.

The USMC Harrier II made its combat debut in Operation Desert Storm in 1991 when it became that service's first tactical strike aircraft to arrive in theatre, operating from expeditionary airfields that brought it close to the front lines of the battlefield. Other aircraft operated from amphibious assault ships.

Since then, the Marine Corps AV-8B fleet has been widely employed in operational theatres, operating over Afghanistan soon after Operation Enduring Freedom was launched in that country. The Harriers flew their first missions in November 2001 from the amphibious assault ship USS *Peleliu*, subsequently also operating from ground bases in Afghanistan.

While fighting in Afghanistan, the USMC Harriers were upgraded with the Litening II targeting pod, typically used in conjunction with laser-guided bombs but which was also used for reconnaissance and overwatch, including at night.

Operation Iraqi Freedom
Marine Harriers were also committed to Operation Iraqi Freedom, the US-led invasion of Iraq that was launched in March 2003. The jets initially operated from bases in Kuwait as well as from amphibious assault ships in the Northern Arabian Gulf. The Harriers remained in action over Iraq during the long counterinsurgency campaign that followed, with a significant upgrade in 2006 adding the ability to employ the GPS-guided Joint Direct Attack Munition (JDAM).

In 2011, the USMC used its Harriers over Libya, flying from the amphibious assault ship USS *Kearsarge* during Operation Odyssey Dawn that was directed against the forces of Libyan dictator Muammar Gaddafi.

Most recently, USMC Harriers have been involved in Operation Inherent Resolve, the fight against so-called Islamic State in Iraq and Syria (ISIS). For the jump-jets, this engagement began with strikes flown from the deck of the USS *Bonhomme Richard* in January 2015. Subsequent deployments were also made to land bases in the region, including Shaikh Isa Air Base in Bahrain.

Currently, the USMC inventory consists of 124 Harriers IIs, comprising 74 Harrier II Plus versions, 34 Night Attack models and 16 TAV-8B trainers. While the USMC is in the process of replacing the Harrier II with the F-35B, the combat-proven AV-8B is scheduled to remain in service until 2028.

Fairchild Republic A-10 Thunderbolt II

Known almost universally as the 'Warthog,' the A-10 is a unique close air support aircraft used exclusively by the US Air Force and developed for the Cold War anti-armour mission over Europe's Central Front.

Since entering service, the air force has made repeated efforts to retire the A-10 by arguing that its niche role can be fulfilled by other types, but the 'Warthog' has excelled in successive combat campaigns, starting with Desert Storm in 1991 and, more recently, operations in Afghanistan and the Middle East. The A-10 originated in the A-X program for a low-cost attack aircraft that was formally launched with a request for proposals in 1967.

Fairchild Republic A-10A Thu

This A-10A is depicted as it appeared when operated by the 510th Fighter Squadron 'Buzzards', part of the 52nd Wing, stationed at Spangdahlem Air Base in Germany, in the 1990s. By this time, the original 'Lizard' camouflage scheme had been replaced with this two-tone grey paintwork, known as 'Compass Ghost'.

'WARTHOG' VERSUS LIGHTNING II

Controversially, the US Air Force plans to replace its A-10s in the close air support, airborne forward air control, and combat search-and-rescue roles with the F-35A. Between April 2018 and March 2019, the service undertook comparative testing of the two types out of Edwards Air Force Base in California, flying a combined total of 117.5 flight hours across 69 sorties. The USAF determined that the F-35A is 'able to conduct all three missions in both low- and medium-threat environments.'

POWERPLANT

The Su-25 is powered by two Soyuz/Moscow R-95Sh turbojets, which are non-afterburning versions of the R-13-300 engine used in the MiG-21. The engines are installed in long nacelles on the fuselage sides. The basic R-95Sh has a thrust output of 40.21kN (9,039lbf), while late-production aircraft use the improved R-195 turbojet developing 44.13kN (9,921lbf). The R-195 also has a lower exhaust gas temperature, which helps reduce the infrared signature.

PRODUCTION
Designed by the Sukhoi Design Bureau in Moscow, manufacture of the Su-25 was initially carried out at the Tbilisi aircraft plant in Georgia (single-seat versions) and the Ulan-Ude aircraft plant in Russia (two-seaters). Production ceased at both plants in 1992 after around 1,320 Su-25s had been built.

COUNTERMEASURES DISPENSERS
The standard countermeasures fit consists of eight ASO-2V chaff/flare dispensers mounted on the upper rear fuselage, at the sides of the tailfin and above the rear engine ducts. These dispensers have capacity for 32 chaff/flare cartridges, each with a diameter of 26mm (1in). Other self-protection equipment includes a Beryoza radar warning receiver and there is provision for a Gvozdika jamming pod.

UNGUIDED ROCKETS
As well as drop tanks, this Su-25 carries B-8M pods for unguided rockets under the wing. The 20-round B-8 launcher is for 80mm (3.15in) S-8 rockets, introduced in the mid-1970s and still widely used. The basic S-8 has a fragmentation warhead, but the rocket can also be armed with shaped-charge/fragmentation, penetrating, flechette or thermobaric warheads.

nderbolt II

ROUGH-FIELD OPERATIONS
Designed to fight on the European Central Front during the Cold War, the A-10 is optimized for short take-offs and landings, including on rougher non-standard surfaces, aided by low-pressure tyres on the undercarriage. While these kinds of operations were seen as essential for survival in a conflict with the Warsaw Pact, current threats in Europe and the Pacific mean that A-10s are once again training to fly in and out of austere locations, including from highways.

RETIREMENT PLAN
The US Air Force is planning to retire the A-10 fleet before the end of the 2020s, if not before. In the meantime, the aircraft are receiving some new capabilities to stay relevant. These include the integration of various new stores, including the ADM-160 Miniature Air-Launched Decoy (MALD) and the 113kg (250lb) GBU-39/B Small Diameter Bomb (SDB), up to 24 of which can be carried.

ARMOUR PROTECTION

Like the US-made A-10, the design of the Su-25 emphasised a high degree of survivability from the outset. The pilot is seated within an armoured 'bathtub' and armour protection extends to critical aircraft systems. The fuel tanks are filled with anti-explosive foam and the control system is partially duplicated with heavy-duty steel pushrods. The engines are widely spaced in stainless steel compartments, to avoid fratricide damage.

UKRAINIAN LOSSES

The Su-25 has been heavily employed by Ukraine in the war following the full-scale Russian invasion. Reflecting the hazardous nature of its missions, 'Frogfoot' losses have been heavy, with at least 23 examples confirmed as having been destroyed or damaged beyond repair as of early 2025.

SIDEWINDERS FOR SELF-DEFENCE

The A-10 routinely carries a pair of AIM-9L/M Sidewinder infrared-guided air-to-air missiles on twin rails fitted to the outboard station under the left wing. The AIM-9L/M versions are not as capable as the latest AIM-9X, but nonetheless offer an all-aspect capability, while the 'M' has improved resistance to infrared countermeasures, enhanced background discrimination capability and a reduced-smoke rocket motor.

A-10A TO A-10C

The most significant upgrade for the Thunderbolt II took place from 2005 onwards and brought the Cold War-era A-10A up to the A-10C standard. In the broadest terms, this upgrade package added precision-guided weapons, a partial glass cockpit and a Sniper or Litening laser designator pod. The A-10C achieved initial operational capability in 2007 and made its combat debut during Operation Iraqi Freedom in the same year.

Sukhoi Su-25 'Frogfoot'

This Ukrainian Air Force Su-25, with the Bort number '31 Blue', is depicted as it appeared at the start of Russia's full-scale invasion of Ukraine, launched in February 2022. The aircraft wears the distinctive pixellated camouflage scheme that the fleet began to receive before the war, in the course of in-depth overhauls. On the intake is the insignia of the 299th Tactical Aviation Brigade, the main Ukrainian Su-25 operator. As the conflict has continued, Ukrainian Su-25s have received large blue and yellow identification panels on their wings, tails and fuselages, to reduce the risk of 'friendly fire' incidents.

FIRE-CONTROL SYSTEM
The basic Su-25 is fitted with a fairly primitive gunsight combined with a Klyon-PS laser rangefinder/target designator. The upgraded Su-25SM has a more sophisticated targeting and navigation suite, the PrNK-25SM Bars, which adds a new head-up display in place of the gunsight, as well as a modernized stores management system.

UKRAINIAN SU-25SM MODERNIZATION
Since around 2010, Ukraine's surviving Su-25s have been put through a mid-life update programme, known as the Su-25M1 (single-seater) and Su-25UBM1 (two-seater). Work is undertaken by the Zaporizhzhia repair plant and new equipment includes a more modern optical sight with a digital computer, combined with a satellite navigation system. A further development is the Su-25M1K upgrade, which adds a DME/TACAN receiver, VOR/ILS navigation system, and other more minor changes.

GUN
The internal gun armament of the Su-25 comprises a twin-barrel 30mm (1.18in) GSh-2-30 (AO-17A) fixed cannon. This is built into the port side of the forward fuselage, below the cockpit and is provided with 250 rounds. The gun has a rate of fire of 3,000 rounds per minute and the entire 250-round belt allows for five seconds of fire. A version of the same gun is also used in the Mi-24P 'Hind-F' attack helicopter.

MISSILE LAUNCH PROCEDURE

To launch one of the 'fire and forget' Maverick missiles, the A-10 pilot first climbs the aircraft to get a good view of the target, then selects a missile. The pilot uses an image transmitted by the Maverick's seeker head to a screen in the cockpit to acquire and designate that target. Once the target is designated, using cross-hairs on the screen, the missile can be launched. The missile holds the designated image in its own memory, guiding itself to impact and allowing the launch aircraft to vacate the area immediately.

GAU-8/A AVENGER CANNON

The A-10 is built around its Avenger gun, a seven-barrel rotary cannon that is driven by a pair of hydraulic motors. The gun is spun up to its full firing rate of 4,200 rounds per minute in 0.55 seconds and has a maximum capacity of 1,350 rounds of 30mm (1.18in) ammunition on a link-less feed system. The ammunition is held in a drum that is 1.85m (6ft 1in) long and 0.85m (2ft 9in) in diameter. The feed system weighs 1,548kg (3,412lb) when loaded, with the gun itself weighing a further 281kg (620lb).

AMMUNITION

The Avenger cannon is provided with three types of ammunition. The PGU-13/B is a high-explosive incendiary (HEI) round, mainly for use against soft targets and non- or lightly armoured vehicles. The PGU-14/B is the armour-piercing incendiary (API) round, primarily used against armour, with a depleted uranium core. Finally, the PGU-15/B is a training practice (TP) round, with no explosive filling.

MAVERICK MISSILE

While the Avenger cannon is the A-10's trademark weapon, for its primary anti-armour role its main weapon was always planned to be the AGM-65 Maverick air-to-ground missile. Measuring 2.49m (8ft 2in) long, with a wingspan of 0.72m (2ft 4in), the Maverick was initially fielded to the A-10 in two main versions. These were the AGM-65B with TV scene magnification seeker, and the AGM-65D with an imaging infrared (IIR) seeker. Both have a shaped-charge high-explosive warhead, to penetrate armour. Another early Maverick variant for the A-10 was the AGM-65G, an IIR weapon with a revised seeker that allows the pilot to designate a specific impact point.

STRIKE AND ATTACK AIRCRAFT

Fairchild Republic's YA-10A ultimately won a competitive fly-off against a Northrop rival, the winning design featuring twin engines in pods mounted high up on the rear of the fuselage and a twin-fin tail unit. Otherwise, the aircraft was essentially built around the huge GAU-8/A Avenger cannon, a seven-barrel 30mm (1.2in) weapon that demanded that the nose landing gear be located offset to accommodate it. Other features included provision for operations from short runways and a titanium 'bathtub' to protect the pilot against ground fire.

The prototype YA-10A first flew on 10 May 1972 and in January the following year was selected as the winner of the A-X competition.

Production deliveries to the US Air Force began in 1979 and the aircraft would also be based in the United Kingdom and South Korea.

Iraq War deployment

As early as 1988, air force officials began proposing replacement of the A-10 with a close support-optimised F-16. The A-10's performance in the Iraq War of 1991 silenced many critics and since then the aircraft has been in demand from ground commanders in particular in various combat theatres around the globe.

In its latest A-10C form, the aircraft has been updated with a cockpit featuring two multifunction colour displays as well as an up-front controller. Surviving aircraft have also been retrofitted with new wings to address structural wear sustained during decades of combat service.

A-10

Weight (maximum take-off): 22,950kg (51,000lb)
Dimensions: Length 16.16m (53ft 4in), Wingspan 17.42m (57ft 6in), Height 4.42m (14ft 8in)
Powerplant: Two General Electric TF34-GE-100 turbofans each providing 40.32kN (9065lb) of thrust
Maximum speed: Mach 0.56
Range: 1287km (800 miles)
Ceiling: 13,636m (45,000ft)
Crew: 1
Armament: One 30mm (1.2in) GAU-8/A seven-barrel Gatling gun plus up to 7200kg (16,000lb) of ordnance on eight underwing and three under-fuselage hardpoints

A-10C Thunderbolt II
Representative of the 'Warthogs' currently in service with the US Air Force is serial number 79-0086, upgraded to A-10C standard and operated by the 104th Fighter Squadron, part of the Maryland Air National Guard. The unit is stationed at Warfield Air National Guard Base and was the longest-deployed Air National Guard fighter squadron at Bagram during the Afghanistan conflict.

A-10A Thunderbolt II
Wearing the original US Air Force colour scheme, serial number 81-0979 was operated by the 509th Tactical Fighter Squadron. The unit flew A-10s from RAF Alconbury, England, until it was inactivated in December 1992. The same aircraft now serves as an A-10C with the 25th Fighter Squadron.

STRIKE AND ATTACK AIRCRAFT

Sukhoi Su-24

The Su-24 was developed beginning in the early 1960s as a long-range tactical bomber able to deliver nuclear and conventional ordnance against critical targets behind the front line.

The aircraft is distinguished by its variable-geometry wings that were chosen to optimise performance at high speed as well as to reduce take-off and landing distances. The pilot and navigator/weapons system officer are seated side-by-side below separate cockpit canopies.

Tigr navigation-attack (nav-attack) system
To carry out its primary mission, the Su-24M 'Fencer-D' strike aircraft is fitted with a Tigr navigation and targeting system that includes air-to-surface radar and a laser/TV daytime sight/target designator. A radar homing and warning pod can be carried to designate targets for anti-radiation missiles, with an alternative datalink pod available for TV/command-guided missiles.

A terrain-following radar is fitted for low-level flying. The comprehensive self-protection system includes radar warning receivers, infrared missile-

STRIKE AND ATTACK AIRCRAFT

launch and approach warning sensors, active radar jammers and chaff/flare dispensers.

Venerable strike aircraft
The T-6-1 initial prototype for the 'Fencer' was first flown on 2 July 1967, originally fitted with a traditional fixed wing and additional lift engines to reduce the take-off run. It flew again with a variable-geometry wing in 1970 and entered Soviet service five years later. The current standard interdictor is the Su-24M 'Fencer-D' that was introduced to production in 1979, adding new precision-guided ordnance and an inflight refuelling capability, and which was also developed in a reconnaissance version, the Su-24MR 'Fencer-E.'

Export version
Before production ended in 1992, more than 1300 'Fencers' of all variants had been completed and the type remains in Russian service today, despite the introduction of the Su-34 'Fullback.' As well as ex-Soviet examples that were inherited by successor states, there was also a dedicated Su-24MK export version acquired by Algeria, Iran, Iraq, Libya and Syria.

Surviving Russian 'Fencer-Ds' have been subject to upgrade, adding modernised avionics to improve navigation and precision-attack capabilities. In this form, the Su-24M has been used extensively by Russia during its participation in the Syrian civil war.

Su-24M2
Weight (maximum take-off): 39,700kg (87,523lb)
Dimensions: Length 24.53m (80ft 6in) with probe, Wingspan 10.37m (34ft) fully swept, Height 6.19m (20ft 3in)
Powerplant: Two Lyulka-Saturn AL-21F3 turbojets, each rated at 108.36kN (24,361lb) thrust with afterburning
Maximum speed: Mach 1.35
Range: 4270km (2653 miles), with one inflight refuelling
Ceiling: 11,500m (37,730ft)
Crew: 2
Armament: One 23mm (0.9in) six-barrel GSh-6-23M cannon, plus a maximum external load of 7500kg (16,535lb) carried on seven external pylons, including tactical nuclear and conventional bombs, precision-guided munitions, submunitions dispensers, rockets and gun pods

Su-24M2
Operated by the 277th Bomber Aviation Regiment, RF-95108 77 is one of a relatively small number of 'Fencers' upgraded to Su-24M2 standard. The aircraft is shown launching an example of the Kh-25ML (AS-10 'Karen') laser-guided air-to-surface missile.

STRIKE AND ATTACK AIRCRAFT

Sukhoi Su-25

Known by the Western reporting name 'Frogfoot,' the Su-25 was developed during the later years of the Cold War specifically as a subsonic close air support aircraft with extensive armour to protect the pilot and important onboard systems.

Su-25UB

The Peruvian Air Force received 10 single-seat Su-25s and eight two-seat Su-25Bs from Belarusian stocks in the mid-1990s. Ten of these have undergone an upgrade and serial number FAP 087 is shown armed with a Kh-58 (AS-11 'Kilter') anti-radiation missile that requires the Fantasmagoria datalink pod to be carried on the centreline.

Work on the future Su-25 began in the late 1960s and the first prototype T-8-1 completed its maiden flight on 22 February 1975. Two test aircraft were deployed to Afghanistan for trials and early production examples were used extensively in the Soviet campaign in that country. In its basic form, the Su-25 provided its pilot with a simple gunsight and a Klyon-PS laser rangefinder/target designator.

A total of around 1320 Su-25s were built, with single-seaters produced at Tbilisi in Georgia and two-seat Su-25UB aircraft at Ulan-Ude in Russia.

The 'Frogfoot' remains in Russian service, where survivors have been upgraded to Su-25SM standard with a new avionics suite that includes inertial and satellite navigation and a head-up display and which provides improved accuracy in air-to-ground missions. The Su-25SM also has improved self-protection equipment, including Pastel radar warning receivers.

Su-25s have also been widely used by other post-Soviet operators and significant numbers have been exported around the world, many of them seeing combat service in a range of mainly counterinsurgency campaigns.

Other variants of the 'Frogfoot' completed in smaller numbers include

Su-25SM
Weight (maximum take-off): 19,000kg (41,888lb)
Dimensions: Length 15.53m (50ft 11.5in), Wingspan 14.36m (47ft 1in), Height 4.80m (15ft 9in)
Powerplant: Two non-afterburning Soyuz/Moscow R-95Sh turbojets each developing 40.21kN (9,039lb) of thrust
Maximum speed: Mach 0.82
Range: 1850km (1450 miles) ferry range with drop tanks
Ceiling: 7000m (22,966ft)
Crew: 1
Armament: One 30mm (1.1in) twin-barrel GSh-2-30 cannon, plus a maximum external load of 4340kg (9568lb) carried on eight main underwing hardpoints and two smaller pylons. Precision ordnance includes laser-guided Kh-25ML (AS-10 'Karen') and Kh-29L (AS-14 'Kedge') air-to-surface missiles and TV-guided KAB-500Kr bombs

Su-25SM
This Russian Air Force Su-25 'Frogfoot-A' was first deployed to Mozdok, in the North Ossetia region, to take part in combat operations over Chechnya in autumn 1999. '27 Red' is armed with a five-round B-13 pod for 122mm (4.80in) S-13 rockets.

STRIKE AND ATTACK AIRCRAFT

the Su-25BM target tug and the Su-25UTG ship-borne trainer used for teaching pilots destined to serve aboard the Russian Navy carrier *Admiral Kuznetsov*. Less successful were efforts to develop a dedicated anti-armour version of the jet, which yielded the Su-25T and Su-25TM with a more sophisticated navigation/attack system, electro-optical sight and provision for anti-tank guided missiles.

Sukhoi Su-34

Derived from the Su-27 interceptor, the Su-34 was developed as a long-range interdictor to supersede the swing-wing Su-24 as the spearhead of Russia's tactical bomber forces.

Su-34

A Russian Aerospace Forces Su-34, '15 Red', as it appeared in August 2019. The 'Fullback' has been involved in several combat operations, beginning with action over Chechnya in the early 2000s. The Su-34 has since been used for offensive operations over Georgia in 2008, and more widely in Syria, where it has been deployed since 2015.

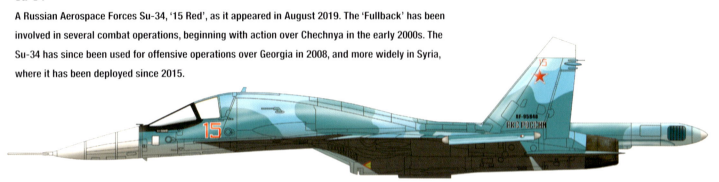

The Su-34 combines an all-new 'platypus' cockpit section with side-by-side seating for two crew with the fuselage of the Su-27. Canard foreplanes and an enlarged tail 'sting' are also fitted.

Work on what became the Su-34 – Western reporting name 'Fullback' – was launched in the late 1970s but it wasn't until 13 April 1990 that the prototype of the Su-27IB (Istrebitel-Bombardirovshchik, meaning fighter-bomber) was flown for the first time.

In 1994 the aircraft received the Su-34 designation and by this time production for the Russian Air Force was underway in Novosibirsk. Compared to the first prototype, the production aircraft had beefed up undercarriage with twin wheels on all three units. Service trials were protracted, however, and it was not until 2014 that the Su-34 was formally commissioned into service.

In the meantime, the aircraft had been combat tested in Moscow's conflicts in Chechnya and Georgia. More recently, Russian Su-34s deployed to Syria have played a significant part in that country's civil war on behalf of local pro-government forces.

Mission avionics are based around the K-102 targeting and navigation suite, including a V004 passive electronically scanned radar that is able to engage four surface targets simultaneously. Data is accessed via a cockpit head-up display and five multifunction displays. A laser and TV sight below the fuselage is used for precision guidance of a wide range of munitions. The aircraft features a comprehensive self-protection system, the Khibiny, which can detect and locate enemy radar and then jam it with electronic countermeasures.

Initially fielded as a tactical interdictor, the Su-34 has subsequently been further developed for the reconnaissance role, for which it can be equipped with a recce suite comprising various external pods, including side-looking radar.

Su-34
Weight (maximum take-off): 45,100kg (99,428lb)
Dimensions: Length 24.8m (81ft 4in), Wingspan 14.7m (48ft 3in), Height 6.08m (19ft 11in)
Powerplant: Two Saturn AL-31F turbofans each rated at 122.58kN (27,558lb) thrust with afterburning
Maximum speed: Mach 1.6
Range: 4000km (2485 miles) ferry range
Ceiling: 15,700m (51,509ft)
Crew: 2
Armament: One GSh-301 30mm (1.1in) cannon, plus up to 8000kg (17,637lb) of external stores on 12 weapons pylons, including Kh-59M (AS-18 'Kazoo') TV-guided missiles, Kh-31P anti-radar and Kh-31A anti-ship missiles (AS-17 'Krypton'), TV- or laser-guided Kh-29T/L (AS-14 'Kedge') air-to-surface missiles and KAB-500 and KAB-1500 guided bombs

STRIKE AND ATTACK AIRCRAFT

Xi'an JH-7

Known by the Western reporting name 'Flounder', the JH-7 is a twin-engine supersonic tactical strike and maritime attack aircraft, development of which began in the mid-1970s. Early development was hampered by the differing requirements of the air force and navy, and it was not until around 1983 that the design was finalised.

The aircraft is powered by WS-9 turbofan engines, which are a licensed version of the Rolls-Royce Spey, and a prototype aircraft completed its first flight in December 1988.

In the meantime, the People's Liberation Army Air Force (PLAAF) began to lose interest in the JH-7, and instead ordered Sukhoi Su-27s and, later, multirole-capable Su-30MKKs from Russia.

Problems with the JH-7's Type 232H multifunction radar also held up the programme and it was not until 1992 that the 'Flounder' finally entered service, the initial production batch all going to the People's Liberation Army Navy Air Force (PLANAF). Subsequent aircraft received an improved JL-10A multi-mode radar, which was retrofitted to the original aircraft.

In July 2002, a much-improved JH-7A version was flown. This features a revised wing, one-piece windshield, additional stores pylons and twin ventral fins below the rear fuselage. More importantly, this version introduced an entirely revised avionics system and cockpit.

The improvements incorporated in the new version attracted the attention of the PLAAF once again and the production run of around 140 aircraft was distributed among both the air force and navy, the aircraft entering service in mid-2004.

Weapons

A wide variety of weapons are available, including YJ-83K/KH anti-ship missiles, KD-88/KD-88A TV/infrared-guided air-to-surface missiles and YJ-91 anti-radiation missiles. The JH-7A also has an electronic attack role and is equipped with external jamming pods.

JH-7

Weight (maximum take-off): 28,475kg (62,777lb)
Dimensions: Length 22.32m (73ft 3in), Wingspan 12.8m (42ft), Height 6.22m (20ft 5in)
Powerplant: Two WS-9 turbofan engines each rated at 91.26kN (20,520lb) thrust with afterburning
Maximum speed: Mach 1.52
Range: around 1760km (1090 miles) with one inflight refuelling
Ceiling: 16,000m (52,000ft)
Crew: 2
Armament: One 23mm (0.9in) twin-barrel GSh-23 cannon plus a maximum of 9000kg (20,000lb) of disposable stores carried on nine hardpoints

JH-7A
This JH-7A, serial number 73270, serves with the People's Liberation Army Air Force's 126th Air Brigade, part of the Nanning Base, within Southern Theatre Command, and stationed at Liuzhou. The creation of the Nanning Base was part of a major overhaul of PLAAF structure, replacing some previous military regions under unified commands.

STRIKE AND ATTACK AIRCRAFT

TA-50 Golden Eagle

The Korea Aerospace Industries (KAI) T-50 family includes supersonic advanced jet trainers, combat-capable trainers and light combat aircraft. It bears some similarity to the F-16 with Lockheed Martin having provided its input into the design of the South Korean jet.

First flown on 20 August 2002, the T-50 Golden Eagle is an advanced training jet offering Mach 1.2 performance, fighter-like handling and a modern glass cockpit with two multifunction displays. In unarmed form, this aircraft fulfils South Korea's advanced training requirements, with 50 aircraft being delivered plus another 10 specifically tailored for the Republic of Korea Air Force's Black Eagles aerobatic display team. The same basic design also lent itself to further development, adding progressively more sophisticated combat capabilities.

The lead-in fighter trainer, or LIFT, version of the aircraft is the TA-50, which has an Israeli-made Elta EL/M-2032 fire-control radar, weapon delivery software, an internal cannon plus external hardpoints for a range of weapons. This variant was ordered by South Korea for tactical and weapons training, while export operators have selected versions of this type to fulfil combat roles. As well as the batch of 22 jets ordered for the Republic of Korea Air Force (ROKAF), the TA-50 has been procured by Indonesia (16), Iraq (24), the Philippines (12) and Thailand (12).

Precision-guided weapons

Very similar to the TA-50 is the FA-50, a dedicated light combat version, with increased internal fuel capacity, improved radar and electronic warfare systems, a Link 16 tactical datalink and compatibility with a wider range of weapons.

South Korea placed orders for a reported 60 FA-50s, which are in the process of replacing a portion of its ageing F-5E/F Tiger IIs. Precision-guided weapons options include the AGM-65 Maverick air-to-ground missile and GBU-38/B Joint Direct Attack Munitions (JDAM).

TA-50
Weight (maximum take-off): 12,300kg (27,117lb)
Dimensions: Length 13.14m (43ft 1in), Wingspan 9.45m (31ft) with wingtip missiles, Height 4.94m (16ft 2in)
Powerplant: Two General Electric F404 turbofans each providing 78.7kN (17,700lb) of thrust with afterburning
Maximum speed: Mach 1.2
Range: 1851km (1150 miles)
Ceiling: 14,630m (48,000ft)
Crew: 2
Armament: One three-barrelled version of the M61 Vulcan 20mm (0.787in) rotary cannon, plus a range of ordnance including bombs, rockets and missiles on five external hardpoints and two wingtip missile rails

T-50i

The Indonesian Air Force received 16 T-50i jets, the first of which entered service in September 2013. Although designated as T-50 trainers, all 16 Indonesian examples are fully combat capable, effectively making them equivalent to TA-50s. The jets operate from Iswahyudi air base and are assigned to Skadron Udara 15.

TRANSPORT AND RECONNAISSANCE

TRANSPORT AND RECONNAISSANCE

As well as the transport aircraft that are needed to move troops and their kit, this chapter includes a range of reconnaissance aircraft, necessary to ensure that timely intelligence is available to combat commanders. These are the airborne early warning and control (AEW&C) aircraft, typically based on transport airframes, that are equipped with radar and increasingly additional sensors to monitor the course of the battle in the air, on the ground and at sea.

This chapter includes the following aircraft:

- Airbus C295
- Airbus A400M Atlas
- Leonardo C-27J Spartan
- Saab Erieye
- Embraer C-390 Millennium
- Lockheed Martin C-130J Hercules
- Boeing C-17 Globemaster III
- Boeing 737 AEW&C
- E-2D Advanced Hawkeye
- Beriev A-50 and KJ-2000
- Mitsubishi C-2
- Shaanxi Y-9
- Xi'an Y-20

An Airbus A400M Atlas four-engined military transport taxis at RAF Fairford, Gloucestershire, UK.

TRANSPORT AND RECONNAISSANCE

Airbus C295

The C295 is one of the world's most widely used new tactical airlifters in the light-to-medium category. Originally manufactured by Construcciones Aeronáuticas SA (CASA), the C295 is now an Airbus product but continues to be built in Spain.

As of 2021, total orders of the C295 exceeded 200 and the aircraft has been acquired by more than 30 countries. A key to its success is its versatillity, which allows it to perform a wide range of missions beyond tactical transport. These include intelligence, surveillance and reconnaissance (ISR), airborne early warning and control (AEW&C), gunship and maritime patrol, with a variety of optional self-protection equipment available for missions in more contested environments. For maritime patrol and other complex missions, the C295 can be fitted with the Fully Integrated Tactical System (FITS), which integrates, controls and displays various different mission sensors.

Hot and high conditions

The latest C295W version is equipped with winglets, improving efficiency and allowing a larger payload to be carried over a longer distance, including in hot and high conditions. The aircraft was designed from the start with a short take-off and landing capability and is able to operate from unprepared airstrips no longer than 670m (2198ft).

A Turkish Air Force C295 takes part in the Sivrihisar SHG Airshow 2020 in Turkey.

Among the most recent variants of the C295 is an aerial tanker, which first demonstrated the type's aerial refuelling capability in 2016 when an appropriately equipped C295W conducted multiple contacts with a standard Spanish Air Force C295. The C295W has also conducted refuelling contacts with a H225M Caracal helicopter. All versions of the C295 feature a glass cockpit with digital avionics, including four liquid-crystal displays that are compatible with night-vision goggles.

C295

Weight (maximum take-off): 21,000kg (46,297lb)
Dimensions: Length 24.46m (80ft 3in), Wingspan 25.81m (84ft 8in), Height 8.66m (28ft 5in)
Powerplant: Two Pratt & Whitney Canada PW127G turboprop engines each rated at 1972kW (2644hp)
Cruising speed: 482km/h (300mph)
Range: 1555km (966 miles), with normal payload
Ceiling: 9145m (30,003ft)
Crew: 2 (plus optional loadmaster)
Capacity: 73 troops, 48 paratroopers, 12 stretcher patients or 7050kg (15,543lb) of cargo

C295

The C295 is one of relatively few Western designs in service today with the Vietnam People's Air Force. A contract for three C295s was announced by Airbus in June 2014 and the first example had been handed over to the VPAF before the end of that year.

ELECTRONIC SUPPORT MEASURES

Australian Wedgetails are equipped with three BAE Australia/ELTA Systems AN/ALR-2001 Odyssey electronic support measures (ESM) systems. These passively detect, locate, classify, and track surface and airborne radio-frequency emitters. ESM contact data is combined with information from other sensors, helping build an accurate threat picture.

AERODYNAMIC MODIFICATIONS

Two ventral fins were added to the rear fuselage of the Wedgetail to provide directional stability, due to the reduction in airflow over the fin and rudder caused by the radar fairing. This is especially important in case of loss of power on one of the engines.

Airbus Military A400M

Wearing the French civilian registration F-RBAV, this A400M is one of around 25 that had been delivered to the French Air and Space Force by early 2025, from a total of 50 aircraft on order. These serve with the 61e *Escadre de Transport* (61st Transport Wing) stationed at Base Aérienne 123 Orléans-Bricy, in north-central France.

AERIAL REFUELLING TANKER

The standard A400M is certified to be rapidly configured as a tanker, with provision for a three-point refuelling system, with centreline hose and drum unit (HDU) system, along with underwing pods. The A400M carries up to 50,800kg (111,995lb) of fuel in its wings and centre wing box, without compromising any cargo hold area and there is also the possibility to install two cargo hold tanks, providing an additional 5,700kg (12,566lb) of fuel each. The cargo-hold tanks also allow for the use of different types of fuel, enabling the A400M to cater for the needs of different types of receiver aircraft.

LAUNCH CUSTOMER

The French Air Force (today the French Air and Space Force) became the first customer to receive the A400M in 2013. Since its service entry, France has used the A400M to support various military campaigns, including Operation Barkhane in Africa's Sahel region and Operation Chammal in the Middle East. The aircraft has also been used to support relief efforts, including after Hurricane Irma in the Caribbean in 2017 and on the Indonesian island of Lombok following an earthquake in 2018.

MESA RADAR

The primary mission sensor of the Wedgetail is the Northrop Grumman Multi-role Electronically Scanned Array (MESA) radar, carried in a large fairing on top of the fuselage. Providing 360° coverage and using active electronically scanned technology, the radar can operate in airborne and maritime threats simultaneously. Meanwhile, the aircraft is fitted with extensive communications and data-sharing capabilities, allowing it to exchange relevant information with other friendly assets in the air, as well as at sea and on the ground.

USAF SENTRY SUCCESSOR

In 2022 the US Air Force announced plans to replace a portion of its fleet of E-3 Sentry Airborne Warning And Control System (AWACS) aircraft with the E-7 Wedgetail. The service determined that the E-7 was 'The only platform capable of meeting the requirements for the Defense Department's tactical battle management, command and control and moving target indication capabilities within the timeframe needed to replace the aging E-3.'

TP400-D6 TURBOPROP

The A400M's TP400-D6 turboprop engine is produced by the multinational Europrop International GmbH consortium, which consists of Rolls-Royce, IPT, MTU Aero Engines and Safran Aircraft Engines. The most powerful turboprop engine in production, the TP400-D6 uses a three-shaft configuration and produces 8,200kW (11,149shp), each engine driving an eight-bladed scimitar propeller. The engine's efficiency is optimised using dual Full Authority Digital Engine Control (FADEC).

INTERMEDIATE TRANSPORT

In terms of performance and capabilities, the A400M falls somewhere between the turbofan-powered C-17 and the turboprop C-130. Thanks to its combination of moderately swept wings and powerful turboprop engines, the A400M is more fuel efficient at lower altitudes than the C-17, while faster at higher altitudes than the Hercules. In terms of payload capacity, it is also intermediate between the C-17 and C-130, although its ability to operate from unprepared or semi-prepared airstrips is superior to the C-17.

Mk 1

RADAR FAIRING

The MESA radar is designed to be lightweight, but it requires a reinforced roof section to be installed. The antennas within the fairing do not rotate, as on the E-3 AWACS. Instead, back-to-back dorsal arrays provide 120° of azimuth coverage on each side of the aircraft, while a 'top hat' array provides 60° of azimuth coverage forward and aft of the aircraft.

INTERIOR LAYOUT

Starting from behind the flight deck and working back, the Wedgetail interior is laid out as follows: toilet; cabinets containing internal communication, satellite, UHF, VHF and Link 11 datalink systems; 10 workstations (six on the left side, four on the right, each with two LCD screens and a situational awareness display); another cabinet with datalink and satellite communications; galley; crew rest area with eight seats; and finally, more cabinets for the ESM and identification friend-or-foe (IFF) systems.

OPERATIONAL USE

The Wedgetail has been used in operational scenarios, primarily by the Royal Australian Air Force, the launch customer, which deployed its E-7A fleet on a rotational basis in support of the mission against ISIS (now Islamic State) in the Middle East. During one such sortie, under Operation *Okra*, one of these aircraft remained airborne for a record 17 hours and 6 minutes, with the aid of two aerial refuelling 'hook-ups'.

FLYING HOSPITAL
The A400M can also be configured for medical evacuation (medevac) operations, in which the aircraft carries six passenger transport units, two of which are equipped for intensive care. Typically, a medevac A400M mission will involve an 11-person onboard medical team who can care for the two intensive care patients, two intermediate-care patients, and two low-care patients.

FIREFIGHTING
Working with the Spanish Air Force, Airbus has been developing a firefighting capability for the A400M. This involved a roll-on/roll-off firefighting kit, which can drop 20,000 litres (4,400 Imp gal) of retardant or water to create high-concentration lines over 400m (1,312ft) long on the ground. The water or retardant is stored in a tank in the cargo hold, which can be filled in less than 10 minutes using standard high-pressure pumps.

PARADROPPING
Initially, there were some significant limitations on the number of paratroopers that the A400M could drop in one go. Early aircraft were only able to deliver 30 paratroopers, but this has now been increased to up to 116. The paratroopers can jump simultaneously from the two rear side doors, with automatic parachute opening, or via the rear ramp, in freefall.

DRONE 'MOTHERSHIP'
In 2022, a Germany A400M launched a Remote Carrier flight-test demonstrator drone from the rear ramp, part of Airbus tests of the A400M as a drone 'mothership'. These experiments are feeding into the Future Combat Air System (FCAS), a multinational European effort that plans to field a crewed New Generation Fighter (NGF) aircraft as well as collaborative drones. The A400M is expected to be able to launch up to 50 small or up to 12 heavy Remote Carrier drones.

Boeing 737 Wedgetail AEW.M

Serial WT001 was the first of three Wedgetail AEW.Mk 1s produced for the Royal Air Force and wears the colours of No. 8 Squadron, which previously flew the E-3D Sentry Airborne Warning and Control System, or AWACS. The squadron badge, a sheathed Arabian dagger known as a *Jambiya*, is displayed prominently on the aircraft's tail. The Wedgetail also wears the emblem of NATO's Airborne Early Warning & Control Force (NAEW&CF).

OPERATOR DIFFERENCES

The South Korean and Turkish Wedgetail aircraft – which were procured under the Peace Eye and Peace Eagle programmes, respectively – feature some different systems, with a proportion of domestically produced equipment. For example, the Turkish E-7 features a locally produced mission computer, VHF/UHF radios, ESM, and electronic warfare self-protection systems. The Korean aircraft also include locally produced electronic mission equipment.

POSEIDON COMMONALITY

The RAF Wedgetail AEW.Mk 1 fleet is located at RAF Lossiemouth, Scotland, alongside the nine-strong fleet of P-8 Poseidon maritime patrol aircraft. Both types are based upon the widely used Boeing 737 Next Generation airframe, reducing the overall maintenance and logistics burden across the two fleets.

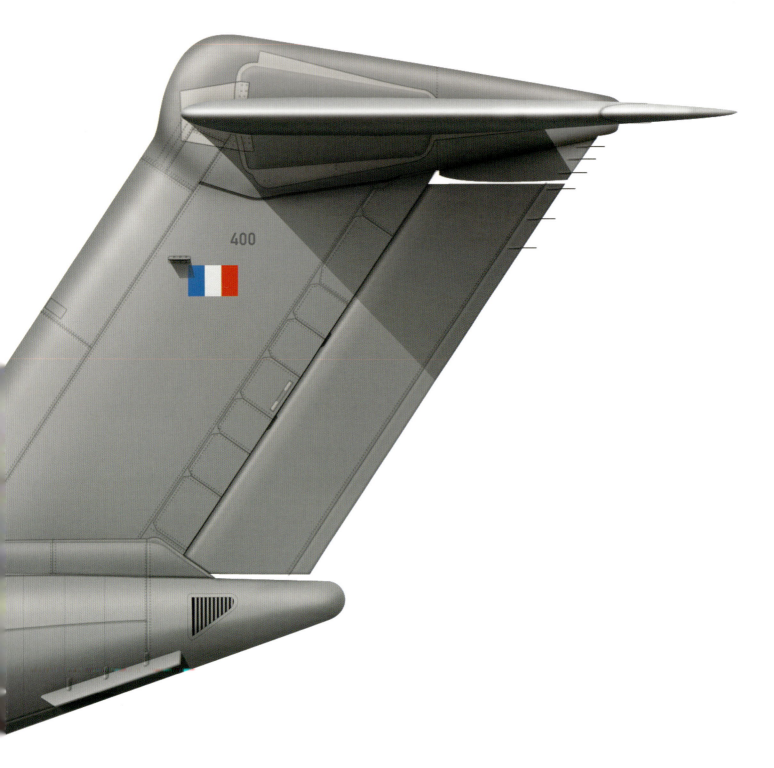

RECORD-BREAKING PARADROP

In 2018, a Royal Air Force A400M delivered a cargo load weighing 23,000kg (50,706lb) tonnes by parachute over the Salisbury Plain training area. This was the largest load ever air-dropped by a British-operated aircraft and was conducted as part of cargo trials by the MoD's Defence Equipment and Support (DE&S). By comparison, the maximum cargo weight deliverable by parachute from a C-130J Hercules is around 15,000kg (33,069lb).

TRANSPORT AND RECONNAISSANCE

Airbus A400M Atlas

A multinational effort, the A400M Atlas programme was launched in 2003 to provide a new airlifter for seven European nations: Belgium, France, Germany, Luxemburg, Spain, Turkey and the United Kingdom.

Subsequently, Malaysia also joined the programme. While final assembly of the A400M takes place in Spain, the wings are manufactured in the UK and the fuselage is made in Germany.

The A400M was designed from the outset to combine the qualities of tactical and strategic military transports, as well as being able to operate as an aerial refuelling tanker. As a result, the aircraft has the long-range performance and internal capacity of a strategic airlifter, but is able to operate from short, semi-prepared airstrips in austere locations. For example, the aircraft can deliver a 25,000kg (55,116lb) cargo load to an unprepared airstrip less than 750m (2461ft) long while carrying enough fuel to complete a 930km (578-mile) return trip.

The A400M recorded its first flight on 11 December 2009 and an initial production aircraft was delivered to the French Air Force in August 2013, entering service the following year.

The outsize military loads that the A400M can accommodate include the CH-47 Chinook helicopter and heavy infantry fighting vehicles. The Atlas can also be configured to deliver paratroopers, with the ability to deliver 116 paratroopers in a single sortie, with 58 jumping from each of two fuselage-side doors.

For aerial tanker missions, the aircraft can be fitted with underwing pods that allow simultaneous refuelling of two fixed-wing aircraft or helicopters.

A Royal Air Force A400M Atlas takes off. The RAF currently operates 20 A400Ms.

A400M Atlas
Weight (maximum take-off): 141,000kg (310,852lb)
Dimensions: Length 45.1m (148ft), Wingspan 42.4m (139ft 1in), Height 14.7m (48ft 3in)
Powerplant: Four Europrop TP400-D6 turboprops each rated at 8200kW (11,000hp)
Maximum speed: Mach 0.72
Range: 8700km (5400 miles), ferry
Ceiling: 12,200m (40,000ft)
Crew: 3 or 4 (2 or 3 pilots, one loadmaster)
Capacity: 116 combat troops or paratroopers, 66 stretcher patients or an equivalent load of cargo

A400M
Germany initially planned to acquire 75 A400Ms, before reducing its order to 60 aircraft, then to 53. At one point, Berlin also planned to try and sell off 13 of its allocated aircraft, but plans were subsequently revised, and all 53 examples will be operated by the Luftwaffe from Wunstorf and Lechfeld air bases. This example serves with the first Luftwaffe unit, Lufttransportgeschwader 62 in Wunstorf, which received its initial A400M in December 2014.

TRANSPORT AND RECONNAISSANCE

Leonardo C-27J Spartan

In service with 16 operators, the C-27J is a thoroughly modernised version of the Aeritalia G.222 transport that was designed in the 1970s and which was optimised for short take-off and landing operations from rough airstrips.

The C-27J differs primarily from its predecessor in having new Rolls-Royce AE 2100 engines driving six-blade propellers and also features a fully digital avionics suite. Compared to the G.222, the new aircraft offers a 35 per cent increase in range and a 15 per cent faster cruising speed.

First flown in prototype form on 24 September 1999, the C-27J is configured primarily for tactical airlift missions, moving troops and cargoes around operational theatres, but can be rapidly reconfigured to undertake other roles, including medical evacuation. Thanks to a range of roll-on/roll-off kits, the aircraft can also be adapted for firefighting, intelligence, surveillance and reconnaissance (ISR), maritime patrol and gunship missions.

The manufacturer claims that the C-27J offers the largest cargo bay in its class as well as the best descent and climb rate. These qualities are combined with a glass cockpit that reduces crew workload, with five colour multifunction displays, a radar and a comprehensive communication suite. For missions in combat environments, the aircraft can be fitted with self-protection equipment, and other options include head-up displays and an air-to-air refuelling probe.

Mission suite

For more demanding tasks, the C-27J can accommodate a more comprehensive mission suite, including optional active electronically scanned array (AESA) search radar, a stabilised electro-optical/infrared (EO/IR) sensor system, electronic support measures (ESM) for ISR and electronic intelligence and a magnetic anomaly detector (MAD), as required.

C-27J Spartan
Weight (maximum take-off): 21,000kg (46,297lb)
Dimensions: Length 22.7m (74ft 6in), Wingspan 28.7m (94ft 2in), Height 9.64m (31ft 8in)
Powerplant: Two Rolls-Royce AE2100-D2A turbo-props each rated at 3458 kW (4637hp)
Maximum speed: 602km/h (374mph)
Range: 5852km (3636 miles), ferry
Ceiling: 9144m (30,000ft)
Crew: 2 (plus optional loadmaster)
Capacity: 60 troops, 46 paratroopers, 36 stretcher patients or equivalent cargo load

C-27J Spartan
The Royal Australian Air Force's No. 35 Squadron operates 10 C-27Js, including serial number A34-005. Acquired via US Foreign Military Sales channels, the first RAAF C-27J took to the air from Alenia Aermacchi's facility in Turin in December 2013 before being delivered to L-3 in Waco, Texas, for fitting out. The first aircraft was officially transferred to the RAAF ownership in November 2014, before aircrew training began in Waco. A first example was delivered to Australia in June 2015.

TRANSPORT AND RECONNAISSANCE

Saab Erieye

Sweden has a relatively long history of airborne early warning and control (AEW&C) development, with the latest mission equipment being based around Saab's popular Erieye system, originally developed by Ericsson to meet a Swedish Air Force requirement.

The Erieye is an active electronically scanned array (AESA) radar that is compact enough to be installed in a business jet-sized airframe. This system began to be tested in the mid-1980s and was then introduced by the Swedish Air Force onboard the Saab 340B twin turboprop, known in Swedish service as the S100 Argus.

Subsequently, the same Erieye radar was adapted for installation in the Saab 2000 twin turboprop and the Embraer EMB-145 regional jet. In these various forms, the export versions of the Erieye have been ordered by Brazil (EMB-145), Greece (EMB-145), Mexico (EMB-145), Pakistan (Saab 2000), Thailand (Saab 340) and the United Arab Emirates (Saab 340).

Air and sea surveillance

The Erieye offers a multi-mission capability, allowing the aircraft to undertake surveillance of air and sea, across an area of over 500,000km^2 (193,051 miles^2) horizontally and over 18,288m (60,000ft) vertically. Targets can range from fighter-sized aircraft to helicopters, cruise missiles and naval contacts as small as jet skis.

The latest iteration of the Erieye is the Erieye ER (Extended Range) that is the cornerstone of the Saab GlobalEye multi-sensor AEW&C platform. The GlobalEye is based on a Bombardier Global 6000/6500 airframe and, as well as the AESA radar installed in Saab's familiar 'balance beam' fairing above the fuselage, the aircraft is also equipped with additional sensors optimised for maritime surveillance. These comprise an electro-optical system and an inverse synthetic aperture radar (ISAR) as well as an automatic identification system (AIS). The launch customer for the GlobalEye is the United Arab Emirates, which has ordered three examples.

Saab 2000 Erieye
Weight (maximum take-off): 13,155kg (29,000lb)
Dimensions: Length 20.57m (67ft 6in), Wingspan 21.44m (70ft 4in), Height 6.97m (22ft 10in)
Powerplant: Two General Electric CT7-9B turbofans each rated at 1390kW (1870hp) thrust
Maximum speed: 487km/h (303mph)
Range: 2858km (1776 miles)
Ceiling: 7620m (25,000ft)
Crew: 2 plus 4 mission personnel

SAAB 2000 Erieye
The Pakistan Air Force was originally set to receive five Saab 2000 Erieye AEW&C aircraft, but this number was later reduced to four, the first two examples being delivered to Pakistan in December 2009 and April 2010, respectively. One of the aircraft had to be repaired after it was damaged in a militant attack on its Minhas base in August 2012. Pakistan has since acquired another three Erieye radars to install on existing Saab 2000 transport variants.

TRANSPORT AND RECONNAISSANCE

Embraer C-390 Millennium

Brazil's Embraer called upon its extensive experience in developing regional commercial aircraft, such as the popular E-Series, to produce a new-generation multi-mission airlifter designed to stress mobility and operational flexibility with low operating costs.

KC-390

As the launch customer for the Millennium, the Brazilian Air Force introduced the KC-390 to service in September 2019. The air arm had announced plans to acquire 28 examples of the tanker/transport to replace its C-130 Hercules fleet. However, in May 2021, as a result of cuts to the defence budget, deliveries were reduced to two aircraft per year, which will likely affect the total number received.

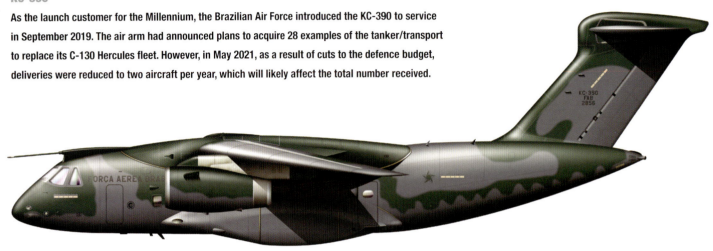

In contrast to most other aircraft in its class, Embraer opted for turbofan propulsion rather than turboprops. The manufacturer asserts that this means the C-390 can fly faster and carry more cargo than similar-sized competitors and that it requires fewer inspections and less intensive maintenance, helping in turn to increase availability levels and bring down life-cycle costs.

Troop transportation

The C-390 is primarily intended to transport troops and cargo but its mission spectrum also includes medical evacuation, search and rescue, humanitarian relief and air-to-air refuelling of both fixed-wing aircraft and helicopters.

First flown on 3 February 2015, the C-390 has been ordered by the Brazilian Air Force, which received the first of a planned 28 examples in September 2019. The aircraft has also been selected by Hungary and Portugal.

The design of the C-390 is based around a generously proportioned hold and a high-mounted wing with various high-lift devices to aid short-field performance. The hold can accommodate two M113 armoured personnel carriers, a Sikorsky H-60 series helicopter, 74 litters with life-support equipment, up to 80 soldiers or 66 fully equipped paratroopers.

The cockpit is equipped with head-up displays as part of an enhanced vision system and includes commercial-standard Rockwell Collins avionics.

KC-390

When operating as a tanker (with the KC-390 designation), the aircraft is fitted with a pair of wing-mounted probe and drogue pods for refuelling operations.

C-390 Millennium
Weight (maximum take-off): 86,999kg (191,800lb)
Dimensions: Length 35.2m (115ft 6in), Wingspan 35.05m (115ft), Height 11.84m (38ft 10in)
Powerplant: Two IAE V2500-E5 turbofans each rated at 139.4kN (31,330lb) thrust
Maximum speed: 988km/h (614mph)
Range: 5820km (3610 miles), with 14,000kg (30,865lb) payload
Ceiling: 11,000m (36,000ft)
Crew: 2
Capacity: 80 troops, 66 paratroopers or equivalent cargo load

TRANSPORT AND RECONNAISSANCE

Lockheed Martin C-130J Hercules

With a longer production run than any other military aircraft, the Hercules remains the Western airlifter of choice and its latest incarnation, the C-130J, continues the aircraft's impressive legacy with the US Air Force and a host of export operators, which fly the aircraft in a wide variety of configurations.

The original C-130A entered production for the US Air Force at what is now Lockheed Martin's Marietta, Georgia, facility in 1953. Since then, the production line has delivered more than 2,500 aircraft, of all variants, to over 60 countries. While 'legacy' versions of the Hercules remain in service around the world, the next-generation Super Hercules, or C-130J, is the major production version, and its development began as a private venture in the early 1990s.

The key features of the C-130J are its new Rolls-Royce AE 2100D3 powerplants and six-blade composite propellers, as well as a fully digital cockpit with four colour multifunction displays and a separate head-up display (HUD) for each pilot. These avionics changes mean the J-model can be flown by a two-person crew, with no requirement for the previous flight engineer and navigator. Thanks to its new engines, the C-130J provides a 40 per cent improvement in range over the 'legacy' Hercules, as well as an increase in speed by 21 per cent and a take-off distance reduced by as much as 41 per cent.

The launch customer for the C-130J was the United Kingdom, which opted for a mix of 15 stretched C-130J-30 and 10 standard-length C-130J models, in 1994. The following year, the US Air Force placed its first orders for the type and on 5 April 1996 the first C-130J (a Dash 30 model) took to the air to begin the flight test programme.

Another long-established Hercules operator, the US Marine Corps then placed its first order for the new type, in the form of the KC-130J, which features an air-to-air refuelling capability.

While the first examples handed over to the US Air Force were standard C-130J transports, delivered in January 1999, the service soon added new variants including the WC-130J 'Hurricane Hunter' for weather reconnaissance and the EC-130J Commando Solo electronic warfare aircraft, equipped to perform psychological operations.

Further US Air Force special-missions derivatives have followed, including the HC-130J Combat King II that was developed to replace the HC-130N/P combat rescue tankers, and the MC-130J Commando II that is a full-spec multi-mission combat transport/special operations tanker, assigned to the Air Force Special Operations Command (AFSOC).

C-130J

Weight (maximum take-off): 70,307kg (155,000lb)
Dimensions: Length 29.79m (97ft 9in), Wingspan 40.41m (132ft 7in), Height 11.84m (38ft 10in)
Powerplant: Four Rolls-Royce AE 2100D3 turboprop engines each rated at 3,458kW (4,637shp)
Maximum speed: 670km/h (417mph)
Range: 3,300km (2,100 miles) with 15,422kg (34,000lb) payload
Ceiling: 12,310m (40,386ft)
Crew: 3 (2 pilots, 1 loadmaster)
Capacity: 92 combat troops, 64 paratroopers, 54 passengers or an equivalent load of cargo

---

C-130J Super Hercules
The California Air National Guard flies this 'stretched' C-130J-30 model, serial number 05-1465. The operating unit is the 115th Airlift Squadron, located at Channel Islands Air National Guard Station, Oxnard, California, as part of the 146th Airlift Wing.

TRANSPORT AND RECONNAISSANCE

A C-130J Hercules approaches Yokota Air Base, Japan, March 2017. Yokota serves as the primary Western Pacific airlift hub for US Air Force peacetime and contingency operations. Missions included tactical air land, airdrop, aeromedical evacuation, special operations, and distinguished visitor airlift.

Perhaps the most radical modification is the AC-130J Ghostrider, the fifth and latest gunship iteration of the Hercules, which is replacing AFSOC's ageing fleet of AC-130U/W gunships. As well as side-mounted 30mm cannon, the AC-130J can deliver ordnance including the AGM-176 Griffin missile and Small Diameter Bombs.

While the US Marine Corps never operated a Hercules gunship, the service's KC-130J has meanwhile been adapted to take on a wider range of missions thanks to the Harvest HAWK (Hercules Airborne Weapons Kit) effort, which adds intelligence, surveillance, and reconnaissance (ISR) equipment as well as precision-guided munitions, including AGM-114 Hellfire and Griffin missiles.

Coast Guard service

The final US military operator is the Coast Guard, which operates the HC-130J that is equipped for long-range maritime surveillance, with dedicated sensors, radios, and workstations.

Following the United Kingdom's lead, the C-130J has gone on to achieve considerable success with export customers, too. As of 2020, the Super Hercules had secured orders from 24 operators in 20 countries, and a global fleet of more than 450 aircraft had recorded more than 2 million flight hours.

EC-130J Commando Solo

EC-130J serial number 01-1935 is flown by the 193rd Special Operations Squadron, a unit of the Pennsylvania Air National Guard located at Harrisburg Air National Guard Base, Middletown, Pennsylvania. The Commando Solo is equipped to fly used psychological operations and can conduct civil affairs broadcast missions over a range of frequencies.

TRANSPORT AND RECONNAISSANCE

Boeing C-17 Globemaster III

The C-17 was developed for the US Air Force as a long-range military transport able to deliver large equipment, supplies and troops directly to small airfields.

CC-177 Globemaster III

In Royal Canadian Air Force service, the C-17A is designated as the CC-177. The first example was delivered to Canadian Forces Base Trenton, Ontario, in August 2007 and a fourth and final aircraft from the original order was handed over in April 2008. In December 2014, Canada announced it was acquiring a fifth Globemaster III, delivered in March 2015.

The first prototype C-17 made its maiden flight on 15 September 1991 and the first production example was delivered to Charleston Air Force Base, South Carolina, in June 1993. The US Air Force declared its first squadron of C-17s operational in early 1995.

Export orders

While the US Air Force is the primary operator with 223 examples delivered, the C-17 has also won important export orders, serving with the United Kingdom, Australia, Canada, Kuwait, Qatar, the United Arab Emirates and India. In addition, NATO's 12-nation Strategic Airlift Capability also operates the type, providing a pool of aircraft to alliance members.

Tactical airlift and airdrop

As well as the rapid strategic delivery of troops and cargo to main operating hubs or directly to forward bases in the deployment area, the C-17 can undertake tactical airlift and airdrop missions as well as aeromedical evacuation. Typical loads include M1 Abrams main battle tanks, armoured vehicles, trucks or trailers loaded and unloaded via a large aft ramp, or up to 102 fully equipped paratroopers.

Short runway operations

The overall design is optimised for operations from small, austere airfields and the aircraft can land and take off from runways as short as 1067m (3500ft), aided by the thrust reversers on all four engines. These provide enough thrust to reverse the aircraft and can also be operated in-flight drag for maximum-rate descents.

An advanced flight deck means the C-17 can be operated by a crew of just three: the pilot and co-pilot in the cockpit, plus a loadmaster.

C-17 Globemaster III
Weight (maximum take-off): 265,352kg (585,000lb)
Dimensions: Length 53m (174ft), Wingspan 51.76m (169ft 10in), Height 16.79m (55ft 1in)
Powerplant: Four Pratt & Whitney F117-PW-100 turbofan engines each rated at 179.9kN (40,440lb) thrust
Maximum speed: Mach 0.875
Range: 4480km (2780 miles) with 71,214kg (157,000lb) payload
Ceiling: 14,000m (45,000ft)
Crew: 3 (2 pilots, 1 loadmaster)
Capacity: 134 troops, 102 paratroopers, 36 stretcher patients or 77,519kg (170,900lb) of cargo

TRANSPORT AND RECONNAISSANCE

Boeing 737 AEW&C

Boeing's latest airborne early warning and control (AEW&C) aircraft is based on the popular Next-Generation 737 airliner that's combined with the Northrop Grumman Multi-role Electronically Scanned Array (MESA) radar carried within a fixed antenna mounted above the fuselage.

Although non-rotating, the MESA radar uses active electronically scanned array (AESA) technology to provide 360-degree coverage and can operate in air and maritime modes out to a range of around 200nm (370km; 230 miles).

Compared to the older E-3 Sentry Airborne Warning and Control System (AWACS), the 737 AEW&C offers increased capabilities coupled with much-reduced operating costs and manpower requirements.

Battle management

In addition to its surveillance function, the 737 AEW&C is able to serve as a battle management tool and communications node, ensuring the effectiveness of joint and coalition forces. Other important features of the advanced radar include sector emphasis, which allows the mission operators to rapidly adjust to changing tactical situations. Thanks to its Open Mission Systems (OMS) design, the 737 AEW&C can be quickly upgraded with new capabilities, including being made compatible with the Battle Management Command and Control (BMC2) system, NATO's latest tactical situational awareness architecture. The aircraft is also fitted with comprehensive self-protection equipment, including programmable chaff and flares.

Export success

The 737 AEW&C has not been acquired by the United States but has a proven track record on the export market, with examples ordered by Australia (as the E-7 Wedgetail), South Korea, Turkey and the United Kingdom. The aircraft has been used in operational scenarios, notably by the Royal Australian Air Force, which deployed its Wedgetail fleet on a rotational basis in support of the mission against ISIS in the Middle East, one of these aircraft remaining aloft during one sortie for a record 17 hours and 6 minutes.

Boeing 737 AEW&C

Weight (maximum take-off): 77,565kg (171,000lb)

Dimensions: Length 33.6m (110ft 4in), Wingspan 35.8m (117ft 2in), Height 12.5m (41ft 2in)

Powerplant: Two CFM International CFM56-7B27A turbofans each rated at 121kN (27,300lb) thrust

Cruising speed: 853km/h (530mph)

Range: 6500km (4000 miles), without in-flight refuelling

Ceiling: 12,500m (41,000ft)

Crew: 2, plus 6–10 mission personnel

E-7A Wedgetail

The first E-7A for the Royal Australian Air Force arrived in Australia in November 2009 and was officially accepted into service in May 2010. The sixth and final example was handed over to the RAAF in May 2012 and initial operational capability was announced in November 2012. The aircraft are operated by No. 2 Squadron at RAAF Base Williamtown.

TRANSPORT AND RECONNAISSANCE

E-2D Advanced Hawkeye

Since the mid-1960s, the US Navy has relied upon successive iterations of the carrier-based E-2 Hawkeye to provide airborne early warning and control (AEW&C) capabilities to ensure the defence of the carrier battle group.

The latest version of the aircraft is the E-2D Advanced Hawkeye that not only serves as the 'eyes and ears' of the fleet but which has also taken on a 'digital quarterback' role, in particular managing complex missions including missile defence.

When employed in the increasingly important missile defence role, the E-2D makes use of the Cooperative Engagement Capability (CEC), which allows it to work in conjunction with Standard Missile SM-6 surface-to-air missiles to tackle various different missile threats, part of an architecture known as Naval Integrated Fire Control-Counter Air (NIFC-CA).

Tactical avionics workstations

The centrepiece of the E-2D's capabilities is the Lockheed Martin AN/APY-9 active electronically scanned array (AESA) radar housed in a rotating radome above the fuselage. This is combined with a new mission computer and tactical workstations for the avionics operators, as well as an all-glass cockpit for the flight crew. The aircraft also boasts an advanced identification friend or foe system and improved electronic support measures.

Compared to earlier Hawkeyes, the E-2D also features an aerial refuelling capability, increasing its potential time on station to five hours and increasing total mission time from four to seven hours.

The first example of the E-2D was delivered to the US Navy's VAW-120 'Greyhawks' at Naval Air Station Norfolk, Virginia, in July 2010 and the type has also been acquired by several export customers, with Egypt, France and Japan all opting to replace their previous Hawkeyes with the latest D-model.

E-2D Advanced Hawkeye

Weight (maximum take-off): 26,082kg (57,500lb)
Dimensions: Length 17.6m (57ft 8.75in), Wingspan 24.56m (80ft 7in), Height 5.58m (18ft 4in)
Powerplant: Two Allison/Rolls-Royce T56-A-427A turboprops each rated at 3,800kW (5100hp)
Maximum speed: 650km/h (400mph)
Range: 2708km (1682 miles), ferry
Ceiling: 10,600m (34,700ft)
Crew: 2 plus 3 mission personnel

E-2D Advanced Hawkeye

This US Navy E-2D, BuNo 168593, is shown in the markings of Carrier Airborne Early Warning Squadron 126 (VAW-126), the 'Seahawks'. Since then, the aircraft has been transferred to VAW-120, which serves as the Fleet Replacement Squadron responsible for training crews on both the E-2 Hawkeye and the C-2 Greyhound.

TRANSPORT AND RECONNAISSANCE

Beriev A-50 and KJ-2000

Russia's primary airborne early warning and control (AEW&C) aircraft is the A-50, known in the West by the reporting name Mainstay, a design that dates back to the Cold War and which is based on the proven airframe of the Ilyushin Il-76MD airlifter.

A-50

The Russian Aerospace Forces operates around 17 survivors from a reported 24 A-50s that were completed for domestic service up until the early 1990s. The type first entered (Soviet) service in June 1984 and the aircraft are now stationed Ivanovo, 250km (155 miles) from Moscow. The first upgraded A-50U was returned to service in October 2011.

The equipment and integration for the A-50 was undertaken by Beriev and the same company continues to upgrade the existing aircraft. Operated by a specialist crew of 10, the A-50's mission avionics are based around the Shmel radar, carried in a rotating dome mounted above the fuselage. The radar can detect aerial and sea targets and has a search range of up to 350km (218 miles) against a fighter-sized target at high altitude. The system can track up to 45 targets simultaneously and can guide up to 12 fighters to intercept them.

Series production aircraft

Development of the A-50 began in the late 1960s and the first prototype took to the air on 19 December 1978. Around 24 series production aircraft were completed, with a handful of the survivors – now operated by the Russian Aerospace Forces – undergoing upgrade to A-50U standard. Beyond this, Beriev is now working on the A-100 as a successor to the A-50, based around an entirely new active electronically scanned array (AESA) radar. The A-100 also features a modernised airframe in the form of the re-engined Il-76MD-90A.

KJ-2000

The original A-50 has been exported to India with Israeli mission systems, while China developed the similar KJ-2000, also based on an Il-76MD airframe, and incorporating indigenous Chinese mission avionics. The KJ-2000 is the largest AEW&C aircraft in Chinese service, but production has been limited by the availability of Il-76MDs for conversion, resulting in the alternative KJ-500 based on the Y-9 airframe.

A-50

Weight (maximum take-off): 190,000kg (418,878lb)
Dimensions: Length 48.27m (158ft 4in) including refuelling probe, Wingspan 50.5m (165ft 8in), Height 14.76m (48ft 5in)
Powerplant: Four Aviadvigatel/Perm D-30KP series 2 turbofans, each rated at 117.68kN (26,455lb) for take-off
Maximum speed: 810km/h (503mph)
Range: 5100km (3169 miles) without inflight refuelling
Ceiling: 12,200m (40,026ft)
Crew: 5 plus 10 mission personnel

Mitsubishi C-2

Japan developed the C-2 as a successor to the Cold War-era Kawasaki C-1 transport, with a greater emphasis on airlift missions in international peacekeeping contexts.

C-2
Following a pair of XC-2 prototypes, orders for 13 production C-2s had been placed on behalf of the Japan Air Self-Defense Force (JASDF) through to Fiscal Year 2019. The two prototypes have since been converted for special missions, one for electronic countermeasures and the other for electronic intelligence (ELINT) missions.

The C-2 is intended to allow the Japan Air Self-Defense Force (JASDF) to support rapid deployment of troops and cargo, as well as to assist in the response to natural disasters and other contingencies. Compared with the C-1, the C-2 has an improved range, increased speed and a larger payload. It also features a range of modern technologies including a tactical flight control system, auto-airdrop system, self-protection equipment and an air-to-air refuelling capability.

The first prototype C-2 took to the air on 26 January 2010 and the JASDF introduced the type to service in early 2017.

Shared design
In order to save time and costs, elements of the C-2's design are shared with the Kawasaki P-1 maritime patrol aircraft, although the fuselage of the cargo aircraft is much enlarged, enabling it to accommodate outsize cargoes such as the Patriot surface-to-air missile system or Mitsubishi H-60 series helicopters.

The modern flight deck is equipped with head-up displays and the flight crew can call upon the tactical flight control system that is combined with fly-by-wire flight controls to ensure safe low-level flying, including in adverse weather.

The C-2 airframe has also been adapted for electronic intelligence gathering, with a single RC-2 version having been converted from the second prototype.

Export models
In a break from previous tradition, the C-2 (and the P-1) have been offered for export, with the aim of challenging competitors such as the A400M and the Il-76, although no foreign sales had been recorded by mid-2021.

C-2
Weight (maximum take-off): 141,400kg (311,734lb)
Dimensions: Length 43.9m (144ft), Wingspan 44.4m (145ft 8in), Height 14.2m (46ft 7in)
Powerplant: Two General Electric CF6-80C2K1F turbofan engines each rated at 265.7kN (59,740lb) thrust
Maximum speed: Mach 0.82
Range: 9800km (6100 miles), ferry
Ceiling: 12,200m (40,000ft)
Crew: 3 (2 pilots, 1 loadmaster)
Capacity: Approximately 120 troops or equivalent cargo load

TRANSPORT AND RECONNAISSANCE

Shaanxi Y-9

Fast becoming China's standard, mid-size tactical airlifter, the Y-9 is a further development of the Y-8, which was itself a licence produced version of the Soviet-designed Antonov An-12.

Y-9
Serial number 10255 is operated by the 4th Division's 10th Air Regiment, within the Western Theatre Command. The unit's new-generation Y-9s serve alongside Y-8Cs based at Chengdu-Qionglai air base.

Originally developed as the Y-8F-600, the aircraft utilises Chinese avionics and engines although its design phase benefitted from input from Antonov and Pratt & Whitney Canada, as well as Western avionics expertise. Compared to the original Y-8/An-12, the new aircraft features redesigned wings and fuselage, which help increase fuel capacity by around 50 per cent.

Development of the Y-9 had begun by 2005 and the prototype completed its first flight on 5 November 2010. As well as the standard transport version, the same airframe is used as the basis for a range of electronic warfare and other special-mission derivatives.

Cargo airdrops

The Y-9 is an altogether more modern and capable transport that its predecessor, with a stretched cargo able to accommodate a range of military vehicles, helicopters, cargo containers or pallets. The aircraft can be used for airdrops of cargo or up to 98 fully equipped paratroopers. In a medical evacuation configuration, the cargo hold has space for 72 casualties plus medical staff.

Cockpit configuration

The four-crew cockpit features six colour multifunction displays and advanced communications equipment, while the reprofiled nosecone accommodates a navigation radar. An electro-optical turret mounted below the nose also enables all-weather, low-altitude operations. Other external changes compared to the Y-8 include small vertical stabilisers on the horizontal tailplanes to improve low-speed stability.

China's People's Liberation Army Air Force received its first production aircraft in 2012, and the aircraft has since entered service with the PLA Army Aviation and Naval Aviation.

Y-9
Weight (maximum take-off): 265,352kg (585,000lb)
Dimensions: Length 36.07m (118ft 4in), Wingspan 38m (124ft 8in), Height 11.3m (37ft 1in)
Powerplant: Four WoJiang WJ-6C turboprop engines each rated at 3805kW (5103hp)
Maximum speed: 650km/h (400mph)
Range: 2200km (1400 miles) with 15,000kg (33,069lb) payload
Ceiling: 10,400m (34,100ft)
Crew: 4
Capacity: 106 paratroopers, 72 medevac patients or 25,000kg (55,116lb) of cargo

TRANSPORT AND RECONNAISSANCE

Xi'an Y-20

The Y-20 has the honour of being China's largest indigenous aircraft, and its long-range heavy-lift capabilities provide a significant advance for the People's Liberation Army Air Force (PLAAF).

Named Kunpeng in China after a giant mythological bird, the Y-20 was intended to supersede the Ilyushin Il-76 in PLAAF service. Design work on the Y-20 benefitted from expertise from the Ukrainian Antonov company, and the aircraft that resulted features dimensions similar to those of the Il-76 but with a wider and taller fuselage that provides more space within the cargo hold for a variety of large-sized cargoes, including the PLA's Type 99A2 main battle tank.

A maiden flight was successfully completed on 26 January 2013 and the aircraft was officially introduced to PLAAF service as the Y-20A in July 2016.

Supercritical aerofoil

In its initial form, the Y-20 is powered by Russian-supplied D-30KP-2 engines, the same as those used in the Il-76, but the latest production aircraft are equipped with indigenous WS-20 high-bypass turbofans offering improved fuel efficiency. These are combined with a wing incorporating a supercritical aerofoil section, which further enhances fuel economy for increased range.

Compared to the Il-76, the Y-20 also uses a greater proportion of composite materials in its construction, and it comes as standard with a modern digital cockpit optimised for a crew of three and featuring digital fly-by-wire controls.

For operations from shorter airstrips or rough-field sites, the Y-20's wing has high-lift devices on the leading and trailing edges.

An aerial refuelling tanker version of the Y-20 has appeared in prototype form and there are multiple reports suggesting that the same airframe will also be used as the basis for a new airborne early warning and control (AEW&C) aircraft, too.

Y-20
Weight (maximum take-off): 180,000kg (396,832lb)
Dimensions: Length 47m (154ft 2in), Wingspan 50m (164ft 1in)
Powerplant: Four Soloviev D-30KP-2 turbofan engines each rated at 117.68kN (26,460lb)
Maximum speed: Mach 0.75
Range: 7800km (4800 miles) with payload of two main battle tanks
Ceiling: 13,000m (43,000ft)
Crew: 3
Capacity: 300 troops, 110 paratroopers, 200 medevac patients or equivalent cargo load

---

Y-20
An early-production Y-20, serial number 11057 is on strength with the 12th Air Regiment of the 4th Division. The aircraft, powered by the original D-30KP-2 low-bypass turbofans, is based at Chengdu-Qionglai.

INDEX

Index

References to illustration captions in **bold**, photographs in *italics*.

Admiral Kuznetsov **46**, 46, 50, **50**,105
Aero Vodochody L-159 ALCA 98
   L-159A 98
   L-159B 98
   L-159T 98
   L-159T+ 98
   L-159T1 98
Afghanistan **16**, 32, **37**, 79, 81, 83, 85, 95, 100, 104
AGM-65 Maverick missile 107
AGM-84 Harpoon missile 45
AGM-84H Harpoon Block II missile 36
AGM-84K SLAM-ER missile 36
AGM-86 missile 82
AGM-88 missile **42**, 45, **94**
AGM-114 Hellfire missile 116
AGM-154 missile 81
AGM-158 missile 45, **78**, 79, 81
AGM-158C missile 79
AGM-176 Griffin missile 116
AIDC F-CK-1 Ching-Kuo 74–5
   F-CK-1A 74
   F-CK-1B 74
   F-CK-1C 74–5
   F-CK-1D 75
AIM-7E Sparrow missile 66
AIM-7M Sparrow missile **35**, 60
AIM-9 Sidewinder missile 60
AIM-9J Sidewinder missile 66
AIM-9M Sidewinder missile **12**
AIM-9P Sidewinder missile 74, **74**
AIM-9X missile 35
AIM-54A Phoenix missile 66
AIM-120 missile 10, 16, 40, 43–4
AIM-120C missile **12**
AIM-120D missile 45
Airbus A400M Atlas *108–9*, 111
Airbus C295 110
   C295W 110
ALARM anti-radar missiles 95
Algeria 47, **47**, 49, 69, 103
ALQ-161 electronic countermeasures system 78
AMX International AMX 97
   A-1A 97
   A-1AM 97
   A-1B 97
   A-11A 97
   A-11B 97
   AMX-T 97
   RA-1 97
   TA-11A 97
   TA-11B 97
AN/AAQ-33 Sniper targeting pod 79
AN/ALQ-99 radar jamming pod 45
AN/ALQ-218(V)2 antenna pod 45
AN/ALR-94 passive receiver system 10

AN/APG-63(V)3 radar 34
AN/APG-63(V)4 radar 35, 36
AN/ APG-68(V)9 radar 40
AN/APG-70 radar 35
AN/APG-73 radar 43, 44, 45
AN/APG-77 radar 10
AN/APG-79(V)4 radar 44
AN/APG- 81 radar 15
AN/APG-82(V)1 radar 38
AN/APG- 83 radar 41–2
AN/APQ-164 radar. 78
AN/AWG-9 radar 66
Angola 48, 73
Armenia 49
ASM-1 60
ASM-2 60
ASM-3 60
ASMP-A missile 32
Australia 17, 44–5, **44**, **112**, 117, 118, **118**

B61 bombs 94, 95
Bahrain 67
Bangladesh **69**
Battle Management Command and Control (BMC2) system 118
Belarus 48, 49
Belgium 17, 39–40
Beriev A-50 and KJ-2000 120
   A-50U 120
   A-100 120
   KJ-500 120
Black Shaheen missile 65
Boeing 737 AEW&C 118
   E-7A Wedgetail 118
Boeing B-52H Stratofortress 82–3
   B-52A 82
Boeing C-17 Globemaster III 117
Boeing F-15 Eagle 34–8
   F-15A 34, 38
   F-15B 34
   F-15C 34, 38
   F-15D 34
   F-15DJ 35
   F-15E Strike Eagle 35–7
   F-15EX Advanced Eagle (Eagle II) 36–7, 38
   F-15F 35
   F-15I 36
   F-15J 35, 38
   F-15K 36
   F-15QA 38
   F-15S 35–6, 38
   F-15SA 36, 38, **38**
   F-15SE Silent Eagle 36
   F-15SG 36
   YF-15A 34
Boeing F/A-18 Hornet and Super Hornet 43–5
   C.15 & CE.15 45
   EA-18G Growler 45
   F/A-18A 43

   F/A-18B 44
   F/A-18C 43–4, 44, 45
   F/A-18D 44, 45
   F/A-18E 43, 44, 45
   F/A-18F 44, 45
   'legacy' Hornets 44
Bonhomme Richard, USS 100
Brazil 28, 64, **64**, 67, **67**, 113
   AMX International AMX 97
   Embraer C-390 Millennium 114
Brazilian Air Force
   1°/10° Grupo de Aviação **97**
Brimstone weapons 26, 95

Canada 17, 44, 45, **117**
Captor-E radar 25–6
Chechnya 85, **104**, 105
Chengdu J-10 54–5
   J-10A 54
   J-10AH 54
   J-10AS 54
   J-10ASH 54
   J-10AY 54
   J-10B 55
   J-10C 55
   J-10SY 54
Chengdu J-20 20–1
   J-20A 20–1
Chile 67
China 49, 53, 73, 74
   Chengdu J-10 54–5
   Chengdu J-20 20–1
   KJ-2000 120
   PAC JF-17 Thunder 56–7
   Shaanxi Y-9 122
   Shenyang J-11 and J-16 57–8
   Shenyang J-15 50–1
   Xi'an H-6 90–1
   Xi'an JH-7 106
   Xi'an Y-20 123
Chinese People's Liberation Army Air Force (PLAAF)
   2nd Division **55**
   4th Division **122**, **123**
   5th Regiment **55**
   9th Brigade 20
   10th Air Regiment **122**
   12th Air Regiment **123**
   16th Air Brigade **57**
   36th Bomber Division **90**, **91**
   98th Air Brigade **58**
   106th Air Brigade **91**
   108th Air Regiment **90**
   126th Air Brigade **106**
   172nd Air Brigade **21**
   176th Brigade 20, **21**
Czech Republic 28
   Aero Vodochody L-159 ALCA 98

Damocles pod 32, 65
Dassault Mirage 2000 64–5
   Mirage 2000-5 (Dash 5) 65

INDEX

Mirage 2000-5 Mk2 65
Mirage 2000-5F 65
Mirage 2000-9 65
Mirage 2000B 64
Mirage 2000C *62–3*, 64, 65
Mirage 2000D 64
Mirage 2000N 64, 65
Dassault Rafale *22–3*, 29–33
  B01 30–1
  Rafale A 29
  Rafale B 32
  Rafale EG 32–3
  Rafale F1 29
  Rafale F2 29, 32
  Rafale F3 29, 32
  Rafale F4 29
  Rafale F5 29
  Rafale M 29, 32
Denmark 17, 39
Draken International 98

E-2D Advanced Hawkeye 119
Egypt 32, 47, **47**, 53, **53**, 64, 119
El Dorado Canyon raids 43
Elbit Display And Sight Helmet 67
Elta EL/M-2032 radar 61, 67, 96, 107
Embraer C-390 Millennium 114
  KC-390 114
Embraer EMB-145 113
Eurofighter Typhoon *7*, 24–7
  DA.1 24
  EF2000 24
  Tranche 1 25, 26
  Tranche 2 25, 26
  Tranche 3 25, 26
  Tranche 3A 25
  Tranche 4 25
Exocet missile 32, 64, 65

Fairchild Republic A-10 Thunderbolt II
  100–1
  A-10A 101
  A-10C 101
  YA-10A 101
Falcon Edge internal electronic
  countermeasures system 40
Ferranti Laser Ranger and Marked
  Target Seeker (LRMTS) 96
Finland 44, 45, **45**
France 111, 119
  Dassault Mirage 2000 *62–3*, 64–5
  Dassault Rafale *22–3*, 29–33
  SEPECAT Jaguar 96
French Navy
  Flottille 12F **29**

GAU-8/A Avenger cannon 101
GBU-31 JDAM 95
GBU-32 JDAM 12
GBU-37 GAM 80
GBU-38/B JDAM 107
GBU-38 JDAM 80
GBU-48 Enhanced Paveway II 26
GBU-57A/B MOP 81
GD-53 Golden Dragon radar 75

Georgia 85, 105
Germany
  Airbus A400M Atlas *108–9*, 111,
    111
  Eurofighter Typhoon 24–7
  Panavia Tornado 94–5
  see also Luftwaffe
Greece 32, 64, 65, 113
Grifo-F/X Plus radar 67
Grifo multi-mode radar 98
Grumman F-14 Tomcat 66
  F-14A 66

HAL LCA Tejas 61
  Mk 1 61
  Mk 1A 61
  Naval LCA 61
Harvest HAWK 116
Honduras 67
Hungary 28, **28**, 114
hydrogen bombs 90

India 19, 32, 46, 47, 48–9, **48**, 64,
    65, 69, 117, 120
  HAL LCA Tejas 61
  SEPECAT Jaguar 96
Indian Air Force
  8 Wing **69**
  No 14 Squadron **96**
  No 18 Squadron **61**
  No 45 Squadron **61**
  No 102 Squadron **48**
Indonesia 49, 73, 107, **107**
Iran 34, 66, **66**, 67, 103
Iraq 32, 66, 79, 81, 82–3, 98, 100,
    101, 103, 107
ISIS 83, 95, 98, 100, 118
Islamic Republic of Iran Air Force
    (IRIAF)
  81st Tactical Fighter Squadron **66**
  82nd Tactical Fighter Squadron **66**
  83rd Tactical Fighter Squadron **66**
Israel 17, 34, 36, 40, **40**, 54
Italy 17, 99
  AMX International AMX 97
  Eurofighter Typhoon 24–7
  Leonardo C-27J Spartan 112
  Panavia Tornado 94–5

J/APG-1 radar 59
Japan 17, 34–5, **38**, 119
  Mitsubishi C-2 121
  Mitsubishi F-2 59–60
Japan Air Self- Defense Force
  3 Hikotai **59**
  8th Air Wing **60**
  21 Hikotai **60**
JBU-32 JDAM weapon **81**
JL-10A multi-mode radar 106
Joint Helmet Mounted Cueing
  System 35, 40, 44, 45
JP233 runway denial system 95

K-102 targeting and navigation suite
  105

Kargil Conflict (1999) 96
Kawasaki P-1 maritime patrol aircraft
  121
Kazakhstan 49, 71
KD-63 missile 91
KD-88 missile 58, 106
Kearsarge, USS 100
Kenya 67
Kh-22 (AS-4 'Kitchen') missile 84, **85**
Kh-25ML (AS-10 'Karen') missile **103**
Kh-29 (AS-14 'Kedge') missile 49
Kh-31A (AS-17 'Krypton') missile 46,
    49
Kh-32 missile 84
Kh-35 (AS-20 'Kayak') missile 46
Kh-55 (AS-15 'Kent') missile 86, 87
Kh-55SM missile 87
Kh-58 (AS-11 'Kilter') missile **104**
Kh-59M (AS-18 'Kazoo') missile 49
Kh-101 missile 87, 89
Kh-102 missile 87
Kh-555 missile 87, 89
Khibiny-M electronic
  countermeasures suite 52–3
Kinzhal ballistic missile 70–1, *71*
KLJ-7A radar 56
KLJ-7(V)2 radar 56
Klyon-PS laser rangefinder/target
  designator 104
Kuwait 26, 44, 45, 117

Leonardo C-27J Spartan 112
Leonardo Grifo-F radar 67
Liaoning (aircraft carrier) 50
Libya 26, 32, **33**, 43, 79, 81, 95, 100,
    103
Link 16 system 26, 79, 94, 107
Litening targeting pods 26, 28, 100
Lockheed Martin 74
  Mitsubishi F-2 59–60
Lockheed Martin AN APY-9 119
Lockheed Martin C-130J Hercules
  115–16
  AC-130J Ghostrider 116
  C-130J-30 115
  EC-130J Commando Solo 115,
    116
  HC-130J Combat King II 115, 116
  KC-130J 115, 116
  MC-130J Commando II 115
  WC-130J 'Hurricane Hunter' 115
Lockheed Martin F-16 Fighting
  Falcon 39–42
  Desert Falcon 40
  F-16A 39, 40–1
  F-16B 40, 40–1
  F-16BM **41**
  F-16C 39, 40, 41
  F-16D 40, 41
  F-16E 40, *41*
  F-16F 40
  F-16I 40
  F-16V 41–2
  KF-16C **42**
  KF-16D **42**

125

INDEX

YF-16 39
Lockheed Martin F-22 Raptor *8–9*, 10–13
Lockheed Martin F-35 Lightning II 14–17
  F-35A 14–15, 16, 17
  F-35B 14, *15*, 16–17
  F-35C 14, 16, 17
  X-32 14
  Lockheed Martin YF-22 10
LS-500J bomb 54, 58
Luftwaffe 24, 25
  Lufttransportgeschwader 62 111
  Taktisches Luftwaffengeschwader 51 94
  Taktisches Luftwaffengeschwader 74 24

Malaysia 44, 45, 49, 69
MBDA ASRAAM missile *26*
MBDA Storm Shadow missile 95
McDonnell Douglas 34–5, 43
McDonnell Douglas AV-8B Harrier II 99–100
  AV-8B Harrier II Plus 99–100
  AV-8B Night Attack 99, 100
  EAV-8B 99
  TAV-8B 99, 100
  VA.2 Matador II 100
  YA-8B 99
Meteor missile 26, 32
Mexico 67, 113
MICA missile 32, 65
Mikoyan MiG-29 68–9
  MiG-29 'Fulcrum-A' 68
  MiG-29 'Fulcrum-C' 68–9
  MiG-29N 69
  MiG-29S 69
  MiG-29SD **68**, 69
  MiG-29SE 68, 69
  MiG-29SM 69
  MiG-29SMT 69
  MiG-29UB 'Fulcrum-B' 68
  MiG-29UBT 69
  MiG-29UPG 69, **69**
Mikoyan MiG-29K and MiG-35 46–7
  MiG-29KR 46–7
  MiG-29KUB 46
  MiG-29KUBR 47
  MiG-29M 47, **47**
  MiG-29M2 47, **47**
  MiG-35D 47
  MiG-35S 47
  MiG-35UB 47
Mikoyan MiG-31 70–1
  'Foxhound-A' 70
  MiG-25MP 70
  MiG-31B 70
  MiG-31BM 70–1
  MiG-31BS 70
  MiG-31D 70
  MiG-31DZ 70
  MiG-31K 70–1
  MiG-31M 'Foxhound-B' 70
MIM-23B missile 66

Mitsubishi 35
Mitsubishi C-2 121
  Kawasaki P-1 maritime patrol aircraft 121
Mitsubishi F-2 59–60
  F-2A 59
  F-2B 59, 60
Mk 80 bombs 66
Mk 84 bombs 80
Morocco 67
Myanmar **57**, 69

N001 pulse-Doppler radar 72–3
N001K radar 50
N010M radar 69
N011M Bars radar 48
N019 pulse-Doppler radar 68
N019M Topaz radar 69
N019ME radar **68**, 69
N019MP radar 69
N041 Zhuk radar 46
N135 Irbis radar 52
Nimitz, USS **43**
Northrop F-5E/F Tiger II 67
  F-5E 67
  F-5E Tigre III 67
  F-5EM/FM 67
  F-5EM Tiger II 67
  F-5F 67
  F-5N 67
  RF-5E 67
  RF-5E Tigereye 67
Northrop Grumman AN/APG-80 radar 40
Northrop Grumman B-2 Spirit 80–1
  B-2A 80, 81
Northrop Grumman B-21 Raider 81
Northrop Grumman MESA radar 118
Northrop/McDonnell Douglas YF-23 10
Norway 17, 39, **41**
Novella radar 89

Oman 26
Operation Allied Force 79, 81, 83
Operation Desert Fox 79
Operation Desert Storm 34, 43, 82, 99, 100
Operation Enduring Freedom 81, 83, 100
Operation Inherent Resolve 95, 97, 100
Operation Iraqi Freedom **39**, 81, 100
Operation Mountain Lion **37**
Operation New Dawn **39**
Operation Northern Watch **39**
Operation Odyssey Dawn 81, 100
Operation Southern Watch **39**
Osina missile-guidance system 86

PAC JF-17 Thunder 56–7
  JF-17A 56
  JF-17B 56
Pakistan 96, **113**
  PAC JF-17 Thunder 56–7

Pakistan Air Force
  26 Squadron **56**
  Combat Commander School (CCS) **56**
Panavia Tornado 94–5
  RET 6-8 95
  Tornado ADV 95
  Tornado GR4 94, 95
  Tornado IDS 94, 95
Pastel radar warning receivers 53, 104
Paveway bomb 26, 32, 95
Peleliu, USS 100
Peru 64, 69, **104**
PL-8 missile 54, 58
PL-10 missile 20, 55, 58
PL-11 missile 54
PL-12 missile 54, 58
PL-15 missile 55, 58
Pod Reco NG 32
Python 3&4 missiles 67

Qatar 26, 32, **32**, 38, 65, 117

R-27 missile 72
R-27R missile 68
R-27R/ER missile 49
R-27T/ ET missile 49
R-33 missile 70
R-33S missile 70
R-37M missile 19, 53, 70
R-40TD missile **70**
R-60M missile 68
R-73 missile 49, 68, **71**, 72
R-74M2 missile 18
R-77 missile 49, **68**, 69, 73
R-77M missile 18
Rafael Derby missile 67
Rafael Litening pod 94
Rafael RecceLite pod 28, 95, 97
Raytheon AN/APG-65 radar 99
Raytheon APG-79 radar 44
RDI radar 64
RDM radar 64
RDY-2 radar 65
RDY multimode radar 65
Republic of China Air Force (ROCAF) 74–5
Rockwell B-1B Lancer 78–9
Ronald Reagan, USS **45**
Royal Air Force 26, *108–9*, **111**
  48th Fighter Wing **36**
  492nd Fighter Squadron 'Bolars' **36**
  No 3(F) Squadron **26**
  No IX (Bomber) Squadron **25**
Royal Australian Air Force
  No 1 Squadron **44**
  No. 2 Squadron **118**
  No 35 Squadron **112**
Russia
  Beriev A-50 120
  Mikoyan MiG-29 68–9
  Mikoyan MiG-29K and MiG-35 46–7

INDEX

Mikoyan MiG-31 70–1
Sukhoi Su-24 102–3
Sukhoi Su-25 *92–3*, 104–5
Sukhoi Su-27 72–3
Sukhoi Su-30 48–9
Sukhoi Su-33 50, *51*
Sukhoi Su-34 105
Sukhoi Su-35 52–3
Sukhoi Su-57 *6*, 18–19
Tupolev Tu-22M 84–5
Tupolev Tu-95MS 86–7
Tupolev Tu-160 *76–7*, 88–9
Russian Air Force
  23rd Fighter Aviation Regiment 19
  31st Guards Fighter Aviation
    Regiment **49**
  121st Heavy Bomber Aviation
    Regiment **88**, **89**
  184th Heavy Bomber Aviation
    Regiment **86**, **87**
  277th Bomber Aviation Regiment
    103
  764th Fighter Aviation Regiment
    70
Russian Navy
  279th Independent Shipborne
    Fighter Aviation Regiment **50**

Saab 340B twin turboprop 113
Saab Erieye 113
  Erieye ER (Extended Range) 113
  Saab 2000 Erieye 113
Saab GlobalEye multi-sensor
  AEW&C platform 113
Saab JAS 39 Gripen 27–8
  39A 28
  39B 28
  39C 27, 28
  39D 28
  39E/F 28
Saudi Arabia 25, 26, **27**, 34, 35–6,
  38, **38**, 95
SCALP missiles 29, 32, 65
Sea Eagle missile 95, 96
Selex ES-05 Raven radar 28
SEPECAT Jaguar 96
  Jaguar IB 96
  Jaguar IS 96
Serbia 79, 81
Shaanxi Y-9 122
  Y-8F-600 122
Shandong (aircraft carrier) 50
Shenyang J-11 and J-16 57–8
  J-11A 57–8
  J-11B 58
  J-11BH 58
  J-11BS 58
  J-11BSH 58
  J-11D 58
  J-16D 58
Shenyang J-15 50–1
  J-15D 51
  J-15S 51
  J-15T 51
Shmel radar 120

Singapore 17, 36
Skyward-G infrared search and track
  system 28
Sniper Advanced Targeting Pod 59,
  79
South Africa 28, 89
South Korea 17, 36, **42**, 67, 118
  TA-50 Golden Eagle 107
Spain 44, 45, 99, **100**
  Airbus A400M Atlas *108–9*, 111
  Airbus C295 110
  Eurofighter Typhoon 24–7
Spectra 32
Sprut missile-guidance system 86–7
Standard Missile SM-6 119
Storm Shadow missile 26, 95
Sudan **68**, 69
Sukhoi Su-24 102–3
  Su-24M 'Fencer-D' 102–3
  Su-24M2 103
  Su-24MK 103
  Su-24MR 'Fencer-E' 103
  T-6-1 103
Sukhoi Su-25 *92–3*, 104–5
  Su-25BM 105
  Su-25SM 104
  Su-25T 105
  Su-25TM 105
  Su-25UB 104
  Su-25UTG 105
  T-8-1 104
Sukhoi Su-27 72–3
  Su-27 'Flanker-B' 72
  Su-27P 72
  Su-27SK 73, **73**
  Su-27SKM 73
  Su-27SM 73
  Su-27SM(3) 73
  Su-27UB 'Flanker-C' 72
  Su-27UBK 73, **73**
  Su-30MK2V **73**
  T-10 72
  T-10S 72
Sukhoi Su-30 48–9
  Su-30K 48
  Su-30KN 48–9
  Su-30M2 49
  Su-30MK 48
  Su-30MK2 49
  Su-30MK2V 49
  Su-30MKA 49
  Su-30MKA(R) 49
  Su-30MKI 48–9
  Su-30MKK 49
  Su-30MKM 49
  Su-30SM 49
Sukhoi Su-33 50, *51*
  Su-27K 50
  Su-27KUB 50
  T-10K-1 50
Sukhoi Su-34 105
Sukhoi Su-35 52–3
  Su-30SM 53
  Su-35BM 52
  Su-35S **52**, 53

Sukhoi Su-57 *6*, 18–19
  SU-57E 19
  Su-57M 19
  T-50-1 19
  T-50-9 **18–19**
Sweden
  Saab Erieye 113
  Saab JAS 39 Gripen 27–8
Switzerland 17, 44, 45, 67
Syria 12, 19, 32, 34, **40**, **46**, **50**, 69,
  79, 83, 85, 87, 89, 100, 103, 105

TA-50 Golden Eagle 107
  FA-50 107
  T-50i 107
Taiwan 65, 67
  AIDC F-CK-1 Ching-Kuo 74–5
Taurus KEPD 350 missile 36, 94
Thailand 28, 107, 113
Thales pods 95
Thales LRMTS 96
Thales RBE2 multimode radar 32
Thales TopSight helmet-mounted
  sight 46
Thomson-CSF Agave radar 96
Tien Chien 2 (TC-2) missile 74, 75
Tien Chien (TC-1) missile 74
Tunisia 67
Tupolev Tu-22M 84–5
  Tu-22M0 85
  Tu-22M1 85
  Tu-22M2 85
  Tu-22M3 84, 85
  Tu-22M3 'Backfire-C' 85
  Tu-22M3M 85
Tupolev Tu-95MS 86–7
  Tu-95MSM 87
  Tu-142 86
Tupolev Tu-160 *76–7*, 88–9
  Tu-160M 89
Turkey **110**, 118
Type 232H radar 106
Type 1473G radar 54
Type 1475 radar 20
Type 1493 radar 58

Uganda 49
Ukraine **73**
United Arab Emirates 40, *41*, 64, 65,
  117
United Kingdom 17, 115, 117, 118
  Airbus A400M Atlas *108–9*, 111
  Eurofighter Typhoon 24–7
  Panavia Tornado 94–5
  SEPECAT Jaguar 96
United States
  Boeing 737 AEW&C 118
  Boeing B-52H Stratofortress 82–3
  Boeing C-17 Globemaster III 117
  Boeing F-15 Eagle 34–8
  Boeing F/A-18 Hornet and Super
    Hornet 43–5
  E-2D Advanced Hawkeye 119
  Fairchild Republic A-10
    Thunderbolt II 100–1

127

INDEX

Grumman F-14 Tomcat 66
Lockheed Martin C-130J Hercules 115–16
Lockheed Martin F-16 Fighting Falcon 39–42
Lockheed Martin F-22 Raptor *8–9*, 10–13
Lockheed Martin F-35 Lightning II 14–17
McDonnell Douglas AV-8B Harrier II 99–100
Northrop F-5E/F Tiger II 67
Northrop Grumman B-2 Spirit 80–1
Northrop Grumman B-21 Raider 81
Rockwell B-1B Lancer 78–9
United States Air Force (USAF)
1st Fighter Wing **11**
2nd Bomb Wing 83, **83**
5th Bomb Wing 83
7th Operations Group **79**
11th Bomb Squadron **83**
13th Bomb Squadron **80, 81**
20th Bomb Squadron **83**
36th Expeditionary Fighter Squadron **37**
40th Flight Test Squadron **37**
52nd Fighter Wing *42*
53rd Test and Evaluation Group **11**
58th Tactical Training Wing 34
90th Fighter Squadron **35**
93rd Bomb Squadron **83**
95th Expeditionary Fighter Squadron *8–9*
104th Fighter Squadron **101**

115th Airlift Squadron **115**
123rd Fighter Squadron **34**
125th Fighter Squadron **39**
138th Fighter Wing **39**
142nd Fighter Wing **34**
149th Fighter Squadron **11**
193rd Special Operations Squadron **116**
307th Bomb Wing 83, **83**
388th Tactical Fighter Wing 39
419th Flight Test Squadron **78**
422nd Test and Evaluation Squadron **11**
509th Bomb Wing **80, 81**
509th Tactical Fighter Squadron **101**
Strike Fighter Squadron 147 (VFA-147) **16**
United States Marines 17, 43, 44, 99–100, 115, 116
3rd Marine Aircraft Wing **16**
Electronic Attack Squadron 141 **45**
Marine Aircraft Group 13 **16**
Marine Attack Squadron 223 **99**
Marine Fighter Attack Squadron 121 **15**
Marine Fighter Attack Squadron 211 **16**
United States Navy 119
Blue Angels display team 44
Carrier Air Wing 2 **16**
Carrier Air Wing 5 **45**
Carrier Airborne Early Warning Squadron 126 **119**
Strike Fighter Squadron 14 **43**
VAW-120 **119**

US Coast Guard 116
V004 radar 105
Venezuela 49, 89
Vietnam 49, **73**, **110**

Wan Chien missile 75, **75**
West Germany, Panavia Tornado 94–5
Xi'an H-6 90–1
H-6A 90, 91
H-6B 91
H-6D 90
H-6E 91
H-6F 91
H-6G 91
H-6H 91
H-6K 90, *91*
H-6L 91
H-6M 91
HU-6D 90–1
Xi'an JH-7 106
JH-7A 106
Xi'an Y-20 123
Y-20A 123
Yemen 69
YJ-6 missile 90
YJ-12 missile 91
YJ-83K missile 91
YJ-83K/KH missile 106
YJ-91 missile 91, 106
Yugoslavia 83

Zaslon radars 70
Zhuk-M2E radar 69

Picture Credits

Photographs:
Alamy: 6 (Artem Alexandrovich/Stocktrek Images), 33 (Abaca Press), 75 (Ann Wang/Reuters)
Alert5: 21 (Creative Commons Attribution-Share Alike 4.0 International License)
Allied Joint Force Command: 65
Dreamstime: 22 (Illuminativisual), 73 (Fotogenix), 76 & 92 (Artyomanikeev), 110 (Bogacerkan)
Eurofighter: 7, 26
Shutterstock: 45 (Grapsole79), 51 & 54 (Fasttailwind), 60 (w_p_o_), 71 (Boris Dianov), 91 (Fasttailwind), 95 (InsectWorld), 108 (Ryan Fletcher), 111 (Joseph Thompson)
U.S. Air Force: 17 (Airman 1st Class Duncan C. Bevan), 35 (Major Gary), 37 (Master Sgt. Lance Cheung), 41 (Tech. Sgt. Michael R. Holzworth), 42 (Staff Sgt. Joshua R. M. Dewberry), 63 (SRA Greg L. Davis), 116 (Yasuo Osakabe)
U.S. Air National Guard: 8 (Staff Sgt. Colton Elliott)
U.S. Marine Corps: 15 (Staff Sgt. Artur Shvartsberg)

Artworks:
Amber Books Ltd: 12–13, 30-31, 81 (bottom)
Rolando Ugolini: 10–11, 24–28, 34–45, 64–67, 80, 81 (top),

82–83, 90–91, 94–96, 99–104, 106, 111–116, 118, 120
Stuart Fowle: 48–53, 57 (bottom), 58, 72–73, 105
Teasel Studio: 14–21, 29, 32–33, 46–47, 55–56, 57 (top), 59–61, 68–71, 74–75, 78–79, 84–89, 97–98, 107, 110, 117, 119, 121–123

Gatefold artwork credits:
Lockheed Martin F-22 Raptor (Amber Books Ltd)
Lockheed Martin F-35 Lightning II (Ugo Crisponi/Aviation Graphics)
General Dynamics F-16C Fighting Falcon (Amber Books Ltd)
McDonnell Douglas CF-18 Hornet (Amber Books Ltd)
Dassault Mirage 2000 (Amber Books Ltd)
Sukhoi Su-27 'Flanker-B' (Amber Books Ltd)
Northrop B-2 Spirit (Amber Books Ltd)
Tuplolev Tu-160 'Blackjack' (Ugo Crisponi/Aviation Graphics)
Fairchild Republic A-10A Thunderbolt II (Amber Books Ltd)
Sukhoi Su-25 'Frogfoot' (Rolando Ugolini)
Airbus A400M (Rolando Ugolini)
Boeing 737 Wedgetail AEW.Mk 1 (Rolando Ugolini)